España Viva

A Spanish course for beginners
on BBC Radio and Television

Course writer

Derek Utley
York Language Training

Language consultant

Maria Assumpta Serarols
Birkbeck College

Researcher

Cristina Lago

Production Assistant

Carol Stanley

Editors

Mick Webb
(Radio Producer)

David Wilson
(Television Producer)

ESPAÑA viva

BBC BOOKS

España Viva is a Spanish course for beginners on BBC Radio and Television, first broadcast in November 1987.

The course consists of

15 Radio and 15 Television programmes

The course book covering all the programmes

Two audio cassettes

A computer software pack

Teachers' Notes are also available

This book accompanies the BBC Television series *España Viva* first broadcast on BBC 1 from November 1987 (produced by David Wilson) and the Radio series of the same name first broadcast on Radio 4 VHF from November 1987 (produced by Mick Webb).

Published to accompany a series of programmes prepared in consultation with the BBC Educational Broadcasting Council

Published by BBC Books
A division of BBC Enterprises Ltd
Woodlands, 80 Wood Lane, London W12 0TT

First published 1987

Reprinted 1988, 1989 (twice), 1990

© The Author and BBC Enterprises Limited 1987

ISBN 0 563 21286 1

This book is set in 9 on 11 point Univers Medium
Printed and bound in England by
Butler & Tanner Ltd, Frome, Somerset
Cover printed by Richard Clay Ltd, Norwich, Norfolk

Contents

Picture acknowledgements

J ALLAN CASH PHOTOLIBRARY pages 54 (left bottom), 64 (right centre), 84 (bottom left), 116 (bottom left), 133 (top), 152 (top right) & 162 (bottom); ARCHIVO ICONOGRAFICO, SA pages 153 & 155 (right); BARNABY'S PICTURE LIBRARY pages 68 (top), 134 (right) & 148; CANTABRIA TOURIST AUTHORITY pages 22 (bottom) & 46; ALEX DUFORT/BBC page 84 (top right); FIRO FOTO page 135; JAIME SUAREZ GARCIA/BBC pages 7 (top), 13, 14, 15, 16, 22 (top), 32 (top & bottom), 38, 44 (right), 48 (right), 49, 54 (right bottom), 56, 65, 66 (top & bottom left), 67, 72 (top & centre), 73, 74, 75, 77, 85, 93, 95, 98, 99, 104, 106 (bottom right), 112, 115, 118, 119, 125, 129 (right), 143 & 162 (top); ERIC HOSKING page 161; IBERFOTO page 155 (left); ANDREW LONGTON pages 36, 86 & 88; MAST WINES AND SPIRITS LTD page 33; STEPHEN MOSS/BBC pages 25, 32 (centre), 34, 35, 37, 45, 47, 57, 68 (centre & bottom), 103 (right) & 106 top); PATRONATO MUNICIPAL DE TURISMO, MADRID pages 24 & 94; PATRONATO PROVINCIAL DE TURISMO, SEVILLA page 123; REX FEATURES page 31; CHRIS RIDGERS/BBC pages 26, 27, 28, 89 & 129 (left); SANTANDER TOURIST BOARD page 54 (right top); JUNTA DE SEVILLA pages 137 & 145; SPANISH NATIONAL TOURIST OFFICE pages 48 (left), 59, 64 (left), 72 (bottom), 134 (right bottom), 152 (left) & 157; SPECTRUM COLOUR LIBRARY pages 39, 54 (left top), 55, 144, 147 & 152 (bottom right); JENNY WALKER page 139; MICK WEBB/BBC pages 63 (right), 76 & 83; ALAN WILDING/BBC pages 66 (bottom right) & 104 (bottom left); DAVID WILSON/BBC pages 7 (bottom), 17, 64 (right bottom), 84 (top left & bottom right), 96, 104 (bottom left), 106 (bottom left), 108, 113, 114, 116 (top), 117, 128, 134 (left) & 156.

Illustration acknowledgements

PAUL CEMMICK cartoons
JOHN GILKES maps and diagrams
OXFORD ILLUSTRATORS line drawings
JOHN SHACKELL graphic symbols
GILLIAN MARTIN front cover

Introduction

THE COURSE

España Viva means 'Living Spain' or 'Spain Alive', and the aim of the course is to give an idea not only of the Spanish language but also of the Spaniards who speak it. Knowing something of the language and of the people should make it easier to appreciate both when you get to meet them.

This course is meant for people who know little or no Spanish and who don't have a great deal of time available to learn it. The points covered in each unit are limited to what could realistically be understood and learnt in an evening. By the end of the course you should be able to handle shopping, ordering meals, asking directions and other everyday situations. You'll also be able to have a simple conversation about work, the weather and yourself.

Isabel Soto

Ⓡ ## THE RADIO PROGRAMMES

Each week's programme will introduce a carefully selected amount of new language. You'll hear how it's used in Spain, and be given a chance to practise yourself. There'll also be a weekly feature on some aspect of Spanish daily life or culture. The recordings were made in several locations, but mostly in Madrid, Barcelona and Mojácar (on the south coast). The interviewers were Isabel Soto and Jordi Roura.

Jordi Roura

Ⓣⓥ ## THE TELEVISION PROGRAMMES

These cover the same topics of language week by week as the radio programmes, but in different settings. Programmes were filmed in three main locations: Santander, on the north coast; Madrid, right in the centre of Spain; and Sevilla, in the far south. Yolanda Vázquez was the interviewer.

Yolanda Vázquez

There are two main parts to each programme. One consists of simple conversations illustrating the basic language to be learnt. The other consists of short film reports on different aspects of local life. These are entirely in Spanish. The idea is to show something of the country and its people, and also to get you used to the sounds of the language. Beginners shouldn't expect to understand much straight away; for this reason the films are subtitled.

THE BOOK

This has 15 units. Each one contains some of the dialogues from the programmes, followed by explanation and exercises. A typical unit consists of:

Spanish Live: a selection of the texts of dialogues presented in the programmes. Sometimes these have been edited for the purposes of the book. Key structures and phrases appear alongside the dialogues. Other new words and phrases that aren't immediately obvious are translated underneath – the translation given applies only to that particular situation.

Spotcheck: a quick question or two in English after each dialogue to check that you've understood.

Keywords: a list of the most important words you'll need to learn for that unit.

How Spanish Works: a brief explanation of the main points of grammar or idiom necessary to understand the language of the dialogues.

Sound Spanish: a quick guide to some of the Spanish sounds that could give difficulty to a speaker of English.

Workout: exercises and practice to get you to use the language of the unit.

About Spain: notes on different subjects mentioned in the programmes – areas and towns of Spain, Spanish customs and behaviour.

At the end of the book are:

Extra Dialogues: a transcript of those dialogues which are presented in the programmes but not printed in the unit.

Grammar in a Nutshell: a summary of the grammar points contained in the dialogues and in the *How Spanish Works* section of each unit.

Pronouncing Spanish: how to recognise and pronounce the sounds of Spanish.

Key: a complete set of answers to the exercises (both *Spotcheck* and *Workout*).

Word Groups: additional lists of words, in English with their Spanish equivalents, organised into themes such as food, numbers, hobbies and sports, etc. Some of these, like numbers, are essential; others may come in useful depending on personal tastes or interests.

Vocabulary: a list of all the Spanish words that appear in the book, with English translations.

THE CASSETTES

These have a separate section for each unit, containing the dialogues in the book units marked with the cassette symbol, together with pronunciation practice and exercises.

THE COMPUTER SOFTWARE

This offers plenty of extra practice in the most important words and phrases taught in the course. There are thirty exercises – two for each unit – on 3 discs, for use with BBC micro-computers.

THE TEACHERS' NOTES

These notes are for teachers using *España Viva* as a course book in their classes. They offer ideas for using the radio and television programmes in class, and for developing more oral and written practice. They also contain complete transcripts of all the Spanish in the programmes, including the television documentary material. The notes can be obtained by sending a cheque or postal order for £2.50, payable to BSS, to: España Viva, PO Box 7, London W3 6XJ.

How to use the book

Try to be methodical, working through the different sections of each unit. But also play to your strengths by doing a lot of what you do well or simply like doing: listening to spoken Spanish, reading texts, doing exercises – even mumbling Spanish to yourself around the house.

If you can possibly join an evening class, you will reap the benefits of expert advice, the opportunity to practise your spoken Spanish, and the chance to share problems. Otherwise, try following the programmes with a friend.

As you work through the course, follow these guidelines if you find they help:

Listen to and watch all the radio and television programmes if you possibly can.

Prepare for the programmes by reading the book first:
■ Read through the printed dialogues in the book and do the *Spotchecks*.
■ Look at the right-hand column of each page of dialogues. These contain the key phrases for each topic – make sure you know them off by heart.
■ Learn the *Keywords*. If you know them, you will have the basic equipment to 'survive' in a particular situation, so it's worth spending time on this, and using as many different techniques as you can: covering up the English word and saying what it is from the Spanish, then vice versa; getting a friend to 'test' you; writing tricky words on memo boards or pieces of paper about the house; using time on the bus, train or tube to run through lists or name any objects you see – in fact, anything that helps you and that you find interesting!

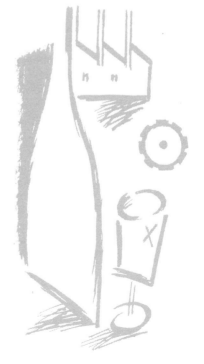

■ Read through *How Spanish Works*. This is not absolutely essential, but it will give you a better understanding of some things in the dialogues that may not have made immediate sense to you. If you want to go further with this, refer to *Grammar in a Nutshell* at the back of the book.

■ Practise the sounds of *Sound Spanish*, using the cassettes if you have them.

■ Work through the exercises of *Workout*. Don't do them all at once – just try a few at a time. In between, go back to *Spanish Live*, *Keywords* or *How Spanish Works*. Check your answers in the *Key* at the back of the book.

■ If you want further practice, have a look at the *Extra Dialogues* at the back of the book. These will give you a chance to test how much you understand and to add a few more words to your vocabulary.

1 ¿Cómo te llamas?

Saying 'hello' and 'goodbye'

Saying who you are

Where you're from

® **1** Helloes and goodbyes can vary according to the time of day. Here's Isabel going into a chemist's shop one morning . . .

Isabel	Hola, buenos días.
Assistant	Hola, buenos días.

. . . and leaving.

Isabel	Hasta luego.
Assistant	Adiós, adiós.

To greet someone:

hola	*hello*
buenos días	*good morning*
buenas tardes	*good afternoon, good evening*
buenas noches	*good evening, goodnight*

Visiting a tourist office in the afternoon . . .

Isabel	Hola, buenas tardes.
Clerk	Hola, buenas tardes.

Isabel	Adiós.
Clerk	Adiós.

. . . and passing a neighbour on the stairs, fairly late one evening.

Neighbour	Hola, buenas noches.
Isabel	Buenas noches.

To say goodbye:

hasta luego	*see you later*
adiós	*goodbye*

▶ Spotcheck 1   Who doesn't Isabel say 'hello' to?

Ⓡ **2**   We started most interviews by asking people their names. Among the people interviewed by Jordi Roura in Barcelona were these two men in their sixties . . .

Jordi	¿Cómo se llama usted?
1st man	Francisco García Torres.

Jordi	¿Cómo se llama usted?
2nd man	Gerónimo Terez Fernández.

. . . and a brother and sister in their twenties.

Jordi	Hola. ¿Cómo te llamas?
Man	Me llamo Santiago, Santiago Peralta Duarte.
Jordi	Hola. ¿Cómo te llamas?
Woman	Me llamo Mercedes Peralta.

To ask someone their name:
¿cómo se llama usted?
¿cómo te llamas?   (less formal)

To say what your name is:
me llamo . . .

Meeting in the street

This businessman from Zaragoza had a very unusual name that Isabel didn't catch first time.

Isabel	¿Cómo se llama usted?
Man	José Luis Causapé.
Isabel	¿Cómo?
Man	Causapé, José Luis Causapé.

To say 'pardon?':
¿cómo?

▶ **Spotcheck 2** Which of the people interviewed was Jordi less formal with?

📺 3 For years, Santander has been a favourite holiday place for Spaniards – but do many foreigners come? Yolanda asked visitors if they were Spanish.

Yolanda	Hola, buenas tardes.
1st woman	Buenas tardes.
Yolanda	¿Cómo se llama?
1st woman	Dorina Muro.
Yolanda	¿Es usted española?
1st woman	Sí, soy española.
Yolanda	¿Cómo se llama?
Man	Manuel Hervás.
Yolanda	¿Es usted español?
Man	Sí, soy español.
Yolanda	¿Es usted española?
2nd woman	Sí, yo soy española.

sí *yes*

To ask a woman if she's Spanish:
¿es usted española?
¿eres española? (less formal)

To ask a man if he's Spanish:
¿es usted español?
¿eres español? (less formal)

To say what nationality you are:
If you're a woman
soy española *I'm Spanish*
soy inglesa *I'm English*

If you're a man
soy español *I'm Spanish*
soy inglés *I'm English*

▶ **Spotcheck 3** How many of these people are Spanish?

Ana

® **4**   It's often said that most people who live in Madrid
weren't actually born there. Isabel tried to find out
if this was true.

Isabel	¿Eres de aquí de Madrid, Ana?
Ana	No.
Isabel	¿De dónde eres?
Ana	Soy de Barcelona.

Isabel	¿Eres de aquí?
Woman	No, no soy de aquí.
Isabel	¿De dónde eres?
Woman	Soy de León.

Isabel	¿Eres de Madrid?
Woman	No. Yo soy de Salamanca.

Isabel	Marga, ¿eres de aquí?
Marga	No.
Isabel	¿Eres española?
Marga	No.
Isabel	¿De dónde eres?
Marga	De Santo Domingo. Es la capital de la República Dominicana.

At last, a native *madrileño* . . .

Isabel	¿De dónde eres?
Jaime	Yo soy de Madrid.

no	*no*
yo	*I*
República Dominicana	*Dominican Republic*

To ask someone if they're from here:
¿es usted de aquí?
¿eres de aquí?   (less formal)

To say where you're from:
soy de . . .

To say where you're *not* from:
no soy de . . .

▶ Spotcheck 4   Who was from Madrid and who was not a Spaniard?

5 The International University at Santander attracts students from all over Spain. Where do they come from?

Palacio de la Magdalena, headquarters of the Universidad Internacional, Santander

Yolanda	¿Eres de aquí de Santander?
1st student	No, no soy de Santander, soy de Madrid.
Yolanda	¿Eres de aquí de Santander?
2nd student	No, soy de León.
3rd student	No, soy de Bilbao.
Yolanda	¿Eres de aquí de Santander?
4th student	No, no soy de Santander.
Yolanda	¿De dónde eres?
4th student	Soy de Segovia.
Yolanda	¿De dónde eres?
5th student	Soy de Sevilla.

To ask someone where they're from:
¿de dónde es usted?
¿de dónde eres? (less formal)

▶ Spotcheck 5 How many people are from the north of Spain and how many from the south?

KEYWORDS

hola	hello
buenos días	good morning
buenas tardes	good afternoon, good evening
buenas noches	good evening, goodnight
adiós	goodbye
hasta luego	see you later
(yo) soy	I am
(usted) es	you are
(tú) eres	you are (less formal)
¿cómo se llama?	what's your name?
¿cómo te llamas?	what's your name? (less formal)
me llamo . . .	my name is . . .

	man	*woman*
Spanish	**español**	**española**
English	**inglés**	**inglesa**
Scottish	**escocés**	**escocesa**
Welsh	**galés**	**galesa**
Irish	**irlandés**	**irlandesa**

(*for more nationalities see p. 210*)

de	from
¿dónde?	where?
¿de dónde?	where from?
aquí	here
¿cómo?	pardon?
sí	yes
no	no

HOW SPANISH WORKS

1 Word-for-word is bad for you

Phrases don't always make sense if you translate them word for word: *me llamo Santiago*, word for word, would be 'myself (I) call Santiago'. So it's often a good idea to learn the meaning of a complete phrase (in this case 'my name is Santiago'), and let the meanings of the individual words come later.

2 Double 'you'

When talking to someone, you must choose one of two words for 'you': *usted* or *tú*. What's the difference? *Tú* is used with people you know, or who are your age or younger; *usted* with older people or in a more formal situation. The tendency nowadays is to use *tú* more and more, but if in doubt – for example, in a shop, bank, and so on – play safe and use *usted*, or listen for a cue from the other person.

3 Missing persons

Spanish, like English, has separate words for 'I', 'you', 'he', 'she', and so on. Unlike in English, though, these words (*yo, tú, usted, él, ella*, etc) are often missed out, eg:

¿de dónde eres? where are you from?
soy de . . . I'm from . . .

When they are used, it's usually for emphasis, contrast, or to avoid confusion: *Alfonso es de Valencia, pero* **yo** *soy de Alicante.*

4 The end of the word

The words for 'English', 'Spanish' and other nationalities have slightly different endings depending on the sex of the person being described. *Española* is used for a Spanish girl or woman, *español* for a Spanish boy or man; and the same thing happens with *inglés, inglesa, escocés, escocesa*, etc. The way gender (masculine or feminine) affects certain words in Spanish is an important part of how Spanish works.

5 Dividing the day

Buenos días is the equivalent of 'good morning'.

Buenas tardes is the greeting used roughly between midday and 9 pm (or nightfall), so it means both 'good afternoon' and 'good evening'. This saves you learning two expressions.

Buenas noches is used in the same way as the English 'goodnight', with one small difference: it can be used when you first meet someone at night as well as when you say 'goodbye'.

You'll often hear people say *Buenas*. It's a shortened form of any one of these three greetings.

SOUND SPANISH

Vowels a – e – o

Spanish vowels are much easier to deal with than English vowels as basically there's only one sound for each letter:

a as in *Ana* is like the English 'a' in 'cat'
e as in *se* is like the English 'e' in 'get'
o as in *yo* is like the English 'o' in 'pot'

Each vowel sound is pronounced clearly and distinctly. For instance, in English the word 'chocolate' is usually pronounced something like CHOCK-ER-LIT. In Spanish it's CHO-CO-LA-TE.

WORKOUT

1 As if you were there

What would you say in these situations?

a In the hotel one morning you greet an elderly man . . .
b You walk into a bar one evening and greet the waiter . . .
c A little boy from the next table wanders over and says *'Hola'* . . .
d You leave some Spanish friends one morning, expecting to be back by lunchtime . . .
e You're just off to bed . . .
f You've just told someone your name and she says *¿Cómo?* . . .

2 Answerback

How would you reply in each case?

a ¡Hola!
b ¿Cómo se llama usted?
c ¿Es usted de Ambridge?
d ¿Eres español(a)?
e ¿Cómo te llamas?
f ¿Eres de aquí de Valencia?

3 Factfinding

Note down two things about each of these short dialogues. Do they take place in the morning (am) or later (pm)? Are the people meeting or leaving each other?

a – Hola, Pepe.
  – Hola, Juan, buenos días.

b – Adiós, Rosa.
  – Adiós, buenas tardes.

c – Buenas tardes, señor García.
  – Hola, buenas tardes.

d – Hasta luego.
  – Hasta luego, Luis. Buenas noches.

4 Bubbles

What's the question that's being asked in each of these situations? Don't forget to choose between *tú* and *usted*.

19

5 Identikit

Read these brief self-portraits. How would each person fill in this form (in English)?

a Pues, me llamo Vicente Zamora, y soy de Sevilla, España.

b Yo soy de Bogotá, Colombia; me llamo Diego Valdano.

c Soy argentino, de Mendoza, y me llamo Eduardo Borges.

d Soy del norte de España, de Vigo precisamente, y me llamo Luisa Núñez.

Surname/apellido ....

First name/nombre ....

Nationality/nacionalidad ....

Place of birth/lugar de nacimiento.................

....

6 Syllablocks

Add one syllable from the right-hand side to complete the sentences.

Me	lla	–	Víc	tor
¿Có	mo	te	lla	– ?
No	soy	de	a	–
¿De	dón	de	e	– ?

mas
mo
res
quí

7 Vertico

Find the phrase written vertically top to bottom, in the darker boxes, by filling in the horizontal phrases with the help of the clues.

Afternoon greeting
Not there
From
English (lady)
Hello!
'Bye for now
Where?
'Bye for longer (maybe)
First part of evening greeting
Said by someone visiting

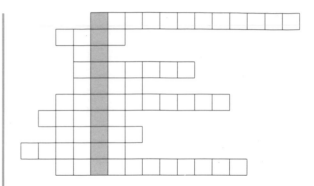

8 Stringalong

Split each string of words up to make a phrase you have learnt. Then add any punctuation.

ERESDEAQUI

COMOTELLAMAS

NONOSOYDEAQUISOYDEMADRID

9 Scriptwriter

With the help of the diagram, complete these radio interviews with people from different parts of Spain.

Interviewer	Hola, buenos días. ¿Cómo te llamas?
....	Hola, me llamo ....
Interviewer	¿Y de dónde eres?
....	Soy de Vitoria.
Interviewer	Y tú, ¿de dónde eres?
Beatriz	Soy de ...., y me llamo Beatriz.
Interviewer	Buenos días, señora, ¿de dónde es usted?
....	Soy de Barcelona.
Interviewer	¿Y cómo se llama?
....	Me llamo ....
Interviewer	Y usted, señor, ¿cómo se llama?
Carlos	Me llamo Carlos, y soy de ....

10 Key Wordsearch

Some of the words you'll find in *Keywords* (p. 18) are contained in this square. They could be separate words, or parts of phrases, and can read in a straight line up, down or across (backwards or forwards). See how many you can find in three minutes (there are at least ten).

```
B U E N A S
U O U S L A
E T S E O I
N U T R H D
O R E E M S
S E D R A T
```

11 Lo típico

The things pictured opposite are associated with particular parts of Spain. Can you match each description with the correct picture?

a   Es una fruta típicamente española, se llama naranja. Sobre todo es de Valencia, en el este de España.

b   Es una iglesia, casi una catedral. Se llama La Sagrada Familia en Barcelona. Es una obra en construcción.

c   Los molinos de viento son de La Mancha, en el interior de España. La Mancha es la región de Don Quijote.

d   Es una playa muy bonita. Se llama La Concha y está en San Sebastián, en la costa norte de España.

e   Es un vino típico del sur de España. Es un tipo de jerez y se llama *fino*.

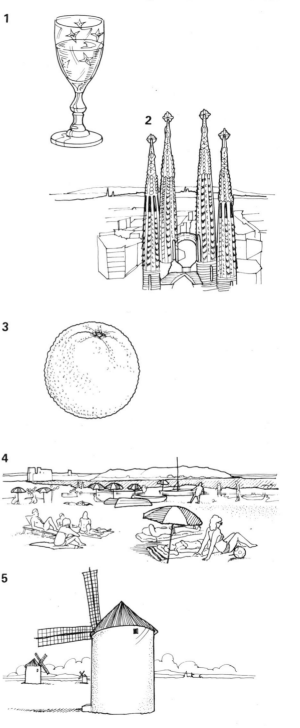

1

2

3

4

5

ABOUT SPAIN

Spanish regions

Regions like the País Vasco (Basque Country), Cataluña (Catalonia) and Galicia have always had their own identity and even their own languages. Now, along with the other Spanish regions, they've been given a certain freedom to run their own political affairs. Altogether there are 17 of these 'communities' (called *comunidades autónomas*), and each one has its own 'capital' with its own local government.

Santander

Santander is a traditional holiday resort for many Spaniards, who come here in the summer to escape the heat of central Spain. It is set in a deep bay fringed by magnificent beaches and looks out to distant mountains. It's also an important port with a large fishing fleet.

Santander is the administrative capital of Cantabria, one of Spain's autonomous communities. The region attracts tourists to its beaches and to its spectacular mountain range, los Picos de Europa. A few miles from the coast are the famous caves of Altamira, which contain some of the most important prehistoric cave paintings in Europe.

Names

Most Spanish people have only one Christian name, sometimes consisting of two parts (*José María, María Rosa*). But everybody has two surnames: the father's first, then the mother's. This means that, instead of being lost on marriage, a woman's family name survives for one more generation in her children. After they are married, women usually keep their own surname, and add their husband's, joined on by *de*. So if *José Hidalgo Pérez* married *Asunción Polo Castillo*, Asunción would become *Asunción Polo de Hidalgo*, and their child would be *Luis Hidalgo Polo*.

Some very common Christian names have a familiar form, so don't be confused if you hear *Paco* instead of *Francisco*, *Lola* instead of *Dolores* or *Pepe* instead of *José*.

El Sardinero beach, Santander

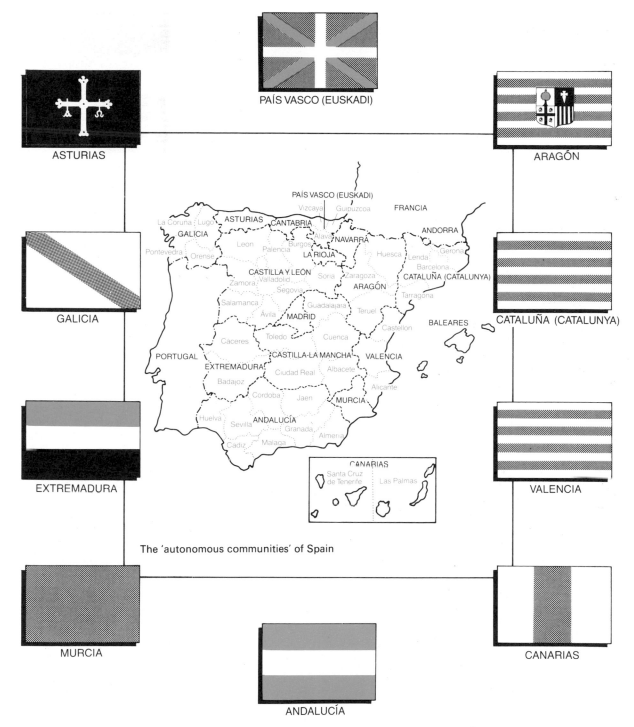

PAÍS VASCO (EUSKADI)

ASTURIAS

ARAGÓN

GALICIA

CATALUÑA (CATALUNYA)

EXTREMADURA

VALENCIA

MURCIA

CANARIAS

ANDALUCÍA

The 'autonomous communities' of Spain

PAÍS VASCO (EUSKADI)
Vizcaya Guipuzcoa
La Coruna Lugo ASTURIAS CANTABRIA
GALICIA Alava NAVARRA
Pontevedra Orense Leon Palencia Burgos
LA RIOJA
CASTILLA Y LEÓN Soria
Zamora Valladolid Zaragoza ARAGÓN
Segovia
Salamanca Guadalajara Teruel
Ávila MADRID
Caceres Toledo Cuenca
PORTUGAL Castellon
CASTILLA-LA MANCHA VALENCIA
EXTREMADURA
Badajoz Ciudad Real Albacete
Cordoba Jaen Alicante
MURCIA
Huelva ANDALUCÍA
Sevilla Granada Almeria
Cadiz Malaga

FRANCIA
ANDORRA
Huesca Lerida Gerona
Barcelona
CATALUÑA (CATALUNYA)
Tarragona
BALEARES

CANARIAS
Santa Cruz de Tenerife Las Palmas

The Plaza Mayor,
Madrid

2 ¡Mucho gusto!

Buying a drink

Meeting people

SPANISH LIVE

1 Three friends with a thirst have just sat down on the terrace of a café in Santander.

Waiter	Buenos días. ¿Qué van a tomar?
Conchi	Pues … una cerveza, por favor.
Luis	Un zumo de tomate.
Carmen	Y una tónica.
Waiter	Una cerveza, un zumo de tomate y una tónica. Muy bien.

¿qué van a tomar?	*what would you like?*
pues	*er …*
y	*and*
una tónica	*a tonic water*
muy bien	*very well, right*

The waiter returns with the drinks.

Waiter	¿El zumo de tomate, por favor?
Luis	Para mí.
Waiter	¿Y la tónica para usted?
Carmen	Sí, gracias.

el zumo	*the juice*
para mí	*for me*
la tónica	*the tonic water*
gracias	*thank you*

▶ Spotcheck 1   How many alcoholic drinks are ordered?

2 Three people sit chatting over drinks in the bar of a Santander restaurant. They are joined by a fourth person, known to his friends as Mann.

Mann	¡Hola! ¿Qué tal, Antonio?
Antonio	*(getting up)* ¿Cómo estás, Mann?

To order a drink:
una cerveza, por favor
   a beer, please
un zumo de tomate, por favor
   a tomato juice, please

Mann	Muy bien.
Antonio	Mira, ésta es Pilar, mi mujer.
Mann	¿Qué tal?
Pilar	¡Hola!
Antonio	Mi hermana, Julia.
Mann	Mucho gusto.
Julia	Encantada.
Pilar	¿Qué tomas?
Mann	Pues ... una cerveza.
Pilar	(*to waiter*) ¡Por favor! Una cerveza para el señor.

To ask how someone is:

¿cómo está?	*how are you?*
¿cómo estás?	
(less formal)	
¿qué tal?	*how are things?*

To say you're fine:
(muy) bien

mira	*look*
mi mujer	*my wife*
mi hermana	*my sister*
encantada	*pleased to meet you*
¿qué tomas?	*what will you have?*
el señor	*the gentleman*

▶Spotcheck 2 a What relation is Julia to Antonio?

b How many people at the table already knew Mann?

Bar in Madrid

® **3** One Sunday afternoon, Isabel goes to Vallecas, a suburb of Madrid, to meet her boyfriend's family for the first time.

Jaime's parents

Jaime	Hola, Isabel, ¿qué tal?
Isabel	Hola, Jaime. (*they kiss on both cheeks*)
Jaime	Anda, venga, te presento a mi familia.
Isabel	Muy bien.
Jaime	Mira, ésta es mi madre.
Isabel	Hola.
Señora Suárez	Hola.
Isabel	¿Qué tal? (*they kiss*)
Señora Suárez	Bien.
Jaime	Mi padre.
Señor Suárez	Encantado.
Isabel	Encantada. (*they kiss*)
Jaime	Esta es mi hermana, Marisa.
Marisa	Hola. (*they kiss*)
Jaime	Y éste es mi cuñado, Julián.
Julián	Hola.
Isabel	Hola. (*they kiss*)
Jaime	Bueno, sentaos.

To introduce a woman:
ésta es ... *this is ...*

To introduce a man:
éste es ... *this is ...*

To say 'pleased to meet you':
mucho gusto
encantada   (said by a woman)
encantado   (said by a man)

anda, venga	*come on*
te presento a	*I'll introduce you*
mi familia	*to my family*
mi madre	*my mother*
mi padre	*my father*
mi cuñado	*my brother-in-law*
bueno	*right*
sentaos	*sit down*

▶ Spotcheck 3   a   How many people does Jaime introduce to Isabel?

b   What is his brother-in-law's name?

® **4**   It's five o'clock on Sunday afternoon. Jaime's
mother offers everyone a drink.

Señora Suárez	¿Qué queréis tomar, café o té? ¿Isabel?
Isabel	Para mí un té, por favor.
Señora Suárez	Vale. ¿Marisa?
Marisa	Yo quiero un té con leche.
Señora Suárez	¿Tú, Julián?
Julián	Café solo.
Señor Suárez	Yo, café con leche.
Señora Suárez	¿Jaime?
Jaime	Yo quiero un café solo.
Señora Suárez	Vale.

¿qué queréis tomar?	*what would you like to drink?*
té (con leche)	*tea (with milk)*
vale	*OK*
yo quiero	*I'd like*
café solo	*black coffee*
café con leche	*white coffee*

▶ Spotcheck 4   How many different kinds of drink are requested?

KEYWORDS

la cerveza	beer
el café (solo)	(black) coffee
el café con leche	white coffee
el zumo de tomate	tomato juice
la tónica	tonic water
el té (con leche)	tea (with milk)

(*for more drinks see p. 206*)

(*for more drinks see p. 206*)

para mí	for me

mucho gusto	
encantado	
(man speaking)	pleased to meet you
encantada	
(woman speaking)	

¿qué tal?	how are things?
¿cómo está?	how are you?
¿cómo estás?	how are you? (less formal)
bien	well

mi	my
la familia	family
la mujer	wife; woman
el marido	husband
la madre	mother
ol padre	father
la hermana	sister
el hermano	brother
la hija	daughter
el hijo	son
la amiga	friend (female)
el amigo	friend (male)
la novia	girlfriend
el novio	boyfriend

por favor	please
gracias	thank you

HOW SPANISH WORKS

1 'A'

Un hermano means 'a brother', and *una hermana* 'a sister'. The word for 'a' (or 'an') depends on the gender of the person.

The words for things are also divided into two groups – *un* is used with some, *una* with others: *un café*, *una cerveza*.

With very few exceptions, words used with *un* are known as 'masculine' nouns, and those used with *una* as 'feminine'. This doesn't mean that Spaniards think of coffee as being particularly virile or beer as rather feminine. It's just a convenient grammatical label.

2 'The'

To say '**the** coffee' or '**the** beer' (or '**the** brother' or '**the** sister'), you also have a choice between two words, *el* or *la* – *el* with masculine words, *la* with feminine ones.

Whenever you learn a new word, make sure you also know whether it is masculine or feminine. One simple rule to help you:
words ending in -*o* are nearly always masculine
words ending in -*a* are nearly always feminine

For example:
un hijo   *una hija*
un amigo   *una amiga*
un zumo   *una cerveza*

3 Discriminating

We've already seen that the ending of words like *española* or *inglés* depends on the gender of the person described. You make the same changes in
encantada   (a woman speaking)
encantado   (a man speaking)
and
ésta es mi hermana
éste es mi hermano

4 Being polite

Por favor ('please') and *gracias* ('thank you') aren't used quite so much in Spanish as in English. This is not a sign of rudeness. When someone does say *gracias* or *muchas gracias* ('thank you very much'), it's normal to reply *de nada* ('don't mention it').

5 Questions and exclamations

You'll have noticed that in a Spanish question like *¿cómo estás?*, there is a question mark written not only at the end of the question but also at the beginning, upside down. The same principle applies to exclamation marks, as in *¡hola!*. This is a very useful way of signalling 'question (or exclamation) on the way'.

SOUND SPANISH

`z` `ce` `ci` as in *cerveza*, *gracias*. Pronounced like the English 'th' of 'thin' or 'theme'. Practise with this phrase: *Cinco cervezas y un zumo de fruta – gracias.*

Notice that c is only pronounced 'th' when it's followed by **e** or **i**. Otherwise it's pronounced like the English c in 'car' or 'crisps': *cinco, un café, una tónica.*

WORKOUT

1 Just imagine

What would you say in the following situations?

a   You meet someone for the first time. She shakes your hand and says *'Encantada'*.

b   You meet a Spanish friend in the street.

c   You're introduced to the local mayor.

d   You're introduced to the young lifeguard on the beach. He says *'Hola. ¿Qué tal?'*.

e   You meet a friend who hasn't been well.

f   You meet the elderly Spanish man from the flat next door. He hasn't been well either.

2 Answerback

Reply to these questions or statements as suggested.

a   A Spanish friend says to you in a bar: *¿Qué quieres tomar?* You'd like a tonic water – what do you say?

b   He asks some of your English-speaking friends too. Tell your friend they'd like a tomato juice, a black coffee and a beer.

c   A friend of the Spaniard's is introduced to you. There are three things you could say – can you remember one of them?

d   You want to introduce some of your friends too. They are Jane, Christine and David – how do you introduce them?

3 The big match

Match the question or statement in the left-hand column with the most likely answer from the right-hand column.

a	¿Qué tomas?	i	Muy bien, gracias.
b	Mucho gusto.	ii	Para mí, por favor.
c	¿Qué tal?	iii	Un zumo de naranja, por favor.
d	Esta es mi mujer, Montse.	iv	Sí, gracias.
e	¿La cerveza?	v	Mucho gusto, Montse.
f	¿Quieres tomar una cerveza?	vi	Encantado.

4 Barred

All the drinks listed in *Keywords* are included in this wordsearch – bar one. Which is it? Read in a straight line, up, down or across, backwards or forwards.

```
E  H  C  E  L  O  M
A  R  N  B  G  S  T
T  O  M  A  T  E  R
C  E  R  V  E  Z  A
A  S  A  N  C  U  P
F  O  N  M  H  M  E
E  L  J  R  E  O  D
D  O  A  S  T  L  N
```

5 Beginnings and ends

Here are some words and phrases with which conversations often begin or end in Spanish – but only the beginnings and ends of the words are given! Can you fill the rest in?

a   B _ _ _ _ s d _ _ s

b   A _ _ _ s

c   H _ _ a

d   H _ _ _ a l _ _ o

e   ¿Q _ é t _ l?

f   B _ _ _ _ s n _ _ _ _ s

6 Family ties

Some words describing family relationships are linked together in this crossword. Try to fill them in with the help of the clues.

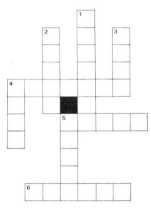

Across
4 My mother's other son
5 My brother's mother
6 The person a woman is married to

Down
1 My father's daughter
2 My mother's husband
3 Male offspring
4 Female offspring
5 The lady I'm married to

7 A question of family

Each member of the Spanish Royal Family introduces some of the other members. Can you work out who's speaking each time?

Elena, Felipe, el Rey Juan Carlos, La Reina Sofía, Cristina

a   Esta es mi hermana, la Princesa Elena, y éste es mi hermano, el Príncipe Felipe.
b   Esta es mi madre, la Reina Sofía, y éstas son mis hermanas.
c   Esta es mi mujer, Reina de España y antes Princesa de Grecia.
d   Esta es mi hermana, la Princesa Cristina, y éste es mi padre, el Rey de España.
e   How would the Queen introduce the rest of her family?

8 Casting

Can you 'script' the dialogue with the waiter so that these five people get the drinks they want?

Waiter	¿El zumo de naranja, por favor?
....	Para mí.
....	¿Y el café solo?
....	Para mí, por favor.
....	¿Las cervezas?
....	Para mí, y para el señor.
....	Y el café con leche para usted, ¿no?
....	Sí, gracias.
Waiter	De nada.

9 Odd one out

a Which of these wouldn't you drink?
   un zumo   una cerveza   un café   una hija

b Which wouldn't you have *con leche*?
   un café   una tónica   un té

c Which phrase wouldn't you use to say 'hello'?
   hola   ¿qué tal?   por favor   buenas noches

d Which of these couldn't be said by a woman?
   soy irlandés   encantada
   mucho gusto   soy española

e Which of these isn't a man?
   novio   hermano   mujer   hijo

ABOUT SPAIN

Introductions

People don't only shake hands when introduced but
also when they meet (or say goodbye to) someone
they already know. Amongst friends it's customary
for a man and a woman or two women to exchange
kisses (one on each cheek).

Titles (what to call people)

It's easy and normal to use first names with someone
you've just met. If you want to use a person's
surname, just put *Señor* or *Señora* in front of it – it's
the equivalent of 'Mr' or 'Mrs'. A respectful way of
addressing someone is to put *Don* or *Doña* in front
of their first name: *Don José, Doña Asunción*. But
it's best not to do this until you've heard someone
else do it first.

Drinks

If you're feeling thirsty, look for the sign *café, cafetería* or *bar*. Drinking hours are much more flexible
than in Britain, cafés staying open till the early hours,
especially in the summer. Having a drink is an
occasion to watch the world go by, especially if
you're outside on the *terraza*; but remember that
here the prices are higher than at the bar (*barra*).
You normally pay after you've had the drink, and
although a 10% tip is not necessarily expected,
people usually leave the small change.

El paseo

A stroll before supper or before Sunday lunch is an
important Spanish custom for people of all ages and
classes. It's a time to be seen, to meet friends and to
chat, and it's often punctuated by brief stops at bars
for *un aperitivo*. The old streets and *plazas* of many
Spanish towns, and broad avenues like Las Ramblas
in Barcelona, are favourite spots for *el paseo*.

Paseo in the Plaza Mayor

Spanish wine

Most Spanish regions produce their own wine, so wherever you go you'll find a cheap local *vino de mesa*, be it *tinto*, *blanco* or *rosado* (red, white or rosé). But if you want something a bit more special then ask for one of the classified wines (labelled *denominado de origen*). The best known amongst these are probably the reds of La Rioja, which get a distinctive flavour from being matured in oak casks; the whites of Penedés in Cataluña; and of course the different kinds of sherry from Jerez. *Finos* are the light, dry sherries that are very popular in the south. Spain's champagne-method wine comes from Cataluña and is called *cava*.

3 De compras

Shopping for food

Talking about family and friends

SPANISH LIVE

1 Concha Rincón is buying fruit and vegetables at a covered market in Santander.

Concha	Hola, buenos días. Un kilo de naranjas, por favor. *(the stallholder weighs the oranges and notes down the price)*
Stallholder	¿Algo más?
Concha	Sí. Medio kilo de tomates. Y también una lechuga.
Stallholder	Muy bien. ¿Algo más?

To ask for something by weight:
un kilo de naranjas, por favor
a kilo of oranges, please
medio kilo de tomates
half a kilo of tomatoes

The open-air market in Santander

Concha	No, eso es todo. ¿Cuánto es?
Stallholder	Doscientas cincuenta pesetas.
	(*Concha pays*)
Concha	Gracias, adiós.
Stallholder	Adiós, buenos días.

¿algo más?	*anything else?*
también	*also*
lechuga	*lettuce*
eso es todo	*that's all*
doscientas	*two hundred and*
cincuenta pesetas	*fifty pesetas*

▶ **Spotcheck 1**   a   How many items does Concha buy?

                   b   How many lettuces does she get?

📺 **2**   Vera Fernández goes to the cold meat and cheese counter in a grocer's – *Mantequerías El Pilar* – in Santander.

> To ask how much it is:
> ¿cuánto es?

Vera	Hola, buenas tardes.
Shopkeeper	Buenas tardes. ¿Qué desea?
Vera	Ciento cincuenta gramos de jamón de York, por favor.
	(*the shopkeeper slices the ham and weighs it*)
Vera	Y cuarto kilo de este queso manchego.
Shopkeeper	(*cuts and weighs the cheese*) ¿Algo más?

The reply may be:

son cincuenta pesetas	*that's 50 pesetas*
son quinientas pesetas	*that's 500 pesetas*
son mil pesetas	*that's 1000 pesetas*

Vera	Sí, una botella de leche.	
Shopkeeper	La leche está allí. *(the shopkeeper gets the milk and joins Vera at the till)*	
Vera	Gracias. ¿Cuánto es todo?	
Shopkeeper	Son quinientas noventa pesetas. *(cashier rings up the total, and Vera pays)*	
Cashier	Gracias.	
Vera	Adiós.	
Shopkeeper	Adiós.	

¿qué desea?	*what would you like?*
ciento cincuenta gramos	*one hundred and fifty grams*
jamón de York	*cooked ham*
cuarto kilo	*a quarter of a kilo*
queso manchego	*cheese from La Mancha*
botella de leche	*bottle of milk*
está allí	*is there*
son	*that's, that comes to*
noventa	*ninety*

▶ **Spotcheck 2**

a Does Vera buy more ham than cheese?

b How much does she pay altogether?

Ⓡ **3** In a grocer's shop in Haro, in the Rioja region, Isabel buys some food and a drink for a picnic.

Isabel	Hola, buenos días.
Shopkeeper	Buenos días.
Isabel	Vamos a ver. ¿Tiene pan?
Shopkeeper	Sí.
Isabel	Pues, una barra mediana, por favor. *(the shopkeeper gets a loaf)* Esa es muy grande. Pues ésta más pequeña, por favor.
Shopkeeper	Muy bien.
Isabel	Eh, ¿qué más? Pues, unas patatas fritas. ¿Tiene patatas fritas?
Shopkeeper	Sí. ¿Bolsa grande o pequeña?
Isabel	Bolsa grande. No, por favor, pequeña.
Shopkeeper	¿Esta?
Isabel	Sí, ésta, por favor.
Shopkeeper	¿Algo más?
Isabel	¿Qué más? Eh, ¿tiene jamón?
Shopkeeper	Sí. ¿De York o serrano?
Isabel	Serrano, por favor. Cien gramos de serrano. *(the shopkeeper slices the ham)*
Shopkeeper	Cien gramos. ¿Algo más?
Isabel	Sí, por favor. Una botella de agua y una botella de vino.

To ask if a shopkeeper has something:

¿tiene pan?	*have you got any bread?*
¿tiene una bolsa?	*have you got a bag?*

The shopkeeper may ask you if you want anything else:
¿algo más? or
¿qué más?

If you don't want anything else:
no, gracias
nada más

Shopkeeper	Vino de Rioja, ¿no?
Isabel	Sí, por favor, sí.
Shopkeeper	¿Blanco o tinto?
Isabel	Tinto.
Shopkeeper	Tinto, muy bien.

vamos a ver	*let's see*
barra mediana	*medium stick-loaf*
muy grande	*very big*
más pequeña	*smaller*
unas patatas fritas	*some crisps*
jamón serrano	*ham (naturally cured)*
cien gramos	*a hundred grams*
agua	*water*
vino	*wine*
blanco o tinto	*white or red (wine)*

▶ Spotcheck 3
a What size loaf did Isabel want?
b How much ham did she buy?

Ⓡ 4 Mamie's a bit young to have a boyfriend, but Isabel asked her anyway.

Isabel	¿Cómo te llamas?
Mamie	Mamie.
Isabel	Mamie. ¿Y cuántos años tienes?
Mamie	Ocho.
Isabel	Dime, Mamie, ¿tienes novio?
Mamie	¡No! No tengo.
Isabel	No tienes. ¿Pero tienes amigos, a que sí?
Mamie	Sí.
Isabel	¿Muchos?
Mamie	Sí, del colegio.
Isabel	Sí. ¿Cómo se llama tu colegio?
Mamie	Arquitecto Gaudí.
Isabel	Arquitecto Gaudí.

To ask someone their age:
¿cuántos años tienes?

And the reply:

tengo diez años	*I'm ten*
tengo veinte años	*I'm twenty*

ocho	*eight*
dime	*tell me*
no tengo	*I haven't*
pero	*but*
a que sí	*I'll bet*
muchos	*a lot*
del colegio	*from school*

▶ Spotcheck 4 What has Mamie got a lot of?

Mamie

Las Ramblas in
Barcelona

® 5 Mercedes Peralta is a single parent, living and
working in Barcelona.

Jordi	Hola. ¿Cómo te llamas?
Mercedes	Me llamo Mercedes Peralta.
Jordi	¿Cuántos años tienes?
Mercedes	Solamente veintiocho.
Jordi	¿Cómo se llaman tus hijos?
Mercedes	Salvador, y Diana.
Jordi	¿Cuántos años tienen Salvador y Diana?
Mercedes	Salvador tiene nueve años y Diana ocho.

solamente	*only*
veintiocho	*twenty-eight*
nueve	*nine*

To ask someone another person's
name:

¿cómo se   *what's your son's/*
  llama su   *daughter's name?*
  hijo/hija?

or less formally:
¿cómo se llama tu hijo/hija?

▶ **Spotcheck 5**   a   What is Mercedes' son called?
                    b   How old is her daughter?

KEYWORDS

el mercado	market
el supermercado	supermarket
el jamón	ham
el queso	cheese
el pan	bread
el vino	wine

(*for more food see p. 207*)

un kilo	a kilo
medio kilo	half a kilo (about a pound)
un cuarto de kilo	a quarter of a kilo (about half a pound)
cien gramos	a hundred grams
la botella	bottle
la bolsa	bag
grande	big, large
pequeño/a	small
nada más	nothing else
¿cuánto?	how much?
¿cuántos/as?	how many?
el año	year
uno	one
dos	two
tres	three
treinta	thirty
cien	a hundred
trescientos	three hundred
mil	a thousand
tres mil	three thousand

(*for numbers see p. 205*)

¿tiene?	do you have?
¿tienes?	do you have? (less formal)
tengo	I have

HOW SPANISH WORKS

1 More than one
When you're talking about more than one of anything, you add

-*s* if the word ends in *a e o*:

naranja	naranjas
tomate	tomates
kilo	kilos

-*es* if it ends in a consonant: *mujer* *mujeres*

The words for 'the' also change:
el *tomate*   **los** *tomates*
la *patata*   **las** *patatas*

2 Missing any?
When asking for something in English we often use the word 'any': 'have you got any oranges?'.
In Spanish you don't need to use a word for 'any': *¿tiene naranjas?*.

3 All shapes and sizes
When you describe a thing (or a person) in Spanish, notice that the describing word generally comes **after** the word it describes: *una bolsa **grande**; queso **manchego**; patatas **fritas***.

4 An age-old question
The way to ask someone their age in Spanish is: *¿cuántos años tienes?*. Word for word this is 'how many years do you have?', so the reply is *tengo dieciocho años* – literally 'I have eighteen years'.

5 Have and have got
There are different ways of saying 'have' or 'has' in Spanish, depending on **who** it is that's doing the having:
'I have' or 'I've got' is *tengo*
'you've got' is *tienes* or *tiene*
'he/she's got' is *tiene*
'they've got' is *tienen*

When you're **asking** if someone's got something – in a shop for instance – you use *¿tiene . . .?* or, less formally, *¿tienes . . .?*.

As usual you don't need a separate word for 'I', 'you', etc.

6 Do it by numbers

There's a table of Spanish numbers on p. 205. Don't try to learn them all at once, but do try to learn, say, five a week. And when you learn, for example, *dos* ('two'), learn also *doscientos* ('two hundred') and *dos mil* ('two thousand').

Notice that
– *un hermano* can mean '**one** brother' as well as 'a brother', and *una hermana* can mean '**one** sister' and 'a sister'

– when used with *pesetas*, the 'hundred' words from 200 onwards end in -*as*: *doscient**as** pesetas; trescient**as** veinte pesetas*

– you don't need the word for 'a' with 100 or 1000: *cien pesetas* – 'a hundred pesetas'; *mil pesetas* – 'a thousand pesetas'.

SOUND SPANISH

j **ge** **gi** as in *naranja, mujer, Gerónimo, ginebra* (gin), *Gijón* (the town). This is pronounced something like an English 'h' said at the back of the throat, or like a Scottish 'ch' in the word 'loch'. Practise with the phrase: *el jamón del bar Gijón es famoso en Gerona.*

Notice that **g** before any letter other than **e** or **i** is pronounced like the English 'g' in 'got': *Granada, Gales, algo.*

WORKOUT

1 As if you were there

Find the right word or phrase for these situations.
a   You walk into a greengrocer's: say 'good morning' and ask the lady behind the counter if she has any oranges.
b   She does. Ask for two kilos.
c   You see some nice tomatoes – ask for half a kilo.
d   The lady serves you, and says: *'Muy bien. ¿Algo más?'*. What do you say if that's all you wanted?
e   Ask how much it is.
f   You hear the reply: *'Doscientas diez pesetas'*. How much change should you expect from a 500 peseta note?
g   Thank the lady and say goodbye.

2 Matching numbers

Match the money in the pictures with the written numbers.
a   Seiscientas cincuenta pesetas.
b   Cuatrocientas setenta y cinco pesetas.
c   Treinta y cinco pesetas.
d   Cincuenta y cinco pesetas.
e   Ochenta y cinco pesetas.
f   Trescientas treinta pesetas.

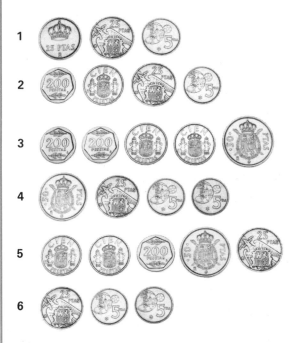

3 Mix-up

Not a mix-up in prices fortunately – simply in the order of the phrases in a shopping dialogue between a customer and a shopkeeper. Try to sort them out and write them down in the right order.

Customer	Nada más, gracias. ¿Cuánto es?
Customer	Buenas tardes. ¿Tiene queso?
Customer	Doscientos cincuenta gramos de queso manchego, por favor.
Customer	Aquí tiene quinientas.
Shopkeeper	¿Serrano o de York?
Shopkeeper	Sí, tenemos queso manchego, queso gallego . . .
Customer	Serrano, por favor.
Shopkeeper	¿Algo más?

Shopkeeper	Manchego, muy bien. ¿Algo más?
Shopkeeper	Buenas tardes.
Customer	Sí, cien gramos de jamón.
Shopkeeper	Son cuatrocientas cuarenta y cinco pesetas.
Shopkeeper	Y cincuenta y cinco son quinientas. Adiós.
Customer	Adiós, buenas tardes.

4 Family tree

Use the family tree to help fill in the gaps in the sentences below.

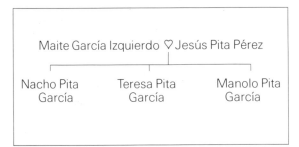

Maite García Izquierdo ♡ Jesús Pita Pérez

Nacho Pita García — Teresa Pita García — Manolo Pita García

a Jesús es el .... de Maite.
b Maite y Jesús tienen .... hijos.
c Tienen dos .... y una ....
d Maite García .... es la .... de Nacho, Teresa y Manolo. Jesús Pita es el ....
e Nacho y Teresa son ....
f Su hermano pequeño es ....

5 Weigh-in

You're making a meal for six people, and go shopping for some of the items. For each item given, select the most likely weight or quantity. Assume average appetites. (The answers in the *Key* are suggestions only!)

a jamón serrano *(for starter)* — cincuenta gramos/trescientos cincuenta gramos
b queso *(final course)* — tres kilos/medio kilo
c naranjas *(part of dessert)* — un cuarto de kilo/un kilo
d limones *(for juice for fish)* — dos/diez
e pan — una barra pequeña/dos barras grandes

6 Sieve

It's easily done! You've been shopping with a well-prepared list, and yet when you come back you find you've forgotten something. Check the items with the list, and make a note of what you may have to go back for.

250g jamón de York
½ kilo de queso
zumo de naranja
vino tinto
melón
botella de leche
lechuga
1 kilo de tomates
limones.
pan. (2 barras)

7 Anagrams

Each of these anagrams is a word or phrase commonly used in shopping. Can you find them all in less than two minutes? To make things easier, accents and question marks have been put in.

a OTESSEDOO
b ROVAFORP
c ¿INEET?
d ASMANDÁ
e ¿GOÁLAMS?
f ¿UTONSECÁ?

8 Overheard

From these snatches of conversation, can you put ages on the family shown?

- ... y mi hermana se llama Mercedes.
- ¿Cuántos años tiene?
- Pues, ella tiene cuatro, y mi hermano Pablo siete.
- ... ¿Mis padres? Pues, mi padre se llama Julio y creo que tiene treinta y siete años.
- ¿Cómo te llamas tú?
- ¿Yo? Amparo. ... mi madre tiene treinta y seis años, y se llama Cristina.
- ... y tú, ¿cuántos años tienes?
- Yo tengo nueve años.

9 Interference

You're sitting in a café, minding your own business, but you can't help overhearing a conversation between the waiter and a young woman at the next table. Unfortunately, the traffic noise drowns some of the words. Fill in the gaps.

Waiter   Hola. ¿Qué quieres?
Woman   Un café con ...., ... favor.
Waiter   ¿......... de aquí?
Woman   No, ... Cuenca.
Waiter   ¿......... familia aquí?
Woman   Sí, ... hermano aquí.

Just then, a small boy and girl run up to the table and sit down ...

Woman   Y éstos son mis ....
Waiter   ¿Cómo se llaman?
Woman   .... Pedro y María.
Waiter   *(to María)* Hola, María. ¿Cuántos .... tienes?
María   .... siete, y mi hermano .... cuatro.
Waiter   *(to their mother)* ¿Qué van a tomar?
Woman   Dos .... de naranja, ...
Waiter   Ahora mismo.

10 Odd one out

a   Which would you buy if you wanted traditional Spanish ham?
jamón serrano   queso manchego   jamón de York

b   You want about a quarter of a pound – which is nearest?
medio kilo   cien gramos
doscientos cincuenta gramos

c   You've got a 50-peseta coin. Is that
quince pesetas   cinco pesetas
cincuenta pesetas

d   You're allergic to dairy produce. Which of these do you buy?
lechuga   leche   queso

e   You want a bottle. Is that
una bolsa   una botella   una barra

f   Which of these wouldn't you put in a salad?
leche   lechuga   tomates

ABOUT SPAIN

Money
The *peseta* is the unit of currency. There are notes for 200, 500, 1000, 2000, 5000 and 10 000 pesetas, and coins for 1, 2, 5, 10, 25, 50, 100 and 200. Eurocheques are easy to cash at banks, as well as traveller's cheques. Credit cards are accepted in large stores and tourist shops, but are less generally used than in Britain (garages rarely accept them, for example).

Weights and measures
The metric system is used for weight and liquid measures. For those who are more used to the Imperial system, some rough equivalents are:
1 kilo = just over 2 lb (2.2)
500 gramos = just over 1 lb
100 gramos = 4 oz
1 litro = just under 2 pints (1.8)
5 litros = just over a gallon

Food and food shops
One of the delights of being in Spain is going to the local market *(el mercado)*. In small towns there's usually a weekly street market, and in larger towns there are permanent covered markets. Supermarkets *(supermercados)* are common. Things to look out for – and at least try – are: *jamón serrano* (naturally cured ham), *queso manchego*, and a range of spicy cooked sausages such as *chorizo, salchichón, longaniza*.

Bread is sold in *panaderías*. Cake shops *(pastelerías)* are sometimes combined with the bread shop. Cakes for special occasions, such as birthdays or Sunday evening, can be elaborate and are beautifully wrapped.

4 ¿Dónde?

Asking where places are

Understanding simple directions

Explaining where you live

SPANISH LIVE

1 Aurelio García arrives in Santander by car, and asks a passer-by where the Hotel Sardinero is.

Aurelio	Por favor, ¿dónde está el Hotel Sardinero?
Passer-by	Sí, mire. Aquí a la derecha, y al final a la izquierda. El hotel está a mano izquierda.
Aurelio	Muy bien. Gracias.
Passer-by	De nada. Adiós.

mire	look
al final	at the end
a mano izquierda	on the left

To ask where something is:
por favor, ¿dónde está ...?

The replies you may hear:
a la derecha   *to the right*
a la izquierda   *to the left*

▶ **Spotcheck 1**   Where does Aurelio have to turn left?

TV 2   A tourist in Santillana is looking for the *parador*
(State-owned hotel).

The parador in
Santillana del Mar

Tourist	Por favor, ¿dónde está el parador?
Passer-by	Mire. Coja la segunda calle a la derecha y la primera a la izquierda, y el parador está en la plaza, a mano izquierda.
Tourist	¿Está lejos?
Passer-by	No, a tres minutos andando.
Tourist	Gracias, adiós.
Passer-by	Adiós.

To ask if something is far:
¿está lejos?

The replies you may hear:
a tres minutos	*three minutes away*
a tres kilómetros	*three kilo- metres away*

coja	*take*
la primera, segunda calle	*the first, second street*
en la plaza	*in the square*
andando	*on foot*

▶Spotcheck 2   a   Which way does the tourist have to turn first?
b   Which side of the square is the *parador* on?

3 José María Pertusa draws up to ask a passer-by the way to a campsite on the edge of Santander.

| José María | Por favor, ¿dónde está el Camping Bellavista? |
| Passer-by | El Camping Bellavista ... ¡Ah, sí! Está cerca del faro. *(she points it out on his map)* Mire, estamos aquí. El Camping Bellavista está aquí. Siga derecho, todo recto, por esta carretera. |

| (todo) recto | |
| (todo) derecho | *straight on* |

el camping	*campsite*
cerca del faro	*near the lighthouse*
siga	*carry on*
por esta carretera	*along this road*

▶ **Spotcheck 3** What landmark is the campsite near?

4 It's likely that the Calle del Prado leads to the Prado Museum, but, just to make sure, Isabel checks with a passer-by.

| Isabel | Por favor, ¿el Museo del Prado? |
| Passer-by | Sí, mire, baja usted por esa calle, que es la calle del Prado. Al final llega usted al Paseo del Prado, y enfrente está el museo. |

baja usted	*you go down*
esa calle	*that street*
llega usted	*you arrive*
enfrente	*opposite*

▶ **Spotcheck 4** Where's the Paseo del Prado?

▲ Isabel asks the way to the Prado

◄ Museo del Prado, Madrid

® 5 In a large restaurant there's no sign of the toilets, so Isabel asks the waitress.

Isabel	¿Dónde están los servicios, por favor?
Waitress	Saliendo del salón, a la derecha, la segunda puerta.
Isabel	O sea, saliendo del salón y la se- . . .
Waitress	Al patio, al patio, a la derecha.
Isabel	La segunda puerta a la derecha.
Waitress	Sí.
Isabel	Muchas gracias, ¿eh?

saliendo del salón	*as you leave the room*
puerta	*door*
o sea	*so*
patio	*courtyard*

To ask where the toilets are:
¿dónde están los servicios?

▶ **Spotcheck 5** Which door leads to the toilets?

Los servicios

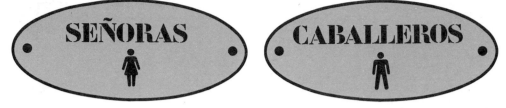

® **6** These three people live in Madrid – they explain whereabouts.

Isabel ¿Dónde vives?

Ana Schöbel Vivo en Madrid, en el barrio de Chamberí. Yo vivo en una calle muy pequeña, que se llama la calle de Españoleto.

Ana Gamarra ¿En qué piso vives?

Isabel Pues mira, vivo en Toledo, la calle Toledo (sí), número cuatro (sí), casi en la Plaza Mayor, piso segundo derecha.

Isabel ¿Y dónde vives, Mamie?

Mamie En Maestro Chapí.

Isabel ¿En dónde?

Mamie Maestro Chapí, veintiuno.

Isabel ¿Y dónde está Maestro Chapí?

Mamie En España.

Isabel ¿En España?

Mamie Sí.

Isabel ¿Y en Madrid?

Mamie Sí.

Isabel ¿Y vives en un piso, Mamie?

Mamie No.

Isabel ¿Dónde vives?

Mamie En un chalet.

Isabel En un chalet. ¿Y tiene jardín?

Mamie Sí.

To ask where someone lives:

¿dónde vive usted?

¿dónde vives?   (less formal)

To say where you live:

vivo en ...

barrio	*district*
¿en qué piso?	*on which floor?*
pues mira	*well*
casi	*almost*
Maestro Chapí	= Calle Maestro Chapí
piso	*flat*
chalet	*(detached) house*
jardín	*garden*

▶Spotcheck 6 a Who lives in a second-floor flat?

b Who lives in a small street?

KEYWORDS

coja	take
siga	follow
(todo) recto	straight on
(todo) derecho	straight on
a la derecha	to/on the right
a la izquierda	to/on the left
lejos (de)	far (from)
cerca (de)	near (to)
primero/a	first
segundo/a	second
tercero/a	third
el minuto	minute
el kilómetro	kilometre
la calle	street
la plaza	square
el centro	centre
las afueras	outskirts
el hotel	hotel
el piso	flat
la casa	house
los servicios	toilets
la ciudad	town, city
el pueblo	small town, village
en	in
vivo	I live
vives	you live
vive	you live or he/she lives
está	is
están	are

HOW SPANISH WORKS

1   Being

Está and *es* can both mean 'is'. *Está* is used to talk about **where** someone (or something) is:
José está en el hotel
or how someone's feeling:
José está bien

The other word, *es*, is used to say who someone is, where he or she is from:
éste es José
José es mi hermano
José es de Madrid

2   Living

In English, if someone asks you 'where do you live?', you might reply 'I live in . . .'. The word 'live' doesn't change whether it's '**you** live' or '**I** live'. But Spanish is different:
*¿dónde viv**es**? – viv**o** en . . .*

In Spanish, all words like this (verbs) change depending on who is being referred to. Remember *tengo, tienes, tiene* (I have, you have, he/she has).

Notice that the part of the verb used with *usted* can also be used to refer to other people:
tiene una casa   you have a house
                    or he has a house
                    or she has a house

There is a pattern to these changes which we'll go into in Unit 7.

3   Joining forces

De can mean either 'from' or 'of' in English:
soy de Santander   I'm **from** Santander
un kilo de naranjas   a kilo **of** oranges

A can also have different English meanings:
a la derecha   **to** the right, **on** the right
a tres kilómetros   three kilometres **away**

If either *a* or *de* is followed by the word *el* ('the'), they join up with it to form just one word:
*saliendo **del** salón*   as you go out **of the** room
***al** final de la calle*   **at the** end of the street

4   Gender benders

Remember that most nouns that end in *-o* are masculine and go with *un* or *el*, and the ones that end in *-a* are feminine and go with *una* or *la*. There are a few exceptions which can be confusing, eg *la mano*, *el mapa*, and other cases where you can't tell, eg *la calle*. So it's best to make a note of the gender as you learn each new noun.

SOUND SPANISH

ll as in *¿cómo te llamas?*. It's very like the 'li' in the English word 'familiar' or 'lli' in 'million'. Practise with: *¿Cómo se llama esta calle?. Se llama calle de Mallorca.*

WORKOUT

1 Getting there

Use *¿dónde está ...?* or *¿dónde están ...?* to ask where these places are:

2 Pathfinder

Match one of the three symbols with each set of directions.

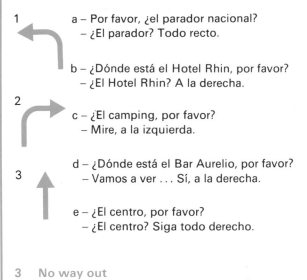

1

a – Por favor, ¿el parador nacional?
– ¿El parador? Todo recto.

b – ¿Dónde está el Hotel Rhin, por favor?
– ¿El Hotel Rhin? A la derecha.

2

c – ¿El camping, por favor?
– Mire, a la izquierda.

d – ¿Dónde está el Bar Aurelio, por favor?
– Vamos a ver ... Sí, a la derecha.

3

e – ¿El centro, por favor?
– ¿El centro? Siga todo derecho.

3 No way out

You're visiting a friend in a big block of flats. The lift doors get stuck. There's an elderly (and rather talkative) Spanish woman with you in the lift. Fill in your part of the conversation in Spanish.

Woman ¿Usted vive aquí?
You (Say no, you have a friend here.)
Woman ¿Cómo se llama?
You (Say he's called Santiago Jiménez. He lives on the second floor.)
Woman Ah sí, el señor Jiménez. Vive con su madre, ¿no es éste?
You (Say no, he has a wife and a daughter.)
Woman Ah sí, el señor Jiménez – en el segundo piso, sí. Mi hermana vive en el segundo piso también.
You (Ask if she has a family.)
Woman Sí, pero no viven aquí. Y usted, ¿de dónde es? Usted no es español, ¿verdad?
You (Say no, you're English and you live in Bristol.)
Woman Tengo un hijo que vive en Inverness. ¿Está cerca de Bristol?
You (Say no, it's in Scotland, 600 kilometres away.)

(At that moment, the lift doors open. You say goodbye and hurry away.)

4 On the map

Which letter on the map identifies the following places?

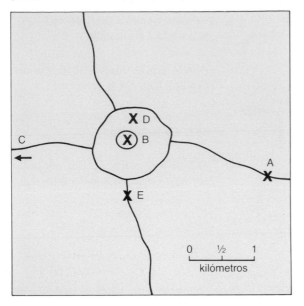

a Está cerca del centro.
b Está a dos kilómetros.
c Está en el centro.
d Está lejos de la ciudad.
e Está a diez minutos andando.

5 Tracking

Start in the top left-hand corner, go in any direction, one letter at a time, to find some advice you might hear from somebody giving you directions.

```
T T O
O C E
D O R
```

6 Break-up

Break up these strings of letters into words to make three phrases you may hear when asking for directions in the street.

COJALAPRIMERACALLEALADERECHA

SIGATODORECTO

ESTACERCADELCENTRO

7 Eavesdropping

From the information given on their visiting cards, can you say who is speaking in each of these snippets of conversation?

1

Eugenio Pérez Vidal
García Camba, 10, 2º
Pontevedra

2

María Arranz de Ballesteros
Malcampo 5, 3º
Madrid

3

Angel Cobo Pérez
Liérganes (Santander)

4

Milagros Castaño Picón
Bami, 6, 2º
Sevilla

a Vivo en la calle Bami, número 6.
b Soy de un pueblo de la provincia de Santander.
c Vivo en el número 10, segundo piso.
d Vivo no muy lejos del centro de Madrid. Estamos en el tercer piso.
e Soy de Madrid, pero vivo en Pontevedra.
f No vivo en el campo, vivo en una ciudad muy grande. La calle se llama Malcampo.

8 On the right track

Only one of the sets of directions given to get from the Tourist Office (*Oficina de Turismo*) to the Hotel Estrella is correct. With the help of the plan, decide which one. You are facing in the direction of the arrow.

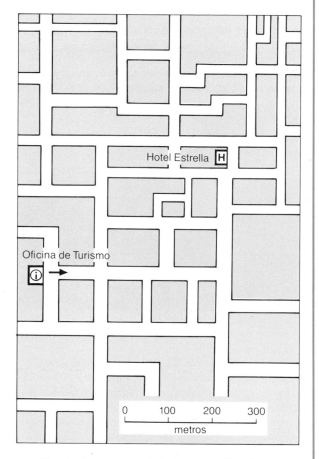

a Siga todo recto y coja la tercera calle a la izquierda. Coja la primera a la derecha, y el hotel está a mano izquierda, a cien metros.

b Siga todo derecho, y coja la primera calle a la izquierda. Luego coja la segunda a la derecha, siga todo recto, coja la segunda a la izquierda, y el hotel está a mano izquierda.

c Siga todo recto y coja la primera calle a la izquierda. Coja la tercera calle a la derecha, y el hotel está al final, a doscientos metros.

9 Odd one out

a It's not very close – which one is it?
aquí cerca   enfrente   lejos

b Where wouldn't you live?
en un supermercado   en una casa   en un piso

c Which of these wouldn't you drive along?
una calle   una carretera   una cerveza

d Where wouldn't you expect a lift to go?
primero   todo recto   segundo

e You want some fresh air – where wouldn't you go?
a los servicios   al jardín   a la calle

f Your hotel's on the edge of town – would that be
en el centro   en las afueras   en los servicios

10 Mmm . . .

Here are five places in Spain, each beginning with M. Match each one with the correct description.

a Está en el centro de España.
b Está cerca de Mallorca. Es una isla.
c Es un pueblo pequeño. Está en la costa, a cincuenta kilómetros de Almería.
d Es una ciudad. Está situada en la Costa del Sol.
e Está en el País Vasco, muy cerca de la ciudad de Vitoria.

ABOUT SPAIN

Madrid

Madrid, in the very centre of Spain, has a population of three and a half million. The old part of the city is to be found around the lovely arcaded square, the *Plaza Mayor*. A short walk away is the *Gran Vía*, which is the main area for shopping and entertainment.

Madrid is divided into districts, each with its own character: for instance, *Chamberí* is a respectable, middle-class area; smart shops are found in *Salamanca*; *Lavapiés* is a traditional working-class district.

One thing Madrid is not famous for is its river, the Manzanares, which is the source of many jokes – but not much water.

Plaza Mayor, centre of old Madrid

Gran Vía, centre of commercial Madrid

Santillana del Mar

Although *mar* means 'sea', Santillana del Mar is in fact tucked away in the rolling green hills behind the Cantabrian coast. It's a small village which grew around an important mediaeval monastery, and despite its size the streets are lined with imposing stone houses built by noble families.

Santillana's inhabitants have adapted to the hordes of summer tourists (up to 15 000 a day – be warned!) by opening a range of hotels and shops. Many little farms and houses sell milk and the local cakes called *sobaos* and *bizcochos*.

La Colegiata, Santillana del Mar

Housing

It's more common in Spain to live in a flat *(piso)* than a house *(casa* or *chalet)*, especially in the towns; and commuting from a distant suburb is a relatively new phenomenon. Blocks of flats in town centres often have a caretaker *(portero* or *portera)* or an intercom system for security.

Addresses can look unfamiliar to British eyes:
Juan Vidal Carrión
c. Alhambra 26, 3º dcha
28012 MADRID

c. = *calle* = street
26 = number of house
3º = third floor
dcha = *derecha* =
   right-hand door
   (izqda = left)
28012 = postcode

De vacaciones

Saying that you're on holiday

What languages you speak

What you think of a place

SPANISH LIVE

®1 In Mojácar during the summer it's surprising to meet people who **aren't** on holiday.

Isabel	¿Está usted de vacaciones?
Woman	No, vivo aquí.
Isabel	Miguel, ¿eres de aquí de Mojácar?
Miguel	Bueno, no soy de Mojácar, soy de Madrid.
Isabel	¿Qué haces aquí en Mojácar? ¿Estás de vacaciones?
Miguel	Bueno, no, no de vacaciones, trabajando.

To ask someone if they're on holiday:
¿está(s) de vacaciones?

In reply you can say

estoy . . .	I'm . . .
. . . de vacaciones	. . . on holiday
. . . trabajando	. . . working
. . . estudiando	. . . studying

Mojácar

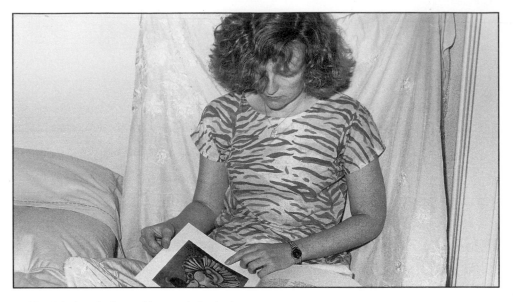

In Madrid, Ana isn't working and she isn't on holiday.

Ana	Yo estoy estudiando.
Isabel	¿Y qué estás estudiando?
Ana	Estoy estudiando restauración de obras de arte para los museos.

bueno	*well*
¿qué haces?	*what are you doing?*
restauración	*restoration*
obras de arte	*works of art*

▶Spotcheck 1   a   Is the woman on holiday?

b   Where is Miguel from?

Ⓡ 2   The official language of Spain is Castilian Spanish, *castellano*. Other regional languages – Basque, Catalan, Galician – are also spoken. This man is from Vich, near Barcelona – so does he speak Catalan?

Isabel	¿Hablas catalán?
Man	Sí, hablo catalán.
Isabel	Entonces, hablas catalán, castellano, ¿y otros idiomas?
Man	Y francés, hablo francés.

What about his girlfriend, who is from León in Castilla?

Isabel	¿Tú hablas catalán?
Woman	No. Estoy aprendiendo.

To ask if someone speaks a foreign language:

¿habla(s)	inglés?
	español?
	francés?

To say what languages you speak:

hablo	inglés
	español
	francés

Isabel	¿Es difícil?
Woman	Sí, es bastante difícil.

And does this passer-by speak any English?

Isabel	¿Hablas inglés?
Woman	Un poquito.

entonces	*so*
otros idiomas	*other languages*
francés	*French*
estoy aprendiendo	*I'm learning*
difícil	*difficult*
bastante	*fairly*
un poquito	*a little bit*

▶ Spotcheck 2   How many of the people claim to speak some English?

📺 3   How well do ordinary Spaniards speak foreign languages? Yolanda goes along the beach at Santander to find out.

Yolanda	¿Qué tal habla inglés?
Holidaymaker 1	Muy mal.
Yolanda	¿Habla idiomas extranjeros?
Holidaymaker 2	Ninguno.
Yolanda	¿Ni un poquito?
Holidaymaker 2	No.

To say how well you speak a language:

bastante bien	*quite well*
un poco	*a bit*
muy mal	*very badly*

Holidaymaker 3	Hablo inglés, hablo francés un poco, alemán un poco e italiano regular.
Yolanda	¿Qué tal hablas inglés?
Holidaymaker 3	Bastante bien.
Yolanda	¿Habla idiomas extranjeros?
Holidaymaker 4	Hablo italiano, portugués, latín.
Yolanda	¿Qué tal habla italiano?
Holidaymaker 4	Bastante regular.
Yolanda	¿Y el portugués?
Holidaymaker 4	Un poco peor.
Yolanda	¿Y el latín?
Holidaymaker 4	Muy bien.

¿qué tal . . . ?	*how well . . . ?*
extranjeros	*foreign*
ninguno	*none*
ni	*not even*
alemán	*German*
e	*and*
regular	*so-so*
peor	*worse*

▶Spotcheck 3 Who speaks most languages?

Ⓡ 4 Isabel asked the woman who ran the *estanco* (tobacconist's) in Mojácar if she liked living there. Her name was Isabel as well – Isabel Alarcón.

Isabel Soto	¿Está usted de vacaciones?
Isabel	No, vivo aquí, justo en la costa.
Isabel Soto	¿Le gusta la playa?
Isabel	¡Muchísimo!
Isabel Soto	¿Le gusta la montaña?
Isabel	También.
Isabel Soto	Aquí en Mojácar tiene las dos cosas. ¿Es usted de aquí de Mojácar?
Isabel	Sí.
Isabel Soto	¿Le gusta el pueblo?
Isabel	Mucho.
Isabel Soto	¿Sí?
Isabel	Sí.

justo	*right*
playa	*beach*
muchísimo	*enormously*
montaña	*mountains*
las dos cosas	*both things*
mucho	*a lot*

To ask if someone likes something:

¿le gusta	la montaña? Mojácar?

and less formally

¿te gusta	la playa? Santillana?

Isabel Alarcón

▶Spotcheck 4 What does Isabel seem to like most?

Valle de Liébana,
Picos de Europa

TV 5 What do visitors to Santander like about the area?
Yolanda stops some to find out.

Yolanda	¿Te gusta Santander?
Passer-by 1	Sí, me gusta mucho Santander.
Yolanda	¿Por qué te gusta?
Passer-by 1	Pues, me gusta Santander porque es muy bonito, es muy divertido.
Passer-by 2	Muy tranquilo, muy verde, un mar muy limpio.

¿por qué?	*why?*
porque	*because*
bonito	*pretty*
divertido	*lively*
tranquilo	*quiet*
verde	*green*
mar	*sea*
limpio	*clean*

To say if you like something:

me gusta	*I like it*
me gusta mucho	*I like it a lot*
no me gusta	*I don't like it*

▶ **Spotcheck 5** Two contrasting descriptions of Santander are given – what are they?

Extra dialogue
p 168

KEYWORDS

las vacaciones	holidays
mal	badly
un poco, un poquito	a little bit
bastante	quite (a lot)
mucho	a lot
el español	Spanish
el inglés	English
el francés	French
(for more languages see p. 210)	
la playa	beach, seaside
la montaña	mountains
el campo	country(side)
el mar	sea
bonito/a	nice, pretty
divertido/a	lively; enjoyable
tranquilo/a	quiet
hablo	I speak
hablas	you speak
habla	you speak or he/she speaks
estoy	I am
estás	you are
está	you are or he/she is
estudiando	studying
trabajando	working
de vacaciones	on holiday
me gusta	I like
te gusta	you like
le gusta	you like or he/she likes

HOW SPANISH WORKS

1   What you're up to

You saw in Unit 4 how *está* is used to describe where a place is: *está a mano izquierda* – 'it's on the left'. The same word is used to talk about what someone **is doing**:

¿está de vacaciones?   are you on holiday?
– and the less formal version is *¿estás de vacaciones?*

When you're answering the question, the key word is *estoy* – 'I'm':

estoy de vacaciones   I'm on holiday
estoy trabajando   I'm working

-ando or *-iendo* at the end of a Spanish word is usually the equivalent of the English '-ing'.

2   As you like it

There's no word-for-word translation of 'I like ...' in Spanish. Instead you have to say '... pleases me'. So 'I like the beach' is: *me gusta la playa*.

To ask if someone else likes it: *¿le gusta la playa?* or *¿te gusta la playa?* (less formal). If more than one thing is involved, use *gustan*: *¿te gustan las ciudades grandes?* – 'do you like big cities?'.

3   Being negative

No, of course, means 'no'. It can also mean 'not':

no estoy trabajando   I'm not working
no soy de aquí   I'm not from here
no hablo francés   I don't speak French

The two meanings of *no* often occur in the same sentence:

¿Eres española? – No, no soy española, soy escocesa

4   Happy endings

A descriptive word like *bonito* (pretty) or *pequeño* (little) has a different ending according to the noun it's describing. The endings *-o* and *-os* go with masculine nouns, *-a* and *-as* with feminine nouns:

un pueblo bonito   *una calle bonita*
pueblos bonitos   *calles bonitas*

But when the descriptive word (adjective) ends in *-e*, like *interesante* or *grande*, the only change you have to make is to add *-s* for the plural:

un hotel grande   *una casa grande*
hoteles grandes   *casas grandes*

SOUND SPANISH

i   as in *vivo*. Pronounced something like the 'ee' in 'teeth'. Practise with: *Sí, San Miguel es divertido y muy bonito.*

u   as in *mucho*. It's like the 'oo' in 'hoot'. Practise with: *mucho gusto.*

Notice that in words like *aquí* and *queso* the **u** isn't pronounced: **qu** is always pronounced like the English 'k' in 'key'. Practise with: *Este queso de aquí no me gusta mucho.*

WORKOUT

1 Wish you were here
Match each of the captions with one of the pictures.

1

2

3

4

5

6

a   Estoy estudiando mucho.
b   Estoy de vacaciones en la playa.
c   No estoy trabajando mucho.
d   Estoy estudiando en la playa.
e   Estoy trabajando en un bar.
f   Estoy de vacaciones en la montaña.

2 As if you were there
You're sitting by the hotel swimming pool. The woman on the next towel starts talking to you. Answer in Spanish. (For the purpose of this exercise you are female.)

Woman	Hola. ¿Hablas español?
You	(*Say yes, you speak a little.*)
Woman	¿Eres inglesa?
You	(*Say no, you're Scottish.*)
Woman	Ah. Me gusta mucho Escocia. ¿De dónde eres?
You	(*Say you're from Dundee – it's a city near Edinburgh. Ask her where she's from.*)
Woman	¿Yo? Soy gallega, pero vivo en Barcelona. Tengo familia aquí en Castro. ¿Te gusta Castro?
You	(*Say you like it very much. The beaches are clean and the countryside is very pretty.*)
Woman	Y el hotel, ¿te gusta?
You	(*Say it's not very quiet but it's quite lively.*)
Woman	¡Pero hablas bien español!
You	(*Smile modestly and say thank you.*)

3 Being negative
You are feeling rather uncooperative. Answer the following questions using *no* in both its meanings ('no' and 'not'). Make sure you change the verbs, eg: *¿Es español? No, no soy español.*

a   ¿Te gusta la playa?
b   ¿Hablas bien español?
c   ¿Eres de aquí?
d   ¿Estás de vacaciones?
e   ¿Vives aquí?
f   ¿Hablas idiomas?
g   ¿Te gusta el vino?
h   ¿Tienes hermanos?

4 Keeping your distance
Now imagine you want to ask someone else the questions in Workout 3, but you feel you must be rather formal about it. Rephrase the questions using the *usted* form.

5 Overheard in a bar in Benidorm

What were the questions that got the following answers?

a Lo siento, no tengo cerveza inglesa.
b Sí, vivo aquí cerca.
c En el centro, no. Tenemos un piso en las afueras.
d No, la playa no me gusta mucho.
e ¿Mi hermano? No, es mi novio.
f Sí, estoy de vacaciones.
g Sí, hablo inglés, pero muy poco.
h No, no soy español, soy de Swansea.

6 Missing words

You receive a letter from a Spanish friend who is studying languages, telling you of his progress. Some words are illegible though. The missing words are below – use them to fill in the gaps.

difícil   hablo   bastante
gustan   aprendiendo   pero

Estoy (1) idiomas en Madrid.

(2) francés un poco (3)

no me gusta mucho. Hablo italiano

muy bien porque no es (4) y

portugués (5) bien. Me (6)

muchísimo estos dos idiomas.

7 Match

The words on the left each start a sentence – complete the sentence with words from the right.
(There's only one way to make them all fit.)

a ¿Habla   i   Paco.
b Estoy   ii de vacaciones?
c ¿Estás   iii española?
d Se llaman   iv español?
e ¿Eres   v   trabajando.
f ¿Es   vi Julio y Ana.
g Se llama   vii usted de aquí?

8 Turismo

a Which of these isn't a language spoken in Spain?
castellano   catalán   chorizo

b Which of these wouldn't you find in Madrid?
el Prado   una playa   un mercado

c Which person doesn't live in the north of Spain?
una gallega   una vasca   una galesa

d Which of these people speaks English well?
Hablo bastante bien inglés.
Hablo inglés un poquito.
Hablo inglés, pero no mucho.

e Which of these people is taking it easy?
Estoy aprendiendo español.
Estoy trabajando en España.
Estoy de vacaciones en España.

f Which of these best describes Barcelona?
una ciudad castellana
una ciudad grande
un pueblo pequeño

9 Going round in circles

In each of these circles, find a starting point, then move clockwise to form a phrase. The first is a question, the second a reply to it. You'll need to add question marks and accents where appropriate.

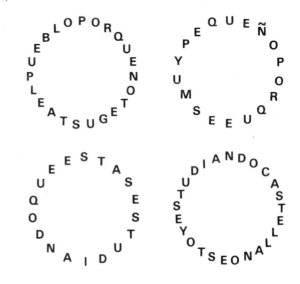

62

10 A matter of taste

Put the correct ending on the word *gust_* in each of the following.

a   Me gust_ muchísimo la montaña.
b   Me gust_ las playas.
c   No me gust_ el vino.
d   Me gust_ el campo.
e   Me gust_ mucho los museos.
f   No me gust_ el jamón.

Who is most likely to have made those statements? Choose from:

a surfer	a vegetarian
a rambler	a mountaineer
an archaeologist	a teetotaller

11 In the wrong place

These are the headings from a pamphlet about Cantabria, but the translations have got mixed up. See if you can guess which is the English equivalent of each Spanish heading.

a   Clima
b   Historia
c   La montaña
d   Direcciones de interés
e   Ríos, lagos y embalses
f   Arqueología y monumentos
g   La capital
h   Alojamientos
i   Gastronomía y folklore
j   Comunicaciones

i   Rivers, lakes and reservoirs
ii   Accommodation
iii The main town
iv   Communications
v   Food and local customs
vi   Useful addresses
vii Climate
viii The mountains
ix   History
x   Archaeology and old buildings

ABOUT SPAIN

Languages of Spain

The Spanish language originated in the part of Spain called Castilla (Castile), and is often referred to as *castellano* (Castilian). Most parts of Spain have their own accent or dialect, and in addition some areas have their own separate language, notably *catalán* in Cataluña, Valencia and the Balearic Islands; *gallego* in Galicia; and *vasco* in the Basque Country. These languages, suppressed under the Franco régime, have flourished enormously in the last few years. Today about 20% of the Spanish population is bilingual in Castilian and one of Spain's other languages.

Catalan car-park signs

Tourism

Each year over 40 million people (about seven million of them British) visit Spain, which is more than Spain's total population. Most of them go to the coast (Spain has 5940 kilometres of it). Tourism is one of Spain's main industries.

Barcelona

Barcelona is Spain's biggest port, its second biggest city, and the capital of the Catalan region. It's very important commercially and culturally, and is also beautifully situated between the hills of Tibidabo and Montjuich and the Mediterranean.

Apart from the wide, tree-lined Ramblas and the fishing port of La Barceloneta, Barcelona is famous for its *barrio gótico* (area of mediaeval streets and buildings) and the focal point of the Plaza de Cataluña.

One of Barcelona's most interesting buildings is *la Sagrada Familia*. Antoni Gaudí began work on this church in 1883, and 60 years after his death it is still unfinished.

Map showing the Sagrada Familia

Port of Barcelona

Outline of the Sagrada Famila church, Barcelona

Mural by Picasso in Barcelona

6 En coche

Getting directions

Buying petrol and maps

Ordering snacks

Talking about what there is to see

DO ORALLY

Ⓡ **1** Finding the right road out of a city isn't always easy. Isabel's looking for the motorway from Madrid towards Zaragoza.

Isabel Perdón, ¿la carretera de Zaragoza, por favor?

Man La carretera de Zaragoza, pues, siga todo recto y al llegar a la calle Arturo Soria, usted gira a la izquierda, y allá empieza la carretera.

Isabel Quo os la carretera de Zaragoza.

Man Exactamente, eso es.

Isabel ¿Es autopista?

Man Sí, sí, es autopista.

Isabel Muy bien. Muchas gracias, ¿eh?

Man Nada, nada.

To ask for the road to a place:
¿la carretera de ...., por favor?

perdón	*excuse me*
al llegar a	*when you get to*
gira	*you turn*
allá	*there*
empieza	*begins*
eso es	*that's right*
autopista	*motorway*

▶**Spotcheck 1** Which way do you turn when you get to Calle Arturo Soria?

Ⓡ **2** And is there a petrol station nearby?

Isabel ¿Y hay una gasolinera cerca?

Man	Sí, un poco antes de . . . de llegar al aeropuerto de Barajas –
Isabel	Sí –
Man	A la derecha tiene usted ya una . . . una gasolinera.
Isabel	Muy bien. ¿Está lejos?
Man	No, ¡qué va!, la tiene usted a siete kilómetros.
Isabel	A siete kilómetros.
Man	Aproximadamente, sí.
Isabel	Vale, muchas gracias, ¿eh?
Man	De nada.

To ask if there's something nearby:

¿hay un hotel	por aquí? cerca?

antes de	*before*
aeropuerto	*airport*
¡qué va!	*not at all!*
la tiene	*you'll find it*
aproximadamente	*more or less*

▶Spotcheck 2   Is the petrol station before you get to the airport or after?

3 A driver pulls into a small petrol station outside Santander.

Attendant	Buenos días.
Driver	Buenos días. Lleno, por favor. ¿Tiene mapas de carreteras?
Attendant	Sí, allí hay algunos.
Driver	Gracias. (*she chooses a map from the rack*) Muy bien, éste mismo. ¿Cuánto le debo?
Attendant	Novecientas treinta y cinco de la gasolina, más trescientas del mapa … mil doscientas treinta y cinco.
Driver	Muchas gracias. Adiós.
Attendant	Adiós. ¡Buen viaje!

To buy petrol:	
lleno	*a full tank*
treinta litros	*thirty litres*
dos mil pesetas	*2000 pesetas' worth*
de súper	*of 4-star*
de normal	*of 2-star*

euos in other bach.

algunos	*some*
éste mismo	*this one*
¿cuánto le debo?	*how much do I owe you?*
gasolina	*petrol*
más	*plus*
¡buen viaje!	*have a good trip!*

▶ **Spotcheck 3** How much does the driver pay for the petrol?

Do you remember how to ask " Have you got?"

4 Two friends are sightseeing in the historic town of Segovia. They stop for a snack.

Waitress	Buenos días. ¿Qué van a tomar?
María	Umm … un agua mineral.
Waitress	¿Con gas?
María	No, sin gas. ¿Tienen helados?
Waitress	Sí, de chocolate, fresa y limón.
María	Uno de chocolate, por favor.
Waitress	(*to Fernando*) ¿Y usted?
Fernando	Un café con leche y … ¿hay bocadillos?
Waitress	Jamón serrano, chorizo y queso.
Fernando	Uno de queso.
Waitress	Muy bien.

con gas	*fizzy*
sin gas	*still*
helados	*ice-creams*
fresa	*strawberry*
limón	*lemon*
bocadillos	*sandwiches*
chorizo	*spicy sausage*

▶ **Spotcheck 4** a What two drinks are ordered?

b What flavours of ice-creams are available?

El Alcázar, Segovia

📼 📺 5 Visiting Segovia, Yolanda finds out what the town
has to offer tourists.

Yolanda	¿Qué hay en Segovia para los turistas?
Passer-by 1	En Segovia hay muchas cosas para los turistas.
Passer-by 2	El acueducto, la catedral, muchas iglesias.
Passer-by 3	Una catedral muy bonita, hay un alcázar muy grande, el acueducto que es muy famoso.

And what is there for the local people?

Yolanda	¿Qué hay en Segovia para los segovianos?
Passer-by 4	Para los segovianos hay muchos bares, muchas discotecas.
Passer-by 5	Hay bibliotecas.
Passer-by 6	Hay festivales, hay cines.
Passer-by 7	Hay restaurantes, hay cafeterías, hay calles preciosas.
Passer-by 8	Muchos monumentos pero pocas diversiones; muchos bares.

iglesias	*churches*
alcázar	*castle*
bibliotecas	*libraries*
cines	*cinemas*
preciosas	*lovely*
pocas diversiones	*not many amusements*

Roman aqueduct, Segovia

▶ **Spotcheck 5** What is said to be very pretty?

Cathedral, Segovia

KEYWORDS

por aquí	near here
gire/gira	turn
antes de	before
después de	after
el cruce	crossroads
el semáforo	traffic lights
la señal	road sign
la autopista	motorway
la carretera	road
la gasolinera	petrol station
la gasolina	petrol
el aceite	oil
lleno	a full tank
un litro	a litre
el coche	car
el mapa	map
el plano	street map
(for more travel vocabulary see p. 209)	
agua mineral con gas	fizzy mineral water
agua mineral sin gas	still mineral water
el helado	ice-cream
el bocadillo	sandwich
el monumento	old building
la iglesia	church
la catedral	cathedral
la oficina de turismo	tourist office
hay	there is, there are
para	for

HOW SPANISH WORKS

1 There is – isn't there?

In this unit, the word *hay* crops up in a number of different places. *Hay* can mean 'there is' or 'there are' and, in a question, 'is there?' or 'are there?':

¿hay una gasolinera?	is there a petrol station?
¿hay bocadillos?	are there/do you have any sandwiches?
hay una catedral	there is a cathedral
hay muchas iglesias	there are a lot of churches

When it's used to ask if there's something available, *¿hay . . . ?* means the same as *¿tiene . . . ?*.

2 Fillings . . .

The English way of describing what's in a sandwich or an ice-cream is to put the filling or flavour first: a *ham* sandwich, a *strawberry* ice-cream. But in Spanish the filling or flavour comes afterwards, and is joined on by *de*: un bocadillo **de** jamón, un helado **de** fresa.

3 . . . and fillers

Every language has one or two words which don't mean a lot but which are useful for 'filling in' and giving you time to think – such as 'well', 'you know' or 'actually' in English. Even if you can't use them at once, here are three Spanish 'fillers' that you may need to recognise:

bueno	well
pues	well, er
o sea	that is, I mean

SOUND SPANISH

$\boxed{\text{v}}$ and $\boxed{\text{b}}$ There's no difference between the **b** and **v** in Spanish. They both sound like an English 'b'. Practise with: *Buen viaje. Balbina vive en Valencia, Viviana vive en Bilbao.*

WORKOUT

1 Nearly there?

Ask if there's one of these nearby:

a   petrol station
b   tourist office
c   bar
d   hotel
e   supermarket

2 Orders

How would you order these things in a café?

a   a ham sandwich
b   a beer
c   two cheese sandwiches
d   a mineral water (no fizz)
e   two white coffees
f   a vanilla ice-cream

3 Directions

Match the picture with the phrase.

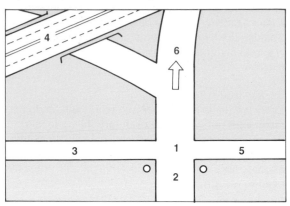

a   En la autopista.
b   En el semáforo.
c   A mano derecha.
d   En el cruce.
e   A mano izquierda.
f   Todo recto.

4 Nice

Use the information on the ice-cream parlour board to help you match the customers' requests to the replies.

a   Un helado grande de fresa.
b   Dos pequeños de limón.
c   ¿Hay helados de vainilla?
d   ¿Cuánto es el pequeño?
e   Tres grandes de chocolate.
f   ¿Hay polos de limón?

i   Doscientas diez pesetas.
ii   No, no hay.
iii   Setenta pesetas.
iv   Sí, hay.
v   Cincuenta pesetas.
vi   Cien pesetas.

•HELADOS•

FRESA
VAINILLA ✖
LIMÓN
CHOCOLATE
TUTTI FRUTTI

50 ptas   50 ptas   70 ptas

5 How far?

Put these places in order – nearest first.

Torrelavega está a unos veintitrés kilómetros; el Hotel Sardinero está a unos trescientos metros; el Bar Marcelino está a mano izquierda, a cien metros; Santillana del Mar está cerca de Torrelavega, a veintisiete kilómetros; y la Playa de la Magdalena está a un kilómetro, o algo así.

6 Getting around

You've arrived in the *plaza mayor* of a Castilian village. You want to find out where there's a hotel, a bar, a tourist office, a campsite and a petrol station, and also how to get to the road for Burgos. Here are the directions – use the map to discover where you're being directed.

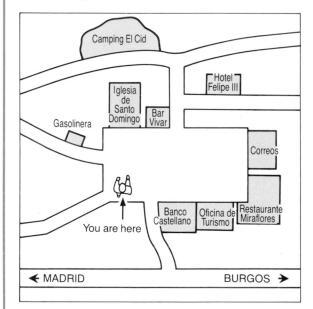

a   Coja la calle de enfrente, y siga todo recto hasta el final. Gire a la izquierda y allí está ....
b   .... está aquí en esta plaza, a mano derecha después del banco.
c   Coja la calle de enfrente. Después gire a la derecha, y a mano izquierda hay ....
d   Coja la calle a la izquierda, y a mano derecha hay ....
e   Aquí enfrente, al lado de la iglesia, hay ....
f   Gire a la derecha, y al final gire a la izquierda y ésa es ....

7 Oddball

Find the odd word out in these groups:

a vainilla, fresa, jamón, limón
b queso, agua mineral, cerveza, vino tinto
c monumento, iglesia, catedral, carretera
d cafetería, gasolinera, café, bar
e gasolina, lleno, súper, queso
f autopista, carretera, bocadillo, señal

8 Do it with numbers

Match the words to the numbers in the drawings.

a ochenta y dos
b trescientas quince
c sesenta
d cuatro mil trescientas doce
e veinticinco
f noventa
g dos mil doscientas

9 City search

Hidden in this block are seven places you might find
in a town. When you have found them (reading in
a straight line, vertically or horizontally), try to spot
the one which is very particular to Segovia.

```
O A D G I R V M E U
T C U A O P A Z S P
C L N S A Z A L P B
U M D O N T N B U D
D I G L E S I A E F
E S R I D Q A R N L
U M O N U M E N T O
C A T E D R A L R R
A S T R H U U A Y S
L B K A J P F V A C
```

10 Forever asking

Ask

a a waiter if there are any sandwiches
b a tourist office clerk if he has a street map of the
city
c a shop assistant if he has any mineral water
d a petrol pump attendant if there are any toilets
e an ice-cream seller if she has any strawberry
ice-creams
f a supermarket assistant if there is any bread.

11 Printout

The hire car desk at Madrid Airport has a computer
which gives a print-out of the directions to most
hotels in the city. The Hotel Las Alondras is not too
difficult to find. Can you work out from the printout:

a The approximate distance to the hotel.
b The first square you come to.
c After you have turned left off the Calle de Ríos
Rosas towards the Glorieta de Quevedo, what is
the next thing you do?

```
2.04 Km   siga a la DERECHA, siga las indicaciones
          a MADRID.
8.0 Km    semaforo, continue en linea recta MARIA
          DE MOLINA.
1.0 Km    PLAZA DEL DOCTOR MARAÑON.
          gire a la DERECHA.tome el CARRIL DE LA
          IZQUIERDA PASEO DE LA CASTELLANA.
0.1 Km    siga las indicaciones a PLAZA DE CRISTO
          REY.
0.2 Km    continue en linea recta CALLE DE RIOS
          ROSAS.
1.3 Km    gire a la IZQUIERDA. siga las indicaciones
          a GLORIETA DE QUEVEDO.
0.3 Km    PRIMERA calle gire a la IZQUIERDA JOSE
          ABASCAL.tome el CARRIL DE LA DERECHA.
0.1 Km    a la DERECHA HOTEL LAS ALONDRAS.
```

ABOUT SPAIN

On the road

Motorists visiting Spain don't officially need an international driving licence, but they are recommended to carry one. Seat belts are not compulsory in built-up areas.

Road distances are measured in kilometres: 1 kilometre (1 km) is approximately 5/8 of a mile so, for example, 100 km = about 60 miles. On most motorways a toll (*peaje*) is paid, depending on the distance covered.

Petrol stations sell two main grades of petrol: *súper* (4-star) and *normal* (2-star). They're relatively infrequent so, if in doubt, fill up. They rarely accept credit cards.

Segovia

Segovia is about 50 miles northwest of Madrid, and is full of buildings of historical interest. Its *Alcázar* (castle), perched on a cliff over the river valley, looks as though it has been lifted from a fairy-tale. It was in fact started by the Moors in the 13th century, finished by the Christians, and then restored after a fire in the 19th century. But it is not the oldest construction in Segovia: this honour goes to the aqueduct, built by the Romans to bring water to the city, its 118 stone arches still spanning one of the main streets of Segovia. The massive cathedral is the most outstanding of many other fine old buildings.

In the hills not far from Segovia is the royal palace of *La Granja*, with its splendid gardens, and the province is full of old castles dating from the days when the Christian kingdoms of Spain battled against the Moors – and against each other!

El Camino de Santiago

One of the oldest and most interesting roads in Spain is the 500-mile-long *Camino de Santiago*, which runs across the north of Spain from the Pyrenees to Santiago de Compostela. For over a thousand years, pilgrims have been travelling to visit the tomb of Santiago (Saint James), which was the most important shrine of the Middle Ages. Even today, in towns like Santo Domingo de la Calzada, pilgrims can stay the night at a special hostel without having to pay.

The M30 motorway around Madrid

Cathedral, Santiago de Compostela

7 El tiempo es oro

Telling the time

Talking about your job

® **1** As a foreign exchange dealer for a Madrid bank, Honorio needs to know the time in different parts of the world.

MADRID   LONDRES   CARACAS   NEW-YORK

Isabel	¿Qué hora es en Madrid?
Honorio	Son las once de la mañana.
Isabel	¿Y en Londres?
Honorio	Son las diez de la mañana.
Isabel	¿En Caracas?
Honorio	Las seis de la mañana.
Isabel	¿En Nueva York?
Honorio	Las cinco de la mañana.
Isabel	¿Y en Hong Kong?
Honorio	Las cinco de la tarde.

de la mañana	*in the morning*
Londres	*London*
Nueva York	*New York*
de la tarde	*in the afternoon*

To ask the time:
¿qué hora es?

To say what time it is:
es la una   *it's one o'clock*
son las dos/   *it's two/three/*
   tres/cuatro   *four o'clock*

To say 'a quarter past' or 'half past':
son las diez y cuarto
son las diez y media

To say 'a quarter to':
son las diez menos cuarto

▶ **Spotcheck 1**   What is the time difference between Madrid and New York?

2 Are Spanish working hours very different from those in Britain?

Yolanda	¿A qué hora empiezas el trabajo?
Passer-by 1	A las nueve de la mañana.
Yolanda	¿A qué hora terminas?
Passer-by 1	Sobre las dos.
Passer-by 2	Por las mañanas empiezo a las nueve, hasta las tres.
Passer-by 3	Por la mañana empiezo a las ocho y media, y termino a las dos. Y por la tarde empiezo a las cinco y termino a las ocho y media.

And what about weekends?

Yolanda	¿Trabaja los fines de semana?
Passer-by 4	Los sábados por la mañana.
Passer-by 5	Los sábados, sí, trabajo. Los domingos, no.
Yolanda	¿Trabaja los fines de semana?
Passer-by 6	No, los sábados y los domingos los tengo libres.

To ask when someone starts or finishes work:

¿a qué hora empieza(s)/ termina(s) el trabajo?

And the reply:

empiezo a . . .
termino a . . .

sobre	about
hasta	until
por la mañana	in the morning
por la tarde	in the afternoon/evening
fines de semana	weekends
sábados	Saturdays
domingos	Sundays
los tengo libres	I'm off ('I have them free')

▶ Spotcheck 2

a　Which people start work at 9 am?

b　Which people work on Saturdays?

Ⓡ 3　Here's a cross-section of the jobs done by people we interviewed for *España Viva*. There's quite a mixed bag: a sociologist, the owner of a bar, an unemployed secretary, a factory worker, and someone studying while she looks for a job.

Jordi　¿En qué trabajas?

María José　Trabajo en el ayuntamiento de Barcelona. Soy socióloga.

Isabel　¿Y qué haces aquí en Mojácar?

Miguel　Pues, tengo un bar y lo llevo con mi mujer.

Isabel　¿En qué trabajas?

Mari Carmen　Actualmente no trabajo porque estoy en paro, pero mi profesión es ser secretaria. También doy clases de español y bueno ... así, algunas cosas más.

Isabel　Julián, ¿en qué trabajas?

Julián　En una fábrica.

Isabel　¿En una fábrica de qué?

Julián　De material eléctrico.

Jordi　¿En qué trabajas?

Ana　No trabajo. Estoy buscando trabajo en estos momentos. Estudio. Estudio idiomas.

To ask what job someone does:
¿en qué trabaja(s)?

To say where you work:

trabajo en	una fábrica un banco

ayuntamiento	town hall
socióloga	sociologist
lo llevo	I run it
actualmente	at the moment
en paro	unemployed
doy clases de	I teach
así	you know
fábrica	factory
material eléctrico	electrical equipment
buscando trabajo	looking for work
en estos momentos	at the moment

▶ Spotcheck 3

a　Who works with his wife?

b　What is Ana doing until she finds a job?

Julián on his way to work

🖭 ⓣⱽ **4** In Madrid most people work in the service industries. Yolanda asked some *madrileños* what jobs they did.

Yolanda	¿Cuál es su profesión?
Passer-by 1	Soy policía municipal.
Yolanda	¿Cuál es su profesión?
Passer-by 2	Soy secretaria de dirección.
Yolanda	¿Cuál es su profesión?
Passer-by 3	Profesor.
Passer-by 4	Soy recepcionista de hotel.
Passer-by 5	Soy directora de empresa.
Passer-by 6	Soy camarero.

To say what your job is:

soy	dentista
	directora

¿cuál es su profesión?	*what's your job?*
secretaria de dirección	*management secretary*
profesor	*teacher*
directora de empresa	*company director*
camarero	*waiter*

🖭 ⓡ **5** Do people enjoy their work? We asked a few of them. Blas is a loom operator in the southern town of Níjar.

Isabel	¿Te gusta tu trabajo?
Blas	Sí.
Isabel	¿Es difícil tu trabajo?
Blas	Es duro.

Isabel runs a tobacconist's – *un estanco*.

Isabel Soto	¿Le gusta su trabajo? ¿Es divertido, es interesante?
Isabel	Bueno, más que divertido, es interesante.

Julián works in an electronics factory.

Isabel	¿Te gusta trabajar, o te gusta tu trabajo?
Julián	Me gusta más el descanso.
Isabel	¿Te gusta más la siesta?
Julián	Sí.

Olga teaches English.

Isabel	¿Y te gusta?
Olga	Sí, me encanta. Es un trabajo que me encanta.

And Luis works in a bank.

Isabel	¿En qué trabajas?
Luis	Yo trabajo en un banco, para mi desgracia.
Isabel	¿Te gusta tu trabajo?
Luis	No me gusta mucho, si soy sincero.

Luis

duro	*hard*
más que	*not so much*
me gusta más	*I prefer*
descanso	*relaxation*
me encanta	*I love it*
para mi desgracia	*unfortunately*
si soy sincero	*if I'm honest, to tell the truth*

▶Spotcheck 5
a Which three people were most positive about their jobs?
b Who preferred *not* to be working?

Drawings of parents at work by children from the Colegio Cardenal Herrera Oria, Madrid

KEYWORDS

¿qué hora es?	what time is it?
¿a qué hora . . .?	(at) what time . . .?
empezar	to start
terminar	to finish
por la mañana	in the morning
por la tarde	in the afternoon/evening
sobre	about
hasta	until
el fin de semana	weekend
el sábado	Saturday
el domingo	Sunday
trabajar	to work
hacer	to do
la empresa	company
la fábrica	factory
la escuela	school
el empleado	employee
el trabajo	work, job
la profesión	job
el paro	unemployment
(*for more jobs see p. 210*)	
difícil	difficult
duro/a	hard
la siesta	afternoon nap

HOW SPANISH WORKS

1 Giving the time

To say what time it is, you start with *es* or *son*. Use *es* only if it's one o'clock: *es la una*. Otherwise: ***son** las dos*, ***son** las tres*, ***son** las ocho*, etc.

When it's a quarter **past** or half **past** the hour, the important word is *y*: *son las nueve **y cuarto**, son las diez **y media*** (literally 'nine and a quarter', 'ten and a half').

When it's a quarter **to** the hour, the important word is *menos*: *las diez **menos cuarto**, la una **menos cuarto*** (literally 'ten minus a quarter', 'one minus a quarter').

2 When?

To ask when or at what time something happens, use *¿a qué hora?*: *¿a qué hora empieza/termina el trabajo?*.

There's also an *a* in the reply: *empiezo a las cinco, termino a las diez*.

To specify whether it's five o'clock in the morning, afternoon or evening, Spanish uses *de*: *las cinco de la mañana, las diez de la tarde, las doce de la noche*.

To say 'in the morning', 'in the afternoon' or 'at night', without specifying a time, use *por*: *por la tarde, por la mañana*.

3 Infinitive wisdom

By now, you've met a number of verbs in different forms: *tengo/tienes/tiene*; *trabajo/trabajas*; *termino/terminas*; *vivo/vives/vive* – and others. But if you want to look up a verb in a dictionary, you'll usually find it listed under a form called the infinitive: *trabajar* – 'to work'; *terminar* – 'to finish'; *vivir* – 'to live'.

You can usually work out the other parts of the verb from the infinitive. All Spanish infinitives end in *-ar*, *-er* or *-ir*. Verbs with infinitives ending in *-ar* follow one pattern; verbs with infinitives ending in *-er* or *-ir* follow a slightly different one:

-ar verbs, eg *hablar* – 'to speak'	
*(yo) habl**o***	I speak
*(tú) habl**as***	you speak
*(usted) habl**a***	you speak

-er and *-ir* verbs, eg *vivir* – 'to live'	
*(yo) viv**o***	I live
*(tú) viv**es***	you live
*(usted) viv**e***	you live

4 Sexism at work

Some words for jobs in Spanish indicate whether the person is male or female:

secretario	secretary (male)
secretaria	secretary (female)
cocinero	cook (male)
cocinera	cook (female)
profesor	teacher (male)
profesora	teacher (female)

Some words don't change:

un or *una recepcionista*   receptionist
un or *una taxista*   taxi driver
un or *una guía*   guide

Note that when you say what job you do, there's no word for 'a': *soy cocinero, soy taxista* – 'I'm a cook', 'I'm a taxi driver'.

SOUND SPANISH

ñ as in *España*. It's pronounced like the 'ni' in 'onion'. It counts as a separate letter in the Spanish alphabet and comes after **n** in dictionaries. Practise with: *una ración pequeña de champiñones para la señora* ('a small portion of mushrooms for the lady').

WORKOUT

1   Got the time?

¿Qué hora es? – What time is it?

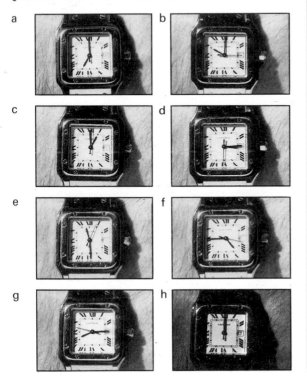

a

b

c

d

e

f

g

h

2   Beginnings . . . and endings

Four people start work at different times. How would they answer the question: *¿a qué hora empieza usted?*.

a   b

c   d

And four others finish at different times. How would they answer the question: *¿a qué hora termina usted?*.

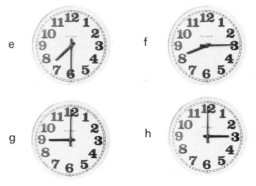

e   f

g   h

3   Confused conversation

Match the answers in the second column with the questions in the first.

a   ¿En qué trabaja?

b   ¿Le gusta su trabajo?

c   ¿Trabaja por la tarde?

d   ¿Cómo se llama?

e   ¿Trabaja los fines de semana?

f   ¿Trabaja en Madrid?

g   ¿Cuántas horas trabaja al día?

i   No, sólo por la mañana.

ii   Siete: de ocho a tres.

iii Soy taxista.

iv   Sí, muchísimo.

v   No, trabajo en Salamanca.

vi   Enrique Bravo.

vii No, sólo los sábados.

4 Getting to know you

A Spaniard you've just met wants to find out a bit about you. Answer in Spanish.

Spaniard	¿De dónde es usted?
You	(*Say you're from York, in England.*)
Spaniard	¿Le gusta York?
You	(*Say yes, you like it a lot.*)
Spaniard	¿Qué hay en York para los turistas?
You	(*Say there's a cathedral, a wall* (una muralla), *and lots of museums.*)
Spaniard	¿York tiene muchos pubs?
You	(*Say yes, lots, and the beer is very good.*)
Spaniard	¿Y cuál es su profesión?
You	(*Say you work in an office.*)
Spaniard	¿A qué hora empieza por la mañana?
You	(*Say you start at 9.15.*)
Spaniard	¿Y a qué hora termina por la tarde?
You	(*Say at 5.30.*)
Spaniard	¿Le gusta su trabajo? ¿Es divertido?
You	(*Say the work isn't much fun, but it's not very difficult.*)

5 Spanish inquisition

Using the *tú* form of the verb, how would you find out the following information from a fellow guest at your hotel?

a What he is called.
b If he is on holiday.
c If he likes the hotel.
d If there's a nice beach nearby.
e If there's a good disco in town.
f Where he is from.
g What job he does.
h What time he finishes work.
i If he's got a car.

6 Vowel trouble

These are all places where someone might work. Fill in the missing letters (which are all vowels) to discover the work place.

a b_nc_
b f_br_c_
c _f_c_n_
d g_s_l_n_r_
e m_s__
f _y_nt_m__nt_
g s_p_rm_rc_d_
h b_r

7 Happy birthday

Using this newspaper's 'birthdays' column, match the names with the right jobs.

a Pilar Miralles
b Elena Terán
c Javier Velarde
d César Fuentes
e Lita Hermida

i juega al fútbol
ii trabaja en un hospital
iii trabaja en cine y teatro
iv diseña casas
v dirige una empresa

CUMPLEAÑOS

Hoy, día 17 de octubre, cumplen años: Pilar Miralles, actriz; Elena Terán, médico; Javier Velarde, arquitecto; César Fuentes, futbolista, y Lita Hermida, empresaria.

Mañana, día 18, cumplen años: Joaquin Galant, diputado del Parlamento valenciano por Alicante, 52; José Sánchez Bueno, diputado del Parlamento andaluz por Málaga, 45; Jaime Ballesteros, político, 55; Kenneth Kaunda, presidente de Zambia, 63; Raúl García Montero, estudiante, 5.

8 What's my line?

When you come across a new Spanish word, you can sometimes guess what it means just by looking at it. See how you get on with these.

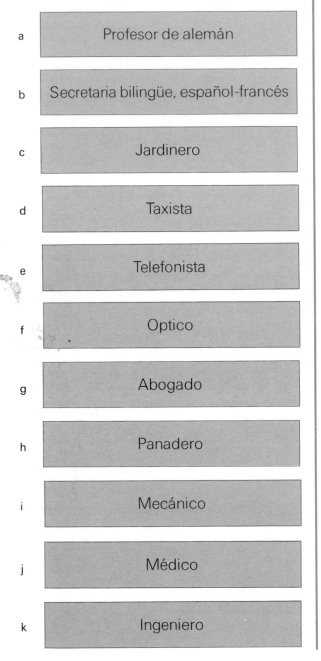

a Profesor de alemán

b Secretaria bilingüe, español-francés

c Jardinero

d Taxista

e Telefonista

f Optico

g Abogado

h Panadero

i Mecánico

j Médico

k Ingeniero

9 Right choice

Choose the correct answer to these questions.

a ¿Te gusta la catedral?
   Sí, me gusta mucho.
   Sí, te gusta.
   Sí, a la derecha.

b ¿A qué hora empiezas el trabajo?
   Termino a las siete.
   Empiezo a las siete de la mañana.
   Empiezo mañana.

c Por favor, ¿el centro ciudad?
   Es divertido.
   Siga recto hasta el puente.
   Un poco.

d ¿Hablas español?
   No, soy electricista.
   No, soy de Madrid.
   No, no me gustan los idiomas.

e ¿Tiene hermanos?
   Sí, tengo siete.
   Para mí, una cerveza.
   Tengo treinta años.

f ¿Cuánto es?
   Son dos hijos y una hija.
   Son las tres y media.
   Son quinientas pesetas.

g ¿Qué hora es?
   Son quinientas pesetas.
   Es la una y cuarto.
   Es la segunda calle.

h ¿Está de vacaciones?
   Sí, estoy trabajando.
   Sí, estoy en el camping aquí cerca.
   Sí, soy de aquí.

ABOUT SPAIN

Working hours and mealtimes

The Spanish day begins about the same time as the British: white-collar workers start about 9 am, blue-collar a bit earlier. But after that, times are different. Many Spaniards work till 1 or 1.30, have lunch about 2.30, and go back to work at 3.30 or 4 pm. Afternoon work tends to go on till 7 or 8, then most of the evening's social activities – cinema, *paseo* or *aperitivo* – take place before the evening meal, which is usually at 10 or 10.30 pm. In summer, especially in the hotter areas, many people work *jornada intensiva*, which involves working through from morning to 3 pm and taking the rest of the day off.

Along with many other Spanish customs, the long lunch break and the famous *siesta* are beginning to disappear as Spain becomes 'Europeanised'.

Employment

Although almost one in five Spaniards still work on the land, Spain is now among the top ten industrial countries in the world, with car-making and ship-building prominent, and electronics developing rapidly. The tourist industry is another important source of employment. Despite all this, though, unemployment is among the highest in Europe.

A great recent change has been in the number of women who have jobs. Nowadays there are some four million women working, which accounts for about a third of the total workforce.

Mojácar

Mojácar depends on tourists for its livelihood, and on the coast nearby new hotels and apartments are still being built. Further inland, the village of Níjar has a more traditional economy based on weaving *jarapas* (a kind of rug), and the town of Tabernas was until recently a centre for film-making – *The Magnificent Seven*, *Once Upon A Time In The West* and even *Lawrence of Arabia* were filmed here in the spectacular desert.

A new source of wealth and work for the province of Almería has been the so-called 'plastic miracle' – the cultivation of fruit, vegetables and flowers in huge plastic greenhouses.

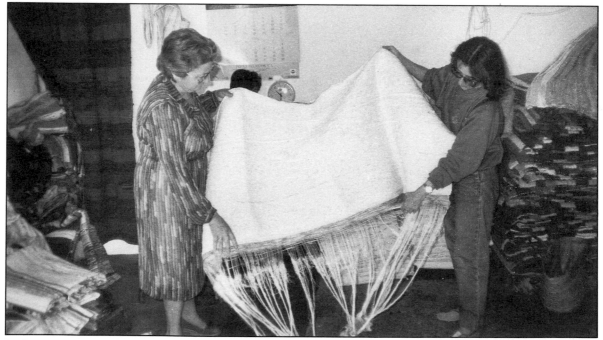

Buying *jarapas* in Níjar

8 ¡Que aproveche!

Ordering food and drink

® 1 Isabel and Luis go for a drink and a *tapa* (appetiser) before a meal.

Waiter	Buenas tardes. ¿Qué van a tomar los señores?
Luis	Yo, gin tonic.
Isabel	Para mí un zumo de naranja. ¿Y qué tapas tiene?
Waiter	Tapas, tiene jamón, queso, patata o aceituna.
Isabel	Pues, una ración de cada.
Waiter	Patata, queso y aceituna.
Isabel	Y jamón.
Waiter	Y jamón.

You may be asked:
¿qué va(n) a tomar?

In reply you can start with:
para mí ... *for me ...*
or
quiero ... *I'd like*

aceituna *olive(s)*
ración *portion*
cada *each (one)*

▶ Spotcheck 1 Which *tapa* does the waiter nearly forget?

A *tapas* bar
in Madrid

📼 📺 2 Emilio and Lali go to a bar for a drink and a *tapa*,
and are joined by Mariano.

Waiter	Buenos días. ¿Qué van a tomar?
Emilio	Umm . . . un fino y un vino blanco, por favor.
	(*as the waiter serves the drinks, Mariano arrives*)
Mariano	¡Hola!
Emilio	¿Qué hay?
Mariano	(*to Lali*) ¿Cómo estás?
Lali	¿Cómo estás?
Emilio	¿Qué tomas?
Mariano	Un vermú.
Emilio	(*to the waiter*) Mmm . . . un vermú. ¿Y qué hay para comer?
Waiter	Hay raciones de queso, de champiñón, de calamares, eh . . . tortilla española, patatas a la brava, patatas alioli.
Emilio	¿Qué tomáis?
Mariano	Para mí nada, gracias.
Lali	Pues, una de champiñones.
Emilio	(*to the waiter*) Umm . . . una ración de champiñones y una de calamares, por favor.

fino	*dry sherry*
¿qué hay?	*how are things?*
vermú	*vermouth*
para comer	*to eat*
champiñón	*mushrooms*
calamares	*squid*
tortilla	*omelette*
patatas a la brava	*potatoes in spicy sauce*
alioli	*garlic mayonnaise*
¿qué tomáis?	*what are you having?*

a   What three drinks are ordered?

▶Spotcheck 2   b   Who is the squid for?

® **3** At a busy restaurant, Isabel Soto and Mick Webb order supper: garlic soup and chops for Mick, and for Isabel . . .

Waiter	Usted, ¿qué va a tomar?
Isabel	Voy a tomar el menú del día. De primero la sopa juliana.
Waiter	Sopa juliana.
Isabel	Y de segundo, el pollo a la parrilla.
Waiter	¿Vino? ¿Agua?
Isabel	Agua mineral con gas. Y además una jarra de agua.

To order the different courses of a meal:

de primero	*as a starter*
de segundo	*for the main course*
de postre	*for pudding/dessert*
para beber	*to drink*

voy a tomar	*I'm going to have*
el menú del día	*the set menu*
sopa juliana	*vegetable soup*
pollo a la parrilla	*grilled chicken*
además	*also*
jarra	*jug*

The soup arrives . . .

Waiter	Sopa de ajo para el señor.
Mick	Ah, muy bien. Gracias.
Waiter	La sopa juliana para la señora, ¡y que les aproveche!
Isabel	Muchísimas gracias.
Waiter	De nada.
Isabel	Bueno, a empezar. ¡Buen provecho!

¡que les aproveche!	*bon appétit, enjoy your meal!*
sopa de ajo	*garlic soup*
a empezar	*let's start*
¡buen provecho!	*bon appétit!*

A waitress comes to check if they'd like a dessert.

Waitress	¿Tomarán postre?
Isabel	¿Qué nos recomienda?
Waitress	Pues, aquí hacen el pudin con chocolate, flan, peras al vino – es un plato típico de aquí de la región. Las manzanas asadas también, es típico de aquí, y el queso de Burgos, pues, con miel, también. Muy rico está todo, así que . . . es difícil la elección.
Mick	Yo voy a tomar las peras al vino.

¿tomarán . . .?	*will you have . . .?*
¿qué nos recomienda?	*what do you recommend?*
hacen	*they make*

flan	*crème caramel*
peras al vino	*pears in wine*
plato	*dish*
manzanas asadas	*baked apples*
miel	*honey*
así que	*so (that)*
elección	*choice*

▶ **Spotcheck 3**   a   What did Isabel have for the first two courses?

b   What did they drink?

📺 **4**   After their *tapas*, Emilio, Lali and Mariano have moved on to a traditional Madrid restaurant, *La Carmencita*.

Waitress	Buenos días.
All	Hola.
Waitress	¿Qué van a tomar los señores?
Emilio	De primero, una sopa de pescado.
Lali	Umm ... para mí también.
Mariano	Para mí ... ¿Qué es la tortilla de Orduña?
Waitress	Pues, es una tortilla de patata, cebolla y manteca.
Mariano	Ya. No, mejor una sopa de ajo.
Waitress	Entonces, son dos sopas de pescado y una de ajo. ¿De segundo?
Emilio	De segundo ... lomo de merluza con almejas.
Lali	Y escalope de ternera para mí.
Mariano	Para mí, un solomillo de cerdo. Y una ensalada para tres.
Waitress	¿Para beber?
Mariano	(*consulting the others*) ¿Vino tinto?
Emilio	Vino.
Lali	Sí.
Mariano	El vino de la casa.
Lali	¡Ah! Y una botella de agua mineral sin gas.
Waitress	Muy bien. Gracias.

pescado	fish
cebolla	onion
manteca	lard
mejor	rather, better
lomo de merluza	hake steak
almejas	clams
escalope de ternera	veal escalope
solomillo de cerdo	pork sirloin
ensalada	salad

▶ **Spotcheck 4**   What first course did Mariano decide against?

Ⓡ **5**   After Sunday lunch at the Suárez household, Marisa offers drinks.

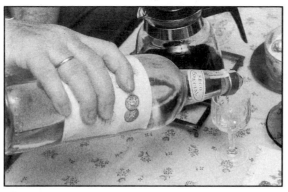

Marisa	¿Quién quiere una copa? Vamos a ver.
Señor Suárez	Yo quiero sol y sombra.
Marisa	Eh, ¿tú?
Jaime	Yo quiero un anís.
Marisa	¿Pero dulce o seco?
Jaime	Dulce.
Marisa	¿Tú, Isabel?
Isabel	Yo un anís dulce también.
Marisa	¿A ver lo que tomas, Julián?
Julián	Un sol y sombra.

¿quién quiere ...?	who would like ...?
copa	glass, drink
sol y sombra	literally 'sun and shade', actually a mixture of anís and coñac
anís	aniseed liqueur
dulce	sweet
seco	dry
¿a ver lo que tomas?	and what are you having?

▶ **Spotcheck 5**   Which drink is chosen by two people?

KEYWORDS

el restaurante	restaurant
quiero	I'd like
el vino blanco	white wine
el vino tinto	red wine
el vino de la casa	house wine
la tapa	appetiser, snack
la ración	portion
el menú del día	set menu
la carta	menu
la cuenta	bill
de primero	as a starter, for the first course
de segundo	for the main course
de postre	for dessert/sweet
la sopa	soup
el pollo	chicken
el ajo	garlic
la tortilla	omelette
la carne	meat
el pescado	fish
los mariscos	shellfish, seafood
las verduras	vegetables
la ensalada	salad
la fruta	fruit

(*for more restaurant items see p. 207*)

rico/a	delicious
la comida	food; meal
la bebida	drink
comer	to eat, to have lunch
cenar	to have supper/dinner

HOW SPANISH WORKS

1 Supercookery

You may be asked if you're enjoying your meal:
¿qué tal la sopa/la tortilla/el pollo?
If something is **very** good, you can say *muy* bueno or *muy* buena.

But there's another way of saying 'very': by adding *-ísimo* to the end of the adjective:
¿qué tal la sopa? – buenísima

Don't forget that the ending of the adjective changes depending on the noun it's describing: *el pollo es riquísimo* but *los calamares son riquísimos*.

2 Changing verbs

Querer means 'to love'; it also means 'to like' and 'to want'. One of its many uses is when ordering food or drinks. The waiter may well ask you: *¿qué **quiere** tomar?*. You could reply: *(yo) quiero . . . .*
(Yo) quiero isn't as blunt as the English 'I want' – it means roughly 'I'd like'.

Notice that with *querer* it's not just the ending of the word that changes with the subject. There's also a change in the middle of the word:

qu*e*rer	to want
qu*ie*ro	I want/would like
qu*ie*res	you want, etc.
qu*ie*re	you want, he/she wants

A number of verbs change in this way. Another you've met is:

emp*e*zar	to start
emp*ie*zo	I start
emp*ie*zas	you start
emp*ie*za	you start, he/she starts

Other verbs that change in this way are shown in the *Vocabulary* like this: *querer (ie)*.

SOUND SPANISH

`r` and `rr` The Spanish **r** is slightly rolled: *gaso-linera, ma*r*iscos*. When the **r** begins or ends a word, or when it's a double **rr**, it is rolled more strongly: *ración, toma*r*, Co*rr*eos*. Practise with: *una ja*rr*a de Rioja, por favor, y una ración de calamares*.

WORKOUT

1 ¿Hay . . . ?

Ask if these *tapas* are available and, assuming they are, order portions of them.

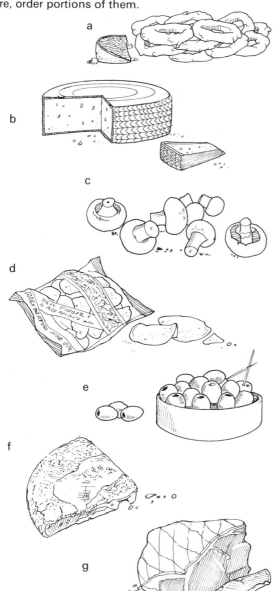

a

b

c

d

e

f

g

2 Going down well

Reply to the following questions, saying that the food you're eating is very good.

a   ¿Qué tal la paella?
b   ¿Qué tal el pollo?
c   ¿Qué tal los calamares?
d   ¿Qué tal el helado de fresa?
e   ¿Qué tal las almejas?
f   ¿Qué tal la tortilla?

3 A perfect match

Each of the words in the left-hand column goes well with one from the right-hand column. Can you make a perfect match?

helados   fritas
vino   española
agua   tinto
patatas   manchego
tortilla   mineral
queso   variados

4 As if you were there

You're in a *cafetería* and the waiter comes to your table.

Waiter Buenos días, señores. ¿Qué van a tomar?
You   (*Give the order – an orange juice, two beers, a red wine and a white wine. Ask if they have any appetisers.*)
Waiter Pues, sí. Hay calamares, patatas a la brava, jamón, queso y aceitunas.
You   (*Ask for a portion of squid, one of cheese and one of olives.*)

The waiter brings the drinks but isn't sure who the red wine is for.

Waiter ¿El vino tinto?
You   (*Say it's for you.*)

A little later on you call the waiter to pay.

You   (*Ask how much it is.*)
Waiter Vamos a ver. Son cinco bebidas y tres tapas. En total, mil cuatrocientas.
You   (*Pay and thank him.*)

How much was it?

5 Don't mix your drinks

Somebody didn't follow this good advice. Can you unscramble the letters to make popular Spanish drinks?

a FECA OSLO
b ET NOC ELCHE
c EVECRAZ
d NOVI NITTO
e MUZO DE JANANRA
f UAAG RAILMEN

6 ¡Buen provecho!

A group of five people went out for supper. Work out who ordered which meal, given that: Ana is a strict vegetarian; Bernarda, on the other hand, can't stand vegetables of any sort; Conchita is very keen on seafood; Diego adores ice-cream; Enrique doesn't like garlic and is allergic to coffee.

Menu A Gambas al ajillo. Merluza. Peras al vino. Café.
Menu B Sopa de ajo. Ensalada mixta de la casa. Una manzana. Café.
Menu C Sopa de cebolla. Filete de cerdo con verduras. Flan. Té.
Menu D Sopa de pescado. Filete de cerdo. Flan. Café.
Menu E Sopa de cebolla. Pollo asado. Flan con helado y fresas. Café.

7 Bad copy

This menu is a very bad photocopy so not all the words have come out well – can you complete them?

```
            MENU DEL D_ _      510 ptas

Primero     Cala _ _ _ _ _ a la romana
            E _ _ _lada mixta
            Tortil _ _ frances_

Segundo     Fil _ _ _ de cerdo
            Po _ _ _ al ajillo
            Pes _ _ do frito

Pos_ _ _    F _ _ _ _ del tiempo
            Fl _ _

            Pa_ y vin_

            Servicio e impuestos incluidos
```

8 Problems, problems!

You're trying to order a meal for two, but it's not going very smoothly.

Waiter ¿Qué van a tomar los señores?
You (*Order a fish soup and a salad as a starter.*)
Waiter No hay sopa de pescado.
You (*Change your order to garlic soup.*)
Waiter Muy bien.
You (*Order paella for two for the main course.*)
Waiter La paella es para cuatro personas mínimo.
You (*Ask if they have seafood.*)
Waiter Sólo calamares.
You (*Order squid and chicken and chips.*)
Waiter ¿Y para beber?
You (*You'd like the house red.*)
Waiter Sólo hay blanco.
You (*Well, a bottle of mineral water.*)
Waiter ¿Grande o pequeña? ¿Con gas o sin gas?
You (*Big, and fizzy please.*)
Waiter ¡Vaya! Esto sí, lo tenemos.

9 All tastes

Six people talk about their likes and dislikes in food. Select the most appropriate dish for each one. (You may need to look up some words in the *Vocabulary*.)

Felipe 'No me gustan los mariscos.'
mejillones marinera   solomillo
gambas al ajillo   almejas en salsa verde

Nicolás 'Me gusta el pescado.'
lomo de cerdo   chuletas de cordero
escalope de ternera   lenguado a la plancha

Lola 'No me gusta el pescado.'
lomo de merluza   trucha con jamón
tortilla de jamón   bonito con tomate

Pilar 'No me gusta la carne.'
pollo a la parrilla   tortilla española
chuletas de cerdo   bistec a la pimienta

Cristina 'Me gusta la fruta.'
entremeses variados   espárragos con mayonesa
piña en almíbar   champiñones al ajo

Ramón 'Me gustan muchísimo los postres.'
ensalada mixta   flan
pollo asado   merluza en salsa verde

ABOUT SPAIN

Tapas

In nearly every bar in Spain there's a display of snacks or *tapas*. When you order a drink you may be served a small portion of crisps (*patatas fritas*) or olives (*aceitunas*) for nothing. If you want something more substantial, you ask for *una ración de ...*

The range of *tapas* may include:
calamares – squid, cut into circles and usually fried in batter (*a la romana*)
gambas – prawns
tortilla – wedge of cold potato omelette
champiñones – mushrooms
ensaladilla rusa – Russian salad (with peas, potatoes and mayonnaise)

A few *raciones* can take the place of a proper meal.

Eating out

Spain has its own traditional version of fast food – *el plato combinado*, a one-course meal which can include meat, fish, vegetables and eggs, all on the same plate. But three courses are the normal thing in most restaurants, and there should be a *menú del día* – a fixed-price meal offering some choice for each course. Service and tax *(servicio e impuestos)* are usually included.

Spanish cookery varies a lot from region to region. There's the *paella* (rice and seafood) of Valencia, and the *gazpacho* (cold tomato soup) of Andalucía. Less well-known abroad are dishes like *fabada asturiana* (a stew of beans and sausages) from Asturias, the *merluza en salsa verde* (hake in garlic and parsley sauce) typical of the Basque Country, and the roast lamb and pork of Castilla.

Department store
in Madrid's main
shopping district

9 De tiendas

Buying postcards and stamps

Buying clothes

Shop opening times

® **1** At an *estanco* in Mojácar, Isabel buys postcards, and stamps to go with them.

Isabel	Hola, buenos días.
Woman	Buenos días.
Isabel	Quiero estas postales.
Woman	Aha. Una, dos, tres, cuatro, cinco, seis, siete, ocho, nueve, diez y once.
Isabel	Y ahora, diez sellos para Inglaterra y un sello para Francia, por favor.
Woman	Ya, de treinta y cinco, para las postales. Muy bien. (*tearing out stamps*) Diez y once. Para Inglaterra y para Francia son el mismo precio.

postales	*postcards*
ahora	*now*
ya	*right*
mismo precio	*same price*

Buying stamps:

diez sellos para	Inglaterra Estados Unidos

For a letter or a postcard:

para	carta postal

▶Spotcheck 1 a How many cards does Isabel buy?

b Where are most of them going to?

Calle de Preciados, Madrid

📼 📺 2 Flora Acero, with her friend Begoña, is looking at shirts in a Madrid boutique, *una tienda de ropa.*

Begoña   ¡Eh, mira! Aquí hay más camisas.
Flora   ¿Qué te parece ésta?
Begoña   No sé. Esta naranja también es bonita, ¿no?
Flora   Sí, pero no me gusta mucho el color.
Assistant ¡Hola!
Flora   ¡Hola! ¿Tienes esta camisa en otros colores?
Assistant ¿Qué talla tienes?
Flora   La cuarenta y dos.
Assistant Sí, mira. *(she shows them more shirts)* La tienes en rojo y en azul. También tienes éstas.
Flora   ¡Huy, no! Es demasiado grande. *(she picks up another one)* Me gusta mucho más esta roja.
Assistant ¿Quieres probártela?
Flora   Sí.
Assistant Los probadores están al fondo, a la derecha.

camisas	*shirts*
no sé	*I don't know*
esta naranja	*this orange one*
la tienes en	*you have it in*
rojo	*red*
azul	*blue*
demasiado	*too*
¿quieres probártela?	*do you want to try it on?*
probadores	*changing rooms*
al fondo	*at the back*

▶ Spotcheck 2   Why doesn't Flora like the first shirt that Begoña suggests?

📼 ® 3 In Mojácar the weather is colder than Isabel expected, so she goes to buy a sweatshirt.

Isabel   Hola, buenos días.
Shopkeeper Hola, buenas.
Isabel   Eh, mira, quiero un suéter, tipo sudadera. ¿Qué colores tienes?
Shopkeeper Pues, en esta talla, que es la más grande, tengo en fucsia, celeste, azul marino, gris, negro, y amarillo.
Isabel   Creo que me gusta la fucsia.
Shopkeeper Si quiere usted, se la puede probar.
Isabel   Muchas gracias. *(Isabel tries it on)* Es tipo chaqueta, ¿verdad?
Shopkeeper Sí, sí, es chaqueta.
Isabel   Bien. ¿Me está bien?
Shopkeeper Mmm, un poquito grande.
Isabel   Claro, es la moda.

To ask what someone thinks of something:

¿qué te/le parece	el hotel*?* la camisa*?*

Talking about sizes:

¿qué talla tiene(s)?	*what size are you?*
la cuarenta	*(size) forty*

To say you'll take something:

me *la* llevo – if it's something feminine, like **la falda**
me *lo* llevo – if it's masculine, like **el suéter**

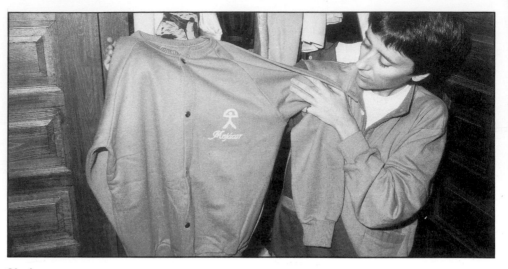

Shopkeeper	Sí, sí.
Isabel	Bien, este color me gusta mucho. ¿Cuánto cuesta?
Shopkeeper	Este modelo, todas las tallas grandes son mil ochocientas cincuenta pesetas.
Isabel	Mil ochocientas cincuenta pesetas. Muy bien. Pues, me la llevo. A ver: mil … quinientas … setecientas … ochocientas, y … cincuenta pesetas.
Shopkeeper	Muchísimas gracias.

suéter, tipo sudadera	*sweatshirt-type sweater*
la más grande	*the biggest*
celeste	*sky blue*
azul marino	*navy blue*
gris	*grey*
negro	*black*
amarillo	*yellow*
creo que	*I think (that)*
se la puede probar	*you can try it on*
chaqueta	*jacket*
¿verdad?	*isn't it?*
¿me está bien?	*is it all right on me?*
claro	*of course*
moda	*fashion*
¿cuánto cuesta?	*how much does it cost?*

▶Spotcheck 3   a   Which colour does Isabel prefer?

b   Why does she take one that's a bit big?

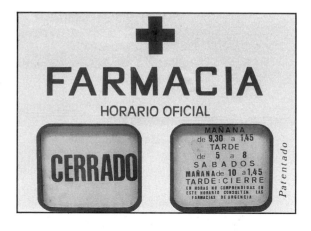

4 Shop opening times in Spain are often different from British ones. Yolanda checked up at two important places: a chemist's and a bank.

Yolanda	¿A qué hora se abre por la mañana?
Chemist	Se abre a las diez menos cuarto.
Yolanda	¿Y a qué hora se cierra?
Chemist	Se cierra a la una y media.
Bank clerk	Por la mañana se abre a las nueve.
Yolanda	¿Y a qué hora se cierra?
Bank clerk	Se cierra a las dos.
Yolanda	¿Y por la tarde?
Chemist	Por la tarde se abre a las cuatro y media y se cierra a las ocho.
Bank clerk	Por la tarde no se abre.

To ask about shop opening times:

¿a qué hora se abre? *what time does it open?*

¿a qué hora se cierra? *what time does it close?*

▶Spotcheck 4 a Which opens first, the chemist's or the bank?
b What's the closing time of the bank?

KEYWORDS

el sello	stamp
la postal	postcard
la carta	letter
el buzón	postbox
Inglaterra	England
Escocia	Scotland
Gales	Wales
Irlanda	Ireland
abrir	to open
cerrar	to close
abierto/a	open
cerrado/a	closed
el lunes	Monday
el martes	Tuesday
el miércoles	Wednesday
el jueves	Thursday
el viernes	Friday
el estanco	tobacconist's
el banco	bank
la tienda	shop
(for shops see p. 208)	
el dinero	money
el cambio	change; exchange
la talla	size
el color	colour
(for colours see p. 209)	
caro/a	dear, expensive
barato/a	cheap
demasiado	too
más	more
probar	to try
¿qué te/le parece ...?	what do you think of ...?
me la/lo llevo	I'll take it

HOW SPANISH WORKS

1 'It' and 'them'

When you say 'I'll take it' in a shop, the word for 'it' will be *lo* or *la*, depending on the gender of the thing you want. If it's a masculine thing, like *un suéter*, use *lo*: *me lo llevo*. If it's a feminine thing, like *una camisa*, use *la*: *me la llevo*.

When there's more than one thing, the word for 'them' is *los* or *las*, again depending on the gender. If they're masculine, like *los tomates*, use *los*: *me los llevo*. If they're feminine, like *las botellas*, use *las*: *me las llevo*.

The other thing to notice about the words for 'it' and 'them' is that, unlike in English, they usually come in front of the verb: *me lo llevo, lo quiero*.

2 This one

Este and *esta* mean 'this': *este suéter, esta camisa*. To say 'this one', just leave out the noun:

este suéter – éste   *esta camisa – ésta*
me gusta éste   *me gusta ésta*

Este and *ésta* can refer to people as well as things (as you saw in Unit 2): *éste es mi amigo, ésta es mi novia*.

The written accent on the *e* doesn't affect the way you say the word – in fact nowadays many Spaniards don't bother to write it.

3 Local colour

The words for colours are like other adjectives. The ending changes slightly, depending on what is being described.

Those ending in *-o/-a*:
una camisa blanca   *dos camisas blancas*
un suéter blanco   *suéteres blancos*

Those ending in other letters:
una bolsa verde   *bolsas verdes*
un coche verde   *coches verdes*

Rojo and *roja* mean 'red'. *El rojo* and *la roja* mean 'the red one'. Which you use depends, as you'd expect, on the gender of the noun:
el suéter rojo – el rojo
la camisa roja – la roja
no me gusta el bikini negro, prefiero el blanco

4 A matter of opinion

¿Qué te parece? ¿Qué le parece? This way of asking someone's opinion works in the same way as *¿te/le gusta?*. Use *te* with someone you'd call *tú*, otherwise *le*.

To give your opinion you can start with *me parece*: *me parece bonito, me parece grande, me parece demasiado pequeña*, etc.

SOUND SPANISH

h The Spanish **h** is never pronounced: *hola* (hello) sounds the same as *ola* (wave).

ch counts as a separate letter in the Spanish alphabet (it comes between **c** and **d**). It's always pronounced like the English 'ch' in 'chop'. Practise with this favourite Spanish breakfast: *un chocolate con churros, por favor*.

WORKOUT

1 As if you were there
You're in an *estanco*.
a Ask if they've got any postcards.
b They have, so when you've chosen some, say 'I'd like these, please'.
c Ask for ten stamps for England and two for the United States.
d Ask how much it comes to.
e Ask if there's a postbox nearby.
f You don't quite understand the directions you're given – what do you say?
g Now you've understood – say thanks and goodbye.

2 Mix and match
These items and their descriptions have got confused – can you rearrange them so that they make sense?
vino para Inglaterra
sellos de queso
gasolina sin gas
agua mineral tinto
bocadillos con leche
menú para ensalada
café normal
tomates del día

3 Going red
In a clothes shop, you are shown a number of things of different colours. But you always like the red ones best! *¿Te gusta esta camisa verde? – Sí, pero me gusta más la roja*.
a ¿Te gusta esta falda blanca?
b ¿Te gustan estas camisas amarillas?
c ¿Te gusta este suéter azul?
d ¿Te gusta esta chaqueta negra?
e ¿Te gusta este pantalón verde?

4 Many a slip
It's easy to make a slip, especially with prices. She was speaking from memory, but did the assistant get any of these items wrong?

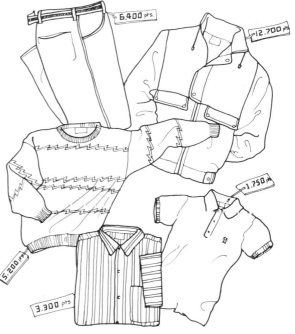

Customer	¿Cuánto cuesta esta camiseta?
Assistant	Mil setecientas cincuenta pesetas.
Customer	¿Y esta camisa?
Assistant	Tres mil trescientas.
Customer	¿Cuánto cuesta este pantalón?
Assistant	Seis mil cuatrocientas pesetas.
Customer	Y esta chaqueta, ¿cuánto cuesta?
Assistant	Doce mil seiscientas.
Customer	¿Y este suéter?
Assistant	Cinco mil doscientas.

5 Right size

Give five answers to the question *¿Qué talla tiene?*.

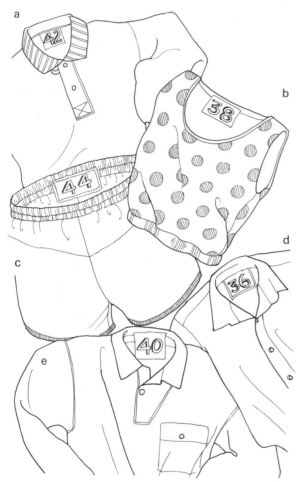

6 Just looking

The shop assistant is showing you some clothes, but you're a difficult customer and would prefer them in another colour or size. Ask if she has what you want – using *lo* or *la* as appropriate.

a Aquí tengo una chaqueta blanca. (*Does she have it in blue?*)

b Aquí tengo una camisa talla cuarenta y dos. (*Size 40?*)

c Aquí tengo un pantalón marrón. (*In black?*)

d Aquí tengo un suéter rojo. (*In yellow?*)

e Aquí tengo una falda talla cuarenta y dos. (*Size 44?*)

7 Over the top

When you're shopping, things aren't always just right first time. Can you answer truthfully the question *¿Qué te parece?* and say what's wrong with these? The first one is done for you.

a Me parece demasiado grande.

8 Opposites

Match up the pairs of opposites.

blanco	todo
abierto	sin
pequeño	mucho
lejos	paro
bien	barato
aquí	negro
con	cerca
trabajo	grande
nada	allí
poco	cerrado
caro	mal

9 Clockwise

With the help of the signs, can you say where these conversations took place?

Oficina de Turismo

lunes a viernes:	10.00 – 2.00
	4.30 – 7.30
sábados, domingos:	10.30 – 1.00

Estanco

lunes a sábado:	9.00 – 1.30
	4.30 – 8.00
domingos:	cerrado

---

a – ¿A qué hora se abre los lunes?
   – Se abre a las diez.
b – ¿Se abre los domingos?
   – No, sólo los sábados.
c – ¿A qué hora se cierra por la tarde?
   – A las ocho.
d – ¿Se abre por la tarde?
   – Sí, de cuatro y media a siete y media.
e – ¿Se cierra a mediodía?
   – Sí, a las dos.
f – ¿A qué hora se abre los sábados?
   – A las diez y media.

ABOUT SPAIN

Postal and telephone services

Correos is the name for a post office. Here you can use the *Lista de Correos* (Poste Restante), and send or collect money, as well as buy stamps.

The most convenient place to buy stamps is *un estanco* (State-controlled tobacconist's). The rate for cards is slightly cheaper than that for letters, so make sure you say what the stamp is for.

An unusual post-box in Santander

Shops

Department stores *(grandes almacenes)* are the same as in Britain, but there are differences between some other Spanish shops and their British equivalents. *Estancos* combine tobacco products, stamps and sometimes stationery, but not sweets or chocolate. For these you'd go to a *confitería* (confectioner's), often attached to a *pastelería* (cake shop).

A *librería*, usually together with a *papelería*, is a bookshop and stationer's, where you can buy postcards, and sometimes newspapers. Newspapers and magazines, however, are more usually on sale in the *quioscos* you'll find in the streets and squares.

A *droguería* is neither a drugstore nor a chemist's but a shop for paints and cleaning materials, often combined with a *perfumería* (perfume and cosmetics shop). A *farmacia* (chemist's) is the place to go for medical products.

Typical shop opening times are 9.30 – 1.30; 4.00 – 7.30.

Fashion

The fashion business is flourishing in Spain. Helped by government investment and the emergence of young and talented designers, it has become important not just nationally but in Europe. Among the best-known names are Sybilla, Roser Marcé of Barcelona, Alfonso Domínguez, a Galician, and Agatha Ruiz de la Prada, who's a product of Madrid's youthful cultural movement, *la movida* – 'the swinging 80s'.

10 Tiempo libre

What you like to do in your spare time

What you're going to do

® 1 Santiago Peralta from Barcelona told Jordi about his leisure pursuits.

Jordi ¿Cuáles son tus aficiones?

Santiago Bueno, la lectura, y como deporte el fútbol.

Jordi ¿Te gusta algún equipo en particular?

Santiago El Español de Barcelona.

To say what sport you're keen on:

| soy aficionado/a | al fútbol
a la nata-
ción |

Football pennant

REAL C. D. ESPAÑOL

Jordi Tú que eres aficionado al fútbol, ¿practicas el fútbol, juegas al fútbol?

Santiago Sí, juego cada domingo, en un equipo del barrio donde vivo.

Jordi ¿Qué equipo es?

Santiago Club Atlético Fortpienc.

aficiones	*hobbies*
lectura	*reading*
como deporte	*by way of sport*
algún	*any*
equipo	*team*
¿practicas . . . ?	*do you do any . . . ?*
¿juegas . . . ?	*do you play?*

▶ **Spotcheck 1**   a   Who does Santiago play for?

             b   Which team does he support?

📺 **2**   Yolanda asked some people in the Retiro park, Madrid, what they liked doing in their spare time.

Yolanda   ¿Qué le gusta hacer en su tiempo libre?

Passer-by 1   Bueno, pues me gusta estudiar y hacer deporte, generalmente.

Amusements in the Retiro park, Madrid

Passer-by 2	Pues, me gusta hacer algo de footing, algo de tenis, natación.
Passer-by 3	Leer, escuchar música.
Passer-by 2	También me gusta leer, también me gusta oír música.
Yolanda	¿Qué te gusta hacer en tu tiempo libre?
Passer-by 4	Pues, dormir, leer.
Passer-by 5	Pues, en mi tiempo libre me gusta mucho, mucho, mucho ir a la piscina, muchísimo.

To say what you like doing:

	hacer deporte
me gusta	leer
	dormir

algo de footing	*a bit of jogging*
natación	*swimming*
leer	*to read*
escuchar	*to listen to*
oír	*to hear*
dormir	*to sleep*
ir	*to go*
piscina	*swimming pool*

▶ **Spotcheck 2** How many people mention sport of some kind?

Ⓡ **3** Four people talk about what they do in their spare time. One of them has a most unusual hobby.

Jordi	¿Cuáles son tus aficiones?
Ana	Pues escuchar música, ver la tele, y viajar.
Jordi	¿Cuáles son tus principales aficiones?
María José	Me gusta ir al cine, me gusta leer, me gusta correr, y me gusta estar con los amigos.
Isabel	Cuando sales para divertirte, ¿qué te gusta hacer?
Jaime	Me gusta mucho ir a cenar a algún sitio con amigos, o a tomar algo de beber o alguna tapa.
Isabel	¿Qué te gusta hacer?
Rubén	Buscar espárragos.
Isabel	Buscar espárragos. ¿Y dónde los buscas?
Rubén	Por los montes.
Isabel	¿Encuentras muchos?
Rubén	Sí.

ver la tele	*to watch the telly*
viajar	*to travel*
correr	*to run*
estar	*to be*
sales para divertirte	*you go out to enjoy yourself*
sitio	*place*
buscar espárragos	*to look for asparagus*
por los montes	*in the hills*
¿encuentras ...?	*do you find ...?*

▶ Spotcheck 3   a   Who doesn't seem to like staying at home?

b   What does Rubén like collecting?

📼   📺 4   It's five o'clock on Sunday afternoon in the Retiro
park. What are people planning to do in the evening?

Yolanda	Esta tarde, ¿qué va a hacer?
Passer-by 1	Voy a ir a casa de unos amigos.
Yolanda	Esta tarde, ¿qué va a hacer?
Passer-by 2	Voy a ir al teatro.
Passer-by 3	Voy a ir a ver una exposición de arte.
Yolanda	¿Qué va a hacer esta tarde?
Passer-by 4	Pues salir con unas amigas a cenar.
Passer-by 5	Pasear un poco.
Passer-by 6	Ver la tele.

To ask what someone's going to do:
¿qué va(s) a hacer?

And to say what you're going to do:

voy a	salir
	jugar al tenis

exposición	*exhibition*
salir	*to go out*
pasear	*to go for a walk*

▶ Spotcheck 4   How many people are going to stay at home?

Cinema in Gran
Vía, Madrid

KEYWORDS

la afición	hobby
el deporte	sport
aficionado/a	keen
la película	film
el cine	cinema
el teatro	theatre
la música	music
la piscina	swimming pool
ir	to go
jugar a	to play
escuchar	to listen to
ver la televisión	to watch television
viajar	to travel
leer	to read
hacer	to do
estudiar	to study
bailar	to dance
dormir	to sleep
preferir	to prefer

(*for more leisure activities see p. 211*)

HOW SPANISH WORKS

1   Like-wise

You saw earlier how to say you **like** something: *me gusta Madrid; me gustan las tapas*. In this unit people talk about what they like **doing**: *me gusta jugar al tenis; me gusta leer*. When you use a verb after *me* (or *te* or *le*) *gusta*, it always ends in *-r* (the infinitive). And the same thing happens with what you **prefer** to do: *¿prefieres estudiar o pasear? – prefiero pasear.*

2   Going to

To say what you're **going** to do, you use *voy a*, followed by the infinitive part of the verb: *voy a ver la tele; voy a dormir*.

Don't forget to put *a* in between *voy/vas/va* and the following verb.

3   Small change

We've seen a number of verbs that change not just at the end of the word but also in the middle:

qu**er**er	to want	qu**ier**o	I want
c**er**rar	to close	c**ier**ra	it closes

As well as the verbs that change to *ie*, there are some that change to *ue*. Two examples in this unit are:

j**u**gar	to play	j**ue**go	I play
d**o**rmir	to sleep	d**ue**rmo	I sleep

4   All change

Some of the most commonly used Spanish verbs change in a much less predictable way than those mentioned above. Three you've already met are:

ser	to be	soy, eres, es
estar	to be	estoy, estás, está
tener	to have	tengo, tienes, tiene

In this unit there are two other very useful verbs:

ir	to go	voy, vas, va
hacer	to do	hago, haces, hace

5   'On' and 'at'

Two words often heard when people talk about hobbies are *aficionado* ('keen') and *juego* ('I play'). A thing to notice about these is that they are both usually followed by the word *a*, which in turn is often linked with *el* to form *al*. For example:

soy aficionado **al** footing	I'm keen on jogging
juego **al** tenis	I play tennis

SOUND SPANISH

Stress

Every Spanish word has a stress on just one of its syllables.

1   If the word ends in a vowel, or *-n* or *-s*, stress the next-to-last syllable:

cinco   pata̱ta   toma̱te   herma̱nos   tie̱nen

2   If the word ends in any other letter, stress the last syllable: *Madri̱d*

3   A written accent over part of a word means that this is the part to stress, whatever the ending:

Má̱laga   Cá̱diz   jamó̱n

WORKOUT

1 Non-trivial

Try to match what each person says about their favourite pursuits with the most likely picture.

a   Me gusta estar con las amigas.
b   A mí me gusta mucho jugar al tenis.
c   Me gusta dormir, nada más.
d   Me gusta el cine; me encanta.
e   A mí me gusta viajar.
f   Me gusta escuchar música.

i

ii

iii

iv

v

vi

2 Preferences

Here is some information about four people's hobbies. How would each one describe his or her favourite? (Use *prefiero*.)

Teresa   No me gustan los deportes.
Soy muy aficionada al cine.
Me gusta bastante el teatro.

Manuel   No me gustan los espectáculos.
No me gusta la televisión.
Me gustan muchísimo los deportes, sobre todo el baloncesto.

Luisa   Me gusta mucho la natación, pero mi gran afición es la lectura.
También me gusta ir al teatro, pero el fútbol no me gusta nada.

Ramón   Me gusta estudiar idiomas.
No me gusta el teatro.
Me encanta hacer footing.
No me gusta la música rock.

3 ¿Qué vas a hacer mañana?

You've written down your evening activities for the week. Match the appropriate verbs to the diary entries, and then tell a friend what you are going to do.

For example: *El lunes, voy a estudiar francés.*

jugar   hacer   ir   cenar
ver   estudiar   tomar

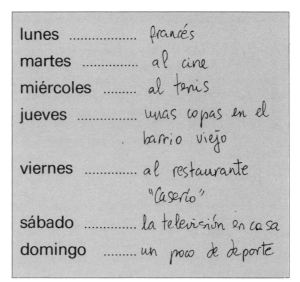

lunes	francés
martes	al cine
miércoles	al tenis
jueves	unas copas en el barrio viejo
viernes	al restaurante "Caserío"
sábado	la televisión en casa
domingo	un poco de deporte

4   As if you were there

You're talking to a fellow guest at the *Hotel Las Gaviotas*. (Use *tú*.)

You	(*Ask what he's going to do this afternoon.*)
Guest	Esta tarde voy a ir al Museo de Arte Abstrac-to.
You	(*Ask if he likes museums.*)
Guest	Sí, bastante. Soy muy aficionado al arte moderno. ¿A tí te gusta?
You	(*Say no, not much. You prefer going to the beach.*)
Guest	Ah, pues, hay una playa muy bonita cerca de aquí. Es muy limpia, y va poca gente.
You	(*Ask where it is.*)
Guest	Está en La Puebla, a veinte minutos en coche.
You	(*Say thanks, you'll go there this afternoon.*)
Guest	¿O sea que te gusta la natación?
You	(*Say well, you don't like swimming – you prefer reading or sleeping.*)

5   Odd one out

a   Which one of these isn't a ball game?
   el fútbol   el golf
   el tenis   la película

b   Which of these doesn't involve moving?
   leer   viajar   bailar   montar en bicicleta

c   Which of these places wouldn't you go to for a night out?
   una discoteca   una biblioteca
   un teatro   un cine

d   Where wouldn't you expect to get a sun tan?
   en la playa   en la montaña
   en una iglesia   en el campo

e   Which wouldn't you do on your day off?
   dormir   bailar   hacer deporte   trabajar

f   Which would you stick on a postcard?
   sello   calle   pollo   tortilla

g   Which wouldn't you put in an omelette?
   queso   patata   carta   champiñones

6   Just say

a   You like playing football.
b   You don't like tennis.
c   You're a football fan.
d   You like listening to music, but you prefer dancing.
e   You like living in the country.
f   You like speaking Spanish.
g   You love travelling in Spain.

7   Ask me another

Match the questions on the left with the most likely answers.

a	¿Qué va a tomar?	i	No, no me gusta el mar.
b	¿Dónde va a ir?	ii	Sí, es muy bonita.
c	¿Te gusta esta camisa?	iii	No, sólo los fines de semana.
d	¿Qué vino prefiere?	iv	Un zumo de tomate.
e	¿Juegas al baloncesto?	v	Sí, vivo aquí, y tengo muchos.
f	¿Practicas el windsurf?	vi	No, prefiero el fútbol.
g	¿Tienes amigos aquí en Alicante?	vii	A la montaña.
h	¿Sales todas las noches?	viii	El tinto de la casa.

8   Routine change

The following people are all going to do something different from their usual routine. How will they explain their change of plan?

a   Me gusta estar tranquilo en casa, pero hoy voy a .... (*go out with my friends*).
b   Me gusta ver películas extranjeras, pero hoy voy a .... (*see a Spanish film*).
c   Me gusta mucho pasear, pero hoy voy a .... (*watch TV*).
d   Me gusta ir al cine, pero hoy .... (*I'm going to go to the theatre*).
e   Me gusta escuchar música, pero esta tarde .... (*I'm going to play football*).
f   Normalmente ceno en una cafetería, pero hoy .... (*I'm going to have dinner at home*).

9 A taste of Spain

At the beginning of 1987, a Spanish newspaper conducted a survey of the preferences of Spaniards. Here are some of the findings.

Para una clara mayoría de españoles (54%), el sábado es el día favorito; el color que más gusta es el azul, sobre todo entre los hombres, y después los colores negro, rojo y gris. Los productos más apreciados son: el coche (14%), joyas (9%), ropa (7%), flores y plantas (6%) y la casa (6%). El plato favorito de los españoles es la paella, y la fruta que más se come es la naranja.

Which of these statements about Spaniards' preferences are true, and which are false?
a Sunday is the most popular day.
b Men's favourite colour is blue.
c Grey is more popular than red.
d A home is valued more than a car.
e Oranges are not popular.

10 Happy days

Using these letters as many times as you like, you can write all the days of the week in Spanish – except one. Which?

A C D E G I J L M N O R S T U V

ABOUT SPAIN

Sport and leisure

Over the last few years there has been an increase in the number of Spaniards who actually take part in some kind of sport, due in some measure to the building of sports centres and government campaigns to make people more aware of health and fitness. Statistics from 1985 show that football is the most popular sport, followed by jogging (*el jogging* or *el footing*), basketball (*el baloncesto*) and cycling (*el ciclismo*).

Football is also the most popular spectator sport and Spaniards are now much more likely to spend Sunday afternoons at a football match (*un partido de fútbol*) than at the traditional entertainment, the bullfight (*la corrida de toros*). Even so, bullfighting continues to draw crowds, particularly in the tourist areas.

The *Retiro*

A large park on the east side of Madrid, the *Retiro* is the place many *madrileños* go to walk, sit, jog, ride, row – or train for a bullfight. With its wide shady walks, its seats, cafés, open-air entertainment, ice-cream stalls and large lake, it offers a haven, within easy reach, for people to get away from the city atmosphere and pressures.

The cinema

In the big cities, there are usually three showings of a film, at about 4.30 pm, 8 pm and 10.30 pm. In smaller towns there may be only the last two. Outside the specialist cinemas, foreign films are usually dubbed into Spanish. In recent years there has been a huge increase in Spanish film production, encouraged by the government. Films such as *Los santos inocentes*, *El sur* and *El amor brujo* have done well abroad, and directors like Mario Camus, Víctor Erice and Carlos Saura have won international prizes.

Spanish music

Spain has had a number of internationally known composers – Granados, Albéniz, de Falla, Rodrigo – but has been best-known for its classical guitarists, such as Segovia and Narciso Yepes, and flamenco guitarists, like Paco de Lucía.

Within Spain, there is still a thriving tradition of folk music and folk dance, which varies greatly from region to region. For instance, Aragón has its *jota* and Cataluña its *sardana*, and in Andalucía of course there's *flamenco*.

Over the past 20 years or so, some of the most popular music has come from the singer–song-writers (*cantautores*) like Joan Manuel Serrat, Luis Llach and Victor Manuel, whose themes are of the social and political variety. Spanish rock music is beginning to find its own identity now as new bands emerge not just from Madrid, but from Barcelona, Galicia and the Basque Country.

A *sardana* in front of Barcelona cathedral

113

Relaxing in
Madrid's Retiro park

11 ¡Buen viaje!

Travelling by public transport:

– asking about times

– buying tickets

Ⓡ **1** Isabel, on her way out to the Madrid suburb of Vallecas, asks a woman if there's a bus.

Isabel Por favor, ¿hay un autobús para Vallecas?
Woman Sí, el cincuenta y siete.
Isabel ¿De dónde sale?
Woman De aquí.
Isabel ¿De esta parada, de aquí?
Woman Sí.

To find out what transport there is:

| ¿hay | un autobús
un tren | para . . . ? |

And where it goes from:
¿de dónde sale?

Isabel	¿Y salen muchos?
Woman	Sí.
Isabel	¿Salen con frecuencia?
Woman	Sí, con frecuencia. Ahí viene uno.
Isabel	Ah sí, es verdad. Muchas gracias.
Woman	De nada.

parada	*stop*
con frecuencia	*regularly*
viene	*comes*
verdad	*true*

▶ Spotcheck 1   a   What number bus does Isabel need?

                 b   Does she have long to wait?

📺 2   Carlos Giménez goes to the information desk at the railway station to ask about train times from Madrid to Sevilla.

Atocha Station, Madrid

SALIDAS		ANDALUCIA LEVANTE		
HORA	CLASE DE TREN	DESTINO	COCHES	OBSERVACIONES
7 3 6	SEMID·TRANVIA	JAEN	2ª	
8 5 0	RAPIDO TALGO	SEVILLA P. A.	1ª-2ª	CAFETERIA
9 1 0	RAPIDO TER	CUENCA-VALENCIA	1ª-2ª BAR	
1 0 4 5	RAPIDO	CADIZ-MALAGA	1ª-2ª	CAFETERIA
1 1 3 0	AUTOMOTOR	CUENCA-VALENCIA	2ª	
1 4 4 1	TALGO PENDULAR	CADIZ-HUELVA	1ª-2ª	RESTAURANTE
1 5 0 2	RAPIDO TALGO	GRANADA-ALMERIA	1ª-2ª	CAFETERIA
1 5 3 0	AUTOMOTOR	CUENCA-VALENCIA-GANDIA	1ª-2ª BAR	
1 6 0 3	SEMID·TRANVIA	LINARES BAEZA	2ª	
1 7 4 5	SEMID·TRANVIA	SANTA CRUZ DE MUDELA	2ª	

Carlos	Buenos días.
Clerk	Buenos días.
Carlos	Por favor, ¿qué trenes hay para Sevilla mañana?
Clerk	¿Por la mañana o por la tarde?
Carlos	Por la tarde.
Clerk	Sí, un momento. (*she consults the timetable*) Hay un Talgo a las catorce cuarenta y dos.
Carlos	¿A qué hora llega a Sevilla?
Clerk	A las veinte treinta y ocho.
Carlos	¿Hay otro tren más tarde?
Clerk	Sí, hay un expreso a las veintiuna cuarenta y cinco que llega a las seis y diecisiete, y otro a las veintitrés horas que llega a las ocho de la mañana.
Carlos	¿Hay restaurante en el Talgo?
Clerk	Sí, sí, hay restaurante.
Carlos	Vale. Muchas gracias, ¿eh?
Clerk	De nada, adiós.

To ask what time something leaves/arrives:
¿a qué hora sale/llega?

mañana	*tomorrow*
Talgo	*fast train*
más tarde	*later*
expreso	*night train*

▶ Spotcheck 2   a   What time does the Talgo get to Sevilla?

b   What time does the last train to Sevilla leave?

Queuing for tickets at Atocha

📻 📺 3   Carlos goes to the ticket office to get a return ticket to Sevilla.

Carlos	Buenos días.
Ticket clerk	Buenos días.
Carlos	Por favor, un billete de segunda clase, ida y vuelta, para Sevilla.
Ticket clerk	¿Para qué tren?
Carlos	Para mañana, para el Talgo de las catorce cuarenta y dos.
Ticket clerk	¿Quiere fumador o no fumador?

To buy a ticket to ....
un billete para ...

single   **de ida**
return   **de ida y vuelta**

Carlos	No fumador.
Ticket clerk	Muy bien, aquí tiene su billete. Son cuatro mil trescientas pesetas.
Carlos	(*he pays*) Gracias. Adiós.
Ticket clerk	Adiós.

de segunda clase   *second class*
(no) fumador   (*non-*)*smoking*

▶Spotcheck 3   a   Does Carlos intend to smoke on the journey?
        b   How much does the ticket cost?

Ⓡ **4**   At the Metro station in the Puerta del Sol, Isabel gets tickets to Gran Vía.

Isabel   Dos, por favor. (*she is given the tickets*) Gracias. Para Gran Vía, ¿qué línea necesito? (*the ticket clerk tells her*) ¿La uno? Gracias.

On the platform, as a train arrives . . .

Isabel	¿Va a Gran Vía?
Man	Sí, va a Gran Vía.
Isabel	Gracias.

Then, as the train pulls in at a station . . .

Isabel	¿Es Gran Vía?
Man	Sí, Gran Vía.
Isabel	Vale.

¿qué línea necesito?   *what line do I need?*

To check you're on the right bus/train:
¿va a . . . ?

▶Spotcheck 4   a   How many tickets does Isabel buy?
        b   What line does she want?

® **5**   Isabel asked a woman living in one of Madrid's
suburbs what the public transport service was like.

Isabel	¿Usted vive en Madrid?
Woman	Vivo en Madrid, en Moratalaz.
Isabel	¿En Moratalaz?
Woman	En Moratalaz.
Isabel	Pero eso está un poco lejos, ¿no?
Woman	¡Hombre!, está un poco retirado del centro, pero hay muy buenas combinaciones.
Isabel	¿Cómo se llega a Moratalaz?
Woman	Pues, se llega ... hay tres autobuses, el treinta y dos, el veinte y el treinta. Y el metro, también hay metro.

To ask how to get to a place:
¿cómo se llega a . . . ?

¡hombre!	*well!*
retirado del centro	*away from the centre*
combinaciones	*connections*

▶ Spotcheck 5   a   How many buses can the woman catch home
from the centre of Madrid?

b   How else can she get home?

KEYWORDS

el tren	train
la estación	station
el avión	plane
el vuelo	flight
el aeropuerto	airport
el barco	boat
el puerto	port
el autocar	coach
el autobús	bus
la parada	stop; rank
el taxi	taxi

(*for more travel vocabulary see p. 209*)

el horario	timetable
el próximo ...	the next ...
el último ...	the last ...
el billete	ticket
de ida	single
de ida y vuelta	return
(no) fumador	(non-)smoking
¿cuándo?	when?
hoy	today
mañana	tomorrow
la salida	departure
la llegada	arrival
salir	to leave
llegar	to arrive
venir	to come
coger	to catch, to take

HOW SPANISH WORKS

1   The third man – or woman, or thing

Most of the verbs you've met so far concern 'I' (*yo*) or 'you' (*tú* or *usted*), known as the 'first person' and the 'second person'. There's also a 'third person': 'he', 'she' or 'it' (*él*/*ella*), or any named person or thing:

¿cuándo viene Pepa?	when's **Pepa** coming?
¿a qué hora sale el tren?	what time does **the train** leave?

¿a qué hora llega?	what time does **it** arrive?

This form of the verb is exactly the same as the form for *usted*. It ends in -*a* (if it's an -*ar* verb) or -*e* (if it's an -*er* or -*ir* verb):

	llegar	tener	salir
(*usted*)	llega	tiene	sale
(*él*/*ella*)	llega	tiene	sale

There is only one exception to these endings – the third person of the verb *ser* is *es*: *Madrid* **es** *grande* (and the *a* of *está* has an accent: *Juan está aquí*).

2   The whole truth

La verdad means 'the truth'. *¿Verdad?* on its own is used at the end of a sentence to check whether something is true or not:

llega a las seis, *¿verdad?*	it arrives at six, doesn't it?
usted se llama Frank, *¿verdad?*	you're called Frank, aren't you?
tienes seis hermanos, *¿verdad?*	you've got six brothers, haven't you?

3   24 hours

The twenty-four-hour clock is used in Spain, as in Britain, when talking about timetables of public transport. You don't need to worry about *y* or *menos* – just give the hours then the minutes:

las catorce veinticinco	1425
las catorce cuarenta	1440

If the time is 1401, 1402 etc, you need to add *cero*: *las catorce cero uno, las catorce cero dos*, etc.

SOUND SPANISH

Two vowels

When two vowels come together in Spanish, you pronounce the two sounds individually, unlike in English where they tend to make a new sound, eg **a** + **i** (pain), **o** + **u** (out). Practise with: *Jaime tiene dieciséis años.*

The only vowel that isn't pronounced is **u** when it comes between a **q** or **g** and an **e** or **i**: *querer, quiero, guitarra.*

WORKOUT

1 Just the ticket

Ask for the following tickets. For example: *Un billete de ida y vuelta para Sevilla, por favor; de segunda clase, no fumador.*

2 Asking the right questions

Where would you be most likely to hear these questions asked? Choose from:

una estación de tren   una gasolinera
una oficina de turismo   una parada de autobús
un aeropuerto

a   Perdón, ¿a qué hora sale el autobús para Vallecas?
b   Dos billetes de ida y vuelta, no fumador, en el expreso a Sevilla, por favor.
c   Perdón, ¿a qué hora llega el avión de Barcelona?
d   ¿La carretera de Mojácar?
e   ¿A qué hora se abre el Museo Picasso, por favor?

3 False start

You ask where the buses start from, but not all the information you're given is accurate. Spot the errors with the aid of the map.

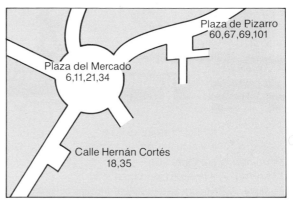

a   – Por favor, ¿de dónde sale el número veintiuno?
    – De la Plaza del Mercado.

b   – El número ciento uno, ¿de dónde sale, por favor?
    – Sale de la Plaza de Pizarro.

c   – Por favor, ¿de dónde sale el número treinta y cinco?
    – El treinta y cinco sale de la Calle Hernán Cortés.

d   – El número sesenta, ¿de dónde sale, por favor?
    – Sale de la Plaza del Mercado.

e   – Por favor, ¿de dónde sale el número sesenta y nueve?
    – De la Plaza de Pizarro.

4 Information

The following sentences contain information about some sort of public transport. Can you work out what question you would have asked to get each answer?

a   El número 33 sale de la Plaza de Cataluña.
b   El expreso llega a Sevilla a las 11.20.
c   No, no hay otro autobús más tarde.
d   La parada del 28 está allí, al otro lado de la calle.
e   No, el tren de Granada no sale hasta mañana.
f   No, no hay restaurante en el expreso.
g   Son diez mil doscientas pesetas.
h   No, no va a Segovia, éste es el tren para Burgos.

5 Getting about

Everyone has their favourite means of transport. Try to match each person with their preference.

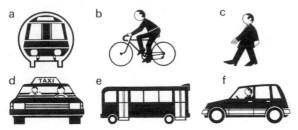

Lola — Prefiero ir en autobús.
Rodrigo — Yo viajo siempre en metro.
Asunción — Para mí el taxi.
Francisco — Yo prefiero ir en bicicleta.
Pastora — Todos los días voy al trabajo en coche.
Juan — A mí me gusta ir andando.

6 Getting there

a Which means of transport wouldn't get you from Barcelona to Palma de Mallorca?
un avión   un autobús   un barco

b Which piece of paper wouldn't help you to get on board a plane?
una postal   un billete   un pasaporte

c Which would tell you about times of Talgos to Valencia?
un mapa de carreteras
un horario de trenes
un plano de la ciudad

d Where would you wait for a bus?
un aeropuerto   una gasolinera   una parada

e Which train should you take if you want to get from Madrid to Almería in time for supper?
el Talgo que llega a las nueve cincuenta
el Talgo que sale a las diecinueve cuarenta
el Talgo que llega a las diecinueve quince

f You're on the train to Granada and you want to have lunch. Which piece of information would you be pleased to hear?
Este tren no tiene restaurante.
Hay restaurante en este tren.
Este tren no va a Granada.

7 As if you were there

You're trying to get to the airport, and it's getting a bit late . . .

You — (Ask a passer-by if there's a bus to the airport.)
Passer-by — Sí, allí en la plaza hay una parada. Sale de allí.
You — (Say thanks, and ask what number it is.)
Passer-by — Lo siento, no sé.
You — (You find the bus stop and a bus arrives. Ask the driver if it goes to the airport.)
Driver — No, al aeropuerto no. Vamos a la estación de tren.
You — (Ask if there is a bus to the airport.)
Driver — Sí, a las cuatro y media.
You — (That's not for another hour – you'll have to get a taxi. Ask if there's a taxi rank around here.)
Driver — Sí, hay una enfrente del Hotel Carlos III.
You — (And where's the Hotel Carlos III?)
Driver — Está bastante cerca. Tiene que cruzar la plaza y coger la avenida.
You — (Ask if the hotel's on the left or the right.)
Driver — A mano izquierda.
You — (Thank him and rush off . . .)

8 Taking flight

You've got a ticket for the Madrid–Barcelona shuttle flight, and you're at the airport information desk.
a Ask what time the next flight leaves.
b The girl at the desk says: Sale a las catorce cuarenta y cinco. It's 2.25 pm now – how much time do you have?
c The man at the check-in desk examines your ticket and says: ¿Fumador o no fumador?. Answer according to your preferences.
d You hear your flight being called: Se ruega a los señores pasajeros que pasen por la puerta número quince. What should you do now?
e At the departure gate, check that this is the flight to Barcelona.
It is – so ¡buen viaje!.

9 Timetables

Convert these times for trains from Gerona from the 24-hour clock to the 12-hour clock – write them out in full in Spanish.

El tren de Gerona llega a las ...

a   a las veintitrés cero cinco
b   a las diecisiete treinta y dos
c   a las dieciocho cuarenta
d   a las trece quince
e   a las diecinueve cincuenta

10 The trains in Spain ...

Travellers are queuing for information at a railway station. Match the questions they ask with the correct replies, using the timetable. The time now is 10.19.

Salida	Destino	Salida	Destino
09.03	Avila	10.38	Avila
09.13	Segovia	10.56	Segovia
10.23	Salamanca	11.09	Salamanca

a   ¿A qué hora sale el próximo tren para Avila, por favor?
   i   Sale a las nueve cero tres.
   ii Sale a las diez treinta y ocho.
b   ¿A qué hora sale el próximo tren para Segovia, por favor?
   i   Sale a las nueve trece.
   ii Sale a las diez cincuenta y seis.
c   ¿A qué hora sale el próximo tren para Salamanca, por favor?
   i   Sale a las diez veintitrés.
   ii Sale a las once nueve.

11 No way out

The word *salida* means 'departure' and 'way out', so it's quite useful when travelling. It also contains some useful letters: prove it by trying to reconstruct these expressions, all taken from this unit, which have had all the letters contained in *salida* removed.

a   no fum _ _ or
b   un b _ _ _ ete
c   _ e pr _ mer _ c _ _ _ e
d   _ e _ _ _ y vue _ t _
e   _ e _ egun _ _ c _ _ _ e
f   _ _ p _ r _ _ _ _ e _ utobú _

ABOUT SPAIN

Sevilla

Sevilla is the capital of Andalucía, and the centre of regional government. It has been the meeting place of many cultures – the Moors, for instance, settled here from North Africa in the 8th century. The *Alcázar* is a monument to that period, with its court-yards, fountains, tiled walls and shady gardens. Just outside the *Alcázar* is the *barrio de Santa Cruz*, the original Jewish quarter of Sevilla – a delightful maze of narrow streets, with typically Mediterranean houses, whitewashed walls, patios and flowers.

In the 15th and 16th centuries Sevilla became one of the richest cities in Europe, the focus of trading activities with the New World. Christopher Columbus was buried here and Magellan prepared his ships here before setting sail.

Today, Sevilla attracts thousands of visitors each spring to its *Semana Santa* (Holy Week) processions and *la Feria de Abril* (the Spring Fair). It is the home of bullfighting and of *flamenco*, an art which is kept very much alive in special schools and *peñas* (flamenco clubs).

The Torre de Oro, Sevilla

Public transport

Buses are frequent and relatively cheap in most towns, and Madrid and Barcelona also have an underground railway system (*metro*). Pay-as-you-enter is the system on the buses, and there is only one fare on buses and underground.

Underground lines are identified by a number and the names of the stations at each end, eg *Línea 5:*

Canillejas – Carabanchel. Bus stops are marked with a sign showing the route, the main stops, and the stop you are at.

Inter-city trains vary in speed. *Un expreso* is not particularly quick, despite the name; it's a night train. The fastest (and most comfortable) trains are the *Talgo* and the *Ter*. You have to pay a supplement to travel on them, and it's worth booking in advance.

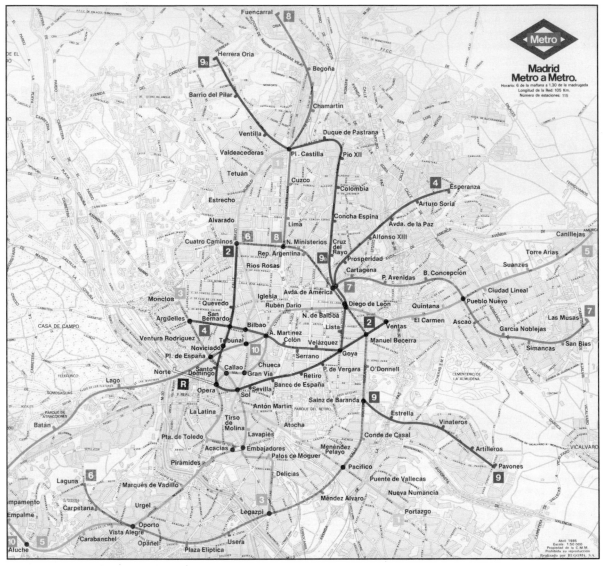

Map of Madrid's Metro

12 Cinco estrellas

Booking in at a hotel

Talking about where you live

® 1 Isabel arrives at a hotel in Madrid where she's already made a reservation.

Isabel	Buenas noches.
Receptionist	Buenas noches, señora.
Isabel	Tengo una habitación reservada a nombre de Isabel Soto.
Receptionist	Sí, señora, un momento, por favor. (*he checks*) Sí, efectivamente. ¿Me deja su pasaporte, por favor?
Isabel	Sí, ¿cómo no?
Receptionist	¿Hace usted el favor de firmar aquí? (*Isabel signs*) Perfecto, muchas gracias. Tiene usted la habitación trescientos nueve.
Isabel	La trescientos nueve.

To say you have a room booked in your name:
tengo una habitación reservada a nombre de . . .

efectivamente	*that's right*
¿me deja . . .?	*can you let me have . . .?*
pasaporte	*passport*
¿cómo no?	*of course*
¿hace usted el favor de . . .?	*will you please . . .?*
firmar	*to sign*

▶ **Spotcheck 1**   What two things is Isabel asked to do?

Ⓣⓥ **2**   Manuel López and his wife Margarita arrive at reception at the Hotel Simón in Sevilla.

Manuel	Buenas tardes.
Receptionist	Buenas tardes.
Manuel	¿Tienen una habitación doble?
Receptionist	¿Para cuántas noches?
Manuel	Para dos noches.
Receptionist	Dos noches. (*he checks the register*) Sí, tenemos habitaciones con baño o con lavabo sólo. ¿Qué prefiere?
Margarita	Mejor con baño. ¿Qué precio tiene?
Receptionist	Son cinco mil pesetas por noche.
Margarita	¿Con desayuno?
Receptionist	No, el desayuno es aparte.
Manuel and Margarita	Muy bien.
Receptionist	Su carnet de identidad, por favor. (*Manuel hands his over*) ¿Me firma aquí? (*Manuel signs*) Aquí tiene su llave: habitación doscientos doce.
Manuel	Gracias.
Receptionist	¿Tienen equipaje?
Manuel	Sí, está en el coche. ¿Tienen ustedes garaje?
Receptionist	No, lo siento, no tenemos.
Manuel	¿Y dónde se puede aparcar?
Receptionist	Hay un aparcamiento cerca, en el Paseo de Colón.
Manuel	Muy bien. Gracias.
Receptionist	Adiós.

To ask for a single/double room:
¿tiene(n) una habitación individual/doble?

To say how long you want to stay:
para una noche   *for one night*
para dos noches   *for two nights*

con baño	*with bathroom*
lavabo	*washbasin*
¿qué precio tiene?	*what price is it?*
por noche	*per night*
desayuno	*breakfast*
aparte	*separate*
carnet de identidad	*identity card*
¿me firma aquí?	*will you sign here?*
llave	*key*
equipaje	*luggage*
lo siento	*I'm sorry*
¿. . . se puede aparcar?	*. . . can I park?*
aparcamiento	*car park*

▶ Spotcheck 2　a　Do Manuel and Margarita take a room with bathroom or just washbasin?

　　b　How much will their bill be (excluding breakfast)?

　　c　Where can they park their car?

Ⓡ **3**　Isabel's checking out of her hotel.

Isabel　Aquí están las llaves, ¿y la cuenta, por favor?

Receptionist　De acuerdo, muy bien. Aquí tiene usted la cuenta. Son quince mil seiscientas trece.

Isabel　Quince mil seiscientas trece. ¿Aceptan ustedes tarjetas de crédito?

Receptionist　Sí, efectivamente, sí, tarjetas de crédito aceptamos, sí.

Isabel　Aquí tiene.

Receptionist　¿Me puede firmar aquí, por favor, si es usted tan amable?

Isabel　Aquí, ¿verdad?

Receptionist　Sí. (*Isabel signs*) Muy bien. Pues, es correcto todo. De acuerdo. Muchas gracias. Adiós, buenos días, y lleven ustedes buen viaje.

Isabel　Muchas gracias. Adiós.

> To ask for the bill:
> la cuenta, por favor

¿aceptan . . .?	*do you accept . . .?*
tarjetas de crédito	*credit cards*
aceptamos	*we accept*
tan amable	*so kind*
de acuerdo	*fine*
lleven ustedes buen viaje	*I hope you have a good trip*

▶ Spotcheck 3　a　How does Isabel pay?

　　b　How much does she pay?

4 Elvira Antón and her husband José are at a table on the patio of the *parador* at Arcos de la Frontera. She calls the waiter over.

Elvira ¡Por favor! (*the waiter comes over*) ¿A qué hora se puede comer?

Waiter El restaurante está abierto desde la una y media hasta las tres y media.

Elvira ¿Y se puede comer aquí en el patio?

Waiter No, no se puede comer. Sólo se puede tomar un aperitivo. ¿Quieren tomar algo?

Elvira Umm . . . un fino para mí.

Waiter (*to José*) ¿Y para usted?

José Un vino blanco. ¡Ah! Y unas aceitunas, por favor.

Waiter Muy bien. Ahora mismo.

Elvira Muchas gracias.

desde	*from*
ahora mismo	*right away*

To ask if something is possible:

¿se puede aparcar?	*is it possible to park?*
¿se puede comer?	*is it possible to eat?*

▶ **Spotcheck 4** a What are the restaurant opening hours?

b What can you have on the patio?

Arcos de la Frontera

® **5** Ana talks about the pros and cons of living in the centre of Madrid.

Madrid: centre and suburbs

Ana Me gusta vivir en el centro porque las tiendas son más numerosas y más baratas. Me gusta también porque hay cines, teatros y restaurantes, y me gusta porque la vida de barrio en Madrid es muy agradable.

Isabel ¿Y qué no se puede hacer en el centro que se puede hacer, por ejemplo, en las afueras?

Ana En las afueras se puede pasear por el campo, los niños pueden jugar en la calle, y se duerme mejor por las noches porque no hay tráfico.

numerosas	*plentiful*
la vida	*life*
agradable	*pleasant*
por ejemplo	*for example*
niños	*children*
pueden	*can*
se duerme	*you sleep*

▶Spotcheck 5 a What is good about the shops in Madrid?
b What are the advantages of living in the suburbs?

KEYWORDS

una habitación doble	a double room
una habitación indi-vidual	a single room
el baño	bath (room)
el lavabo	washbasin
la ducha	shower
el desayuno	breakfast
el pasaporte	passport
firmar	to sign
la tarjeta de crédito	credit card
la llave	key
el equipaje	luggage
el aparcamiento	car park
el aire acondicionado	air conditioning
el ascensor	lift
el teléfono	telephone

(*for more accommodation vocabulary see p. 209*)

¿se puede . . .?	is it possible . . .?
lo siento	I'm sorry
la vida	life
agradable	pleasant

HOW SPANISH WORKS

1   We . . .

The ending -*mos* on a Spanish verb tells you that the subject of the verb is 'we':

aceptamos tarjetas de crédito we accept credit cards

tenemos una habitación we have a room

The 'we' part of the verb is usually formed like this:
-*ar* verbs like *trabajar* *trabajamos*
-*er* verbs like *comer* *comemos*
-*ir* verbs like *vivir* *vivimos*

The main exceptions are *vamos* (we go) from *ir*, and *somos* (we are) from *ser*.

The word for 'we', usually omitted, is *nosotros* or *nosotras*.

2   . . . and you

The verb endings -*an* and -*en* are the ones that go with *ustedes*, and this is the formal way of saying 'you' to more than one person:
¿aceptan ustedes . . .? do you accept . . .?
¿viven aquí? do you live here?

The *ustedes* part of the verb is usually formed like this:
trabajar *trabajan*
comer *comen*
vivir *viven*

The main exceptions are *son* (you are) and *van* (you go).

The more informal way of saying 'you' is covered in the next unit.

3   Possible or not possible

¿Se puede? – this is a useful way of asking if it's possible to do something, or if it's allowed:
¿se puede aparcar aquí?
¿se puede fumar?
¿a qué hora se puede comer?

Se can be used with words other than *puede*, as in *se vive bien* or *en España se come muy bien*. Here it means 'you live well', 'people eat well in Spain'. You've also come across *se* in Unit 9 in *se cierra, se abre*: *¿a qué hora se abre?* – 'what time do you open?'.

SOUND SPANISH

$\boxed{\text{y}}$ It's usually like the 'y' in the English 'yes', eg *desayuno*, but when it comes at the beginning of a word it has a touch of the 'j' as in English 'jam', eg *ya, yo*.

When the **y** is on its own (meaning 'and') it has another sound, like 'ee' in the English 'me'.

Practise with: *yo estoy muy bien hoy*.

WORKOUT

1 Somewhere to sleep

Ask for the following hotel rooms.

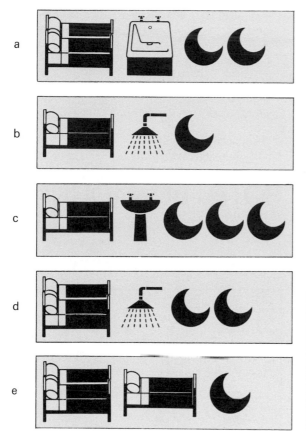

a

b

c

d

e

2 As if you were there

Imagine you've been travelling all day, and at about 7 pm you see a reasonable-looking hotel and decide you'd like to spend the night there before moving on. Could you cope in Spanish?

a You walk into the hotel, greet the receptionist and ask if they have a double room.

b You're in luck! The receptionist asks: *¿Para cuántas noches?* What do you reply?

c Say you would like a room with a bathroom.

d Still no problem. But what about the price?

e He replies: *Cinco mil novecientas pesetas por noche.* How much is that?

f Ask if that's with breakfast.

3 Matchmaker

Match each question on the left-hand side with the correct answer from the right.

a ¿Tienen habitaciones?

b ¿Qué precio tiene?

c ¿Incluye el desayuno?

d ¿Tiene baño?

e ¿Qué numéro tiene la habitación?

f ¿Se puede cenar?

i Cinco mil novecientas pesetas por noche.

ii La ciento seis; aquí tiene la llave.

iii Sí, ¿doble o individual?

iv Sí, de nueve a once.

v Sí, todas las habitaciones tienen.

vi No, es aparte.

4 Cans and can'ts

Match each of the signs with the most likely caption or phrase.

a Se puede tomar algo aquí.

b Se puede fumar aquí.

c Se puede comer aquí.

d No se puede aparcar aquí.

e Se puede pagar con tarjetas de crédito.

f Se puede aparcar aquí.

g No se puede hacer fotos.

h No se puede fumar aquí.

i Se puede telefonear aquí.

5 Missing link

In each of these questions from the hotel receptionist, there's a key word (the verb!) missing. In each case, can you supply it from the list? And how many people is he speaking to – one, or more?

viajan deja tienen vive firman quiere

a ¿......... equipaje?
b ¿......... en España?
c ¿Me .... su pasaporte?
d ¿......... cenar?
e ¿......... en coche?
f ¿Me .... aquí?

6 We ...

Change the following statements to refer to 'we' instead of just 'I'.

a Voy a Portugal.
b Tengo un piso en el centro.
c Hago muchas cosas.
d Soy profesor de alemán.
e Acepto todas las tarjetas de crédito.
f Vivo en el sur de Inglaterra.
g Estoy muy bien.
h Juego al baloncesto.

7 All mod cons

You and your family (spouse and three children) are driving round Spain. You arrive in a town and go to the local information office to find out about hotels – which facilities will you need?

a Which combination of rooms would suit you best (bearing in mind that you're not made of money)?
cinco habitaciones individuales
una habitación doble y tres individuales
una habitación doble y una con tres camas

b It's the middle of July and you want to make sure the heat won't stop you sleeping. Do you want a hotel with
teléfono aire acondicionado aparcamiento

c You're hot and tired after driving all day and you all want a bath. Do you want rooms with
baño lavabo agua mineral

d One of the children has twisted an ankle and can't walk upstairs easily. To get to your rooms on the fourth floor do you need
una llave un aparcamiento un ascensor

e You want supper, so you choose a hotel that offers
desayuno incluido cena de 8 a 10.30
bar y tapas

f You need to leave the car somewhere safe overnight. Do you want
un ascensor un garaje una ducha

8 Short stay

From this hotel bill, work out:

HOTEL DEL MOLINO

POTES (Cantabria)
Teléfono 73 73 18 4 18   ✶ ✶   Nº 000404

Habitación n.º 213

[2][ ][ ]

Sr. D. _____

Mes de ABU 1986	Dia 4 Pesetas	Dia 5 Pesetas	Dia 6 Pesetas	Dia Pesetas	Dia Pesetas	TOTALES Pesetas
Habitación.	3.600	3.600				7.200
Pensión alimenticia						
Desayunos		600	600			1.200
Almuerzos	3.025	3.420				6.445
Cenas.						
Cafetería	530					530
Extras						
Lavado y planch.						
Supletoria.						
Telef. y telegramas						
Total del día						15.375
Suma anterior.						
Abonos a cuenta.						
T O T A L.						
I V A 6 %						890
Teléfono.						
TOTAL.						16.265

a the room number
b the number of nights stayed
c the amount paid for drinks
d the amount paid for main meals
e how much tax was paid
f what cost 1200 pesetas

9 Hotel information

Many hotels have their information sheets written in English as well as Spanish – but if yours didn't, could you work them out? Try matching these typical phrases with the brief summary in English of what they mean.

a Horario de desayunos.

b Si desea desayunar en la habitación, por favor, cuelgue esta tarjeta en su puerta antes de las siete de la mañana.

c La dirección del hotel no responde de los objetos y valores no depositados en los cofres individuales de Recepción.

d Se ruega a los señores clientes anuncien su salida antes del mediodía, y dejen libres sus habitaciones antes de las doce horas. En caso contrario, les será cargado el importe de ese día.

e Desayuno completo.

f Se aplican precios máximos en Navidad, Semana Santa, Fiestas locales.

g Habitación doble para una persona: 80% de su importe.

h Precio diario de esta habitación: ....

i Por favor entregue la llave.

i Full continental breakfast.

ii Hang this note on door by 7 for breakfast in room.

iii Price of room per day.

iv Please leave by 12, or room will be charged.

v Breakfast times.

vi Please hand in your key.

vii One person in double room charged 80% of room price.

viii No responsibility accepted for valuables not left in safe.

ix Full prices on certain special days.

ABOUT SPAIN

Hotels

Hotels are generally good value in Spain. There is an official system for categorising hotels, from one to five stars, and for describing the more modest *hostales*, from one to three stars. *Pensiones* are good for simple, inexpensive accommodation.

One special category consists of the *paradores*, special State-owned hotels, which are often away from the main towns, sometimes in historic buildings. They're in the four to five-star category, with restaurants that usually specialise in regional cuisine.

All establishments must by law have a complaints book (*libro de reclamaciones*) for customers who are dissatisfied in some way.

Telephoning

Most public telephones now display the sign
urbano, interurbano, internacional, which means
they can be used for all calls, including international.
Coins of 50 pesetas or more are placed into a groove
over the slot, and these are used as the call is made.
The code 07 44 will get you through to Britain, and
then remember to remove the 0 from the British area
code. For example, to ring York, dial 07 44 904 (not
0904) and then the subscriber's number.

If you prefer, calls can be made from the central
teléfonos, where you book the call from a telephonist and pay once the call is completed. Phone calls
made from hotels tend to incur a hefty supplement.

Moorish Spain

At the beginning of the 8th century, Spain was
almost completely taken over by the Moors –
Moslem Arabs from North Africa who ruled in Spain
up to the 15th century. For almost 800 years the
Christians fought intermittently to drive the Moors
out of Spain, finally succeeding at Granada in 1492,
the year in which Spanish efforts turned to the New
World.

Moorish civilisation was extremely advanced in
learning, architecture and agriculture, and its traces
can still be found in Spain today, particularly in
Andalucía. The palace of the Alhambra in Granada
and the Great Mosque of Córdoba are two superb
examples of Moorish architecture; the irrigation
system of the coastal plain around Valencia was also
initially planned by the Moors; and the Spanish
language is full of Moorish-derived words like
alcázar (castle), *alcachofa* (artichoke), *albaricoque*
(apricot). *Al-* at the beginning of a place name
shows that it was once Moorish, eg *Alicante, Almería*.

The Alhambra, Granada

The Mezquita, Córdoba

13 Sol y sombra

Buying things at the chemist's

Talking about weather and climate

SPANISH LIVE

📺 1 Rafael Arcimiega visits a chemist's in Sevilla.

Rafael	Buenos días.
Chemist	Buenos días.
Rafael	¿Tiene algo para las quemaduras de sol?
Chemist	Sí. (*she brings two jars*) Tenemos esta crema, que es muy buena. ¿Prefiere tamaño grande o pequeño?
Rafael	¿Cuánto cuesta el grande?
Chemist	Cuatrocientas cuarenta pesetas.

To ask for something at a chemist's:
¿tiene algo para ...?
do you have anything for ...?

Rafael	Pues ése mismo. ¿Y algo para el dolor de cabeza? Es para un niño pequeño.
Chemist	¿Cuántos años tiene?
Rafael	Cuatro años.
Chemist	¿Tabletas o supositorios?
Rafael	Mejor tabletas.
Chemist	(she produces a packet) ¿Algo más?
Rafael	Nada más, gracias. ¿Cuánto es?
Chemist	Cuatrocientas cuarenta, más noventa . . . Son quinientas treinta pesetas.
Rafael	Aquí tiene. Muchas gracias.
Chemist	Adiós. Buenos días.
Rafael	Adiós.

quemaduras de sol	sunburn
crema	cream
tamaño	size
ése mismo	that one
dolor de cabeza	headache
tabletas	pills
supositorios	suppositories

▶ **Spotcheck 1** a What size of cream does Rafael take?

b Who are the pills for?

📺 2 Sevilla is one of the hottest cities in Europe. Yolanda asked some local people about the weather, first in summer . . .

Yolanda	¿Qué tiempo hace aquí en verano?
Passer-by 1	En verano hace mucho calor.
Passer-by 2	¿En verano? ¡Uf, es horroroso!
Passer-by 3	¡Uf, horrible!

. . . and then in winter.

Yolanda	¿Qué tiempo hace aquí en invierno?
Passer-by 1	En invierno hace frío y llueve, pero no demasiado.
Passer-by 2	En invierno no hace tanto frío.
Passer-by 3	¿En invierno? Muy, muy húmedo.
Yolanda	¿Y en qué mes hace más frío?
Passer-by 4	Diciembre, enero.
Passer-by 5	Quizás enero, febrero.
Passer-by 6	Creo que en diciembre.

verano	summer
horroroso	awful
invierno	winter

To ask what the weather is like:
¿qué tiempo hace?

To say what it's like:
hace calor	it's hot
hace frío	it's cold
llueve	it rains

tanto	*so*
húmedo	*damp*
mes	*month*
diciembre	*December*
enero	*January*
quizás	*maybe*
febrero	*February*

▶Spotcheck 2   a   What two things are generally agreed about the summer weather?

b   What two features of the winter weather are mentioned?

Écija, near Sevilla, known as the hottest town in Spain

③ **3**   When Isabel was in Mojácar it was late spring. She asked Isabel at the *estanco* what the weather was like in midsummer and midwinter.

Isabel Soto   ¿Hace mucho calor en Mojácar en verano?
Isabel   Bastante, en agosto mucho.
Isabel Soto   Por ejemplo, ¿qué temperaturas se alcanzan?
Isabel   Pues, de treinta a treinta y cinco. A veces pasa, treinta y ocho grados (*sí*) . . . al sol. Es mucho.
Isabel Soto   ¿Y en invierno hace frío?
Isabel   No. No, generalmente no. Un poco, pero una temperatura bastante buena.
Isabel Soto   ¿Cuántos grados, por ejemplo?
Isabel   Por ejemplo, enero, es fantástico porque hace una temperatura de hasta quince grados.

agosto	*August*
se alcanzan	*are reached*
a veces	*sometimes*
pasa	*it goes higher*
grados	*degrees* (*Celsius*)
al sol	*in the sun*

▶Spotcheck 3 a   What is the highest temperature mentioned?

b   Which month does Isabel seem to prefer?

Ⓡ **4**   The weather in Madrid is not ideal – there's a saying: *nueve meses de invierno, tres meses de infierno* (nine months of winter, three months of hell). When's the best time then? Isabel asked two people for their views.

Isabel   ¿Cuál es el mejor mes en Madrid, Marisa?

Marisa   Para mí el mejor mes es junio.

Isabel   ¿Por qué?

Marisa   Porque no hace el calor del verano ni el frío del invierno.

Isabel   ¿Qué prefieres, el verano o el invierno?

Marisa   El verano.

Isabel   ¿Es más difícil trabajar en verano?

Marisa   ¡Ay! ¡Como estoy en paro no lo sé!

Isabel   Julián, ¿cuál es el mejor mes en Madrid?

Julián   El mejor mes es febrero.

Isabel   ¿Por qué?

Julián   Es el mes que tiene menos días y se trabaja menos.

Isabel   ¿No te gusta el verano?

Julián   Hace excesivo calor.

Isabel   ¿Cambia la vida en verano?

Julián   Sí, se duerme un poco más.

Isabel   ¿Se duerme un poco más?

Julián   Sí, porque se practica el deporte nacional, que es la siesta.

Isabel   ¿Te gusta la siesta?

Julián   ¡Me encanta!

junio	*June*
ni	*nor*
como	*as*
no lo sé	*I don't know*
menos días	*fewest days*
se trabaja menos	*you work least*
¿cambia la vida?	*does life change?*

▶Spotcheck 4 a   What does Marisa like about June?

b   What does Julián seem to prefer doing?

Vines at Jerez
ripen in the
southern sun

KEYWORDS

estar bien/mal	to be well/unwell
la farmacia	chemist's
algo	anything
las quemaduras de sol	sunburn
el dolor de cabeza	headache
el dolor de estómago	stomach-ache
me duele	it hurts
(for parts of the body see p. 211)	
el tiempo	weather
hace sol	it's sunny
hace calor	it's hot
hace frío	it's cold
llueve	it rains
húmedo	damp
el verano	summer
el invierno	winter
la primavera	spring
el otoño	autumn
el mes	month
(for days, months and seasons see p. 205)	
la temperatura	temperature
el grado	degree (Celsius)
¿por qué?	why?
porque	because
menos	less; least
mejor	better; best

llueve	it rains (*or* it's raining)
está lloviendo	it's raining
nieva	it snows (*or* it's snowing)
está nevando	it's snowing

HOW SPANISH WORKS

1 The rain in Spain . . .

To talk about the weather, you generally use the verb *hacer*:

¿qué tiempo hace en Inglaterra?	what's the weather like in England?
hace frío	it's cold
hace calor	it's hot
hace sol	it's sunny

And to say that it's **very** hot, cold or sunny, just add *mucho*: *hace **mucho** calor, hace **mucho** frío*, etc.

However, for rain or snow, you don't need *hace*:

2 Being under the weather

One way of explaining aches and pains is:

tengo dolor de . . .	I have a pain in the . . .
. . . cabeza/estómago	. . . head/stomach, etc.

Or you can say *me duele*. On its own this means 'it hurts', and you can also use it to say **what** hurts:

me duele	*la cabeza*
	la garganta
	el estómago

3 More or less

Más and *menos* mean 'more' and 'less':

en enero hace menos calor y llueve más	in January it's less warm and it rains more

Sometimes *más* is equivalent to '-er' in English:

es más grande	it's bigg**er**
es más pequeño	it's small**er**

Or even '-est':

el más caro es éste	the dear**est** is this one

The word *mejor* can mean 'better' or 'best':

el verano es mejor que el invierno	summer is better than winter
el mejor mes es febrero	the best month is February

4 The present

A word like *vive* can have different English equivalents:

¿dónde vive?	where **does** she **live**?
	or where **is** she **living**?
(ella) vive en Vallecas	she **lives** in Vallecas
	or she **is living** in Vallecas

This is called the present tense, and is used to say what **happens** or what **is happening**.

The only form of the present tense we haven't explained so far is the one that goes with *vosotros/as* (the plural of *tú*). The ending for this form is *-áis*, *-éis* or *-ís*.

Here's the typical pattern for the present tense of the three types of verbs:

trabajar	trabaj-**o**	-**as**	-**a**	-**amos**	-**áis**	-**an**
comer	com-**o**	-**es**	-**e**	-**emos**	-**éis**	-**en**
vivir	viv-**o**	-**es**	-**e**	-**imos**	-**ís**	-**en**

The other *-ar*, *-er* and *-ir* verbs follow these patterns, except for the unusual ones like *hacer, tener, estar, ser, ir*. You'll find a list of these on p. 186.

SOUND SPANISH

d This is pronounced like an English 'd' when it comes at the beginning of a word, but when it comes in the middle or at the end of a word it's more like the 'th' sound in the English word 'the'. Practise with: *Daniel desayuna cada día, ¿verdad?*.

WORKOUT

1 Today's weather

Here are the symbols used by one Spanish newspaper for its weather forecast. Match each symbol with the most suitable description.

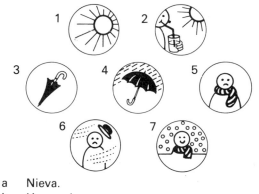

a Nieva.
b Hace sol.
c Llueve.
d Hace frío.
e Hace calor.
f Posibilidad de lluvia.
g Hace viento.

2 Who says?

Who's making the following statements?

a Aquí llueve todos los días.
b Hace calor, ¿verdad?
c Me duele la cabeza.
d Me duele el estómago.
e ¡Está muy fría el agua!
f ¡Qué frío hace hoy!

141

3   Feeling bad

How would you say

a   I've got a stomach-ache.

b   I've got a headache.

c   It hurts (me) here.

d   My son's not well.

e   Have you got anything for sunburn?

f   It hurts, but not too much.

4   The three Ms

In each of these sentences there's a word missing beginning with the letter M: *más, menos* or *mejor*. Try to put the right one in.

a   El .... mes del año para el esquí es enero.

b   Junio es .... húmedo que noviembre.

c   Llueve .... en abril que en agosto.

d   Nieva .... en los Pirineos que en Sevilla.

e   El verano es .... que el invierno para los turistas.

f   Hace .... sol en Santander que en Sevilla.

5   Which?

Choose the right way of . . .

a   Asking a couple of friends out for supper.
¿Quieres cenar?   ¿Queréis cenar?
Quiero cenar.

b   Saying you and your friend are going to the cinema.
Voy al cine.   Vamos al cine.   Van al cine.

c   Saying that some friends live near here.
Viven cerca de aquí.
Vivimos cerca de aquí.
Vives cerca de aquí.

d   Asking an elderly receptionist about hotel rooms.
¿Tienes habitaciones?   Tengo habitaciones.
¿Tiene habitaciones?

e   Saying you and your friends are from Folkestone.
Somos de Folkestone.   Soy de Folkestone.
Eres de Folkestone.

f   Describing where the toilets are.
Estamos allí al fondo.   Están allí al fondo.
Estás allí al fondo.

g   Asking a couple of children if they live here.
¿Vives aquí?   ¿Vivimos aquí?   ¿Vivís aquí?

6   Split months

Can you join up the halves to make six months?

ag	embre
ab	yo
feb	osto
ma	ril
ju	rero
dici	nio

7   As if you were there

You're in a taxi in Madrid, discussing the weather.

You	(*Say it's hot, isn't it?*)
Taxi-driver	Bueno, no mucho, son sólo treinta grados.
You	(*Say it's too hot for you.*)
Taxi-driver	¿No le gusta el calor? A veces alcanza los cuarenta grados.
You	(*Say that you don't like the heat.*)
Taxi-driver	¿Prefiere el clima de Inglaterra? Allí llueve mucho, ¿no?
You	(*Say yes, it does rain quite a lot.*)
Taxi-driver	¿Llueve todo el año o sólo en invierno?
You	(*Say it rains more in the winter, but it rains in the summer as well.*)
Taxi-driver	Es como en el norte de España. En la Costa Cantábrica el clima es muy húmedo.

8   Timesearch

Missing from this wordsearch are one of the seasons and two of the months. Which?

9 All weathers

The weather in December can vary greatly from one part of Spain to another. These four people explain how they're going to spend a weekend. Where would the weather be most suitable for each of them?

Juan García	Yo voy a ir a la montaña, a esquiar.
Luis Gómez	Voy a pasear, a visitar el nuevo parque.
Teresa Vázquez	Voy a ir a la playa, a tomar el sol.
Elvira Zapata	No quiero salir. Voy a quedarme en casa.

	Tiempo	Temperatura
Islas Canarias	Calor	25°
Barcelona	Sol	9°
Madrid	Frío; llueve	5°
Pirineos	Frío; nieva	0°

10 Opposites

Match the opposites.

Hace mucho calor.	En el sur.
En invierno.	Estoy mal.
Llega el tren.	La noche.
En el norte.	Hace mucho frío.
Estoy bien.	El pequeño.
Un poco más.	En verano.
El grande.	Sale el tren.
El día.	Un poco menos.

ABOUT SPAIN

The climate

Those who see Spain as a land of sun, heat and blue skies are right – but only partly. The east coast has a Mediterranean climate – a lot of sunshine most of the year, little rainfall, and summer temperatures of around 30° Celsius.

Away from this area, however, the story is slightly different. The north coast can be wet and quite mild in summer. Most of the interior is high (around 2500 feet), so it's extremely hot in summer but bitingly cold in winter. And although the south has mild winters, the summer temperatures, regularly in the mid-thirties, can be difficult to take – unless you're close to a swimming pool.

It's the mountains that provide the key to Spain's geography: they not only affect the climate, they are also a great barrier to communication, with the different ranges cutting across the country, sending roads and railways in long loops and causing difficult driving conditions in winter.

Madrid in the rain

Medical services

Under EEC regulations, Spain has a reciprocal free medical service with the UK – full details from your local DHSS office. Most people also include medical costs as part of the normal holiday insurance policy.

Spanish doctors tend to specialise more than their British counterparts, so if you're very ill you'll probably see a specialist. The most likely thing, however, is that you'll just need some advice about colds or minor complaints, and for this Spanish chemists are well qualified and helpful.

The Pyrenees, a
favourite place for
winter sports

14 Viajes y vacaciones

Talking about holidays: those you've had and those you're planning

SPANISH LIVE

TV 1 Yolanda asked some *sevillanos* where they went last
year on holiday.

Yolanda	¿Adónde fue el año pasado?
Passer-by 1	El año pasado fui a Marruecos.
Yolanda	¿Adónde fuiste el año pasado?
Passer-by 2	El año pasado fui a Inglaterra.

Cádiz

Yolanda	¿Adónde fue el año pasado?
Passer-by 3	A Cádiz.
Passer-by 4	A Málaga, Torremolinos.
Passer-by 5	Estuve en Málaga.
Passer-by 6	Pues estuve en Marruecos.
Passer-by 7	Fui a la playa, estuve en la costa.

And how long did they stay there?

Yolanda	¿Cuánto tiempo estuviste allí?
Passer-by 7	Estuve veinticinco días, creo.
Yolanda	¿Cuánto tiempo estuviste allí?
Passer-by 6	Estuve quince días.
Passer-by 1	Estuve sólo diez días.
Yolanda	¿Cuánto tiempo estuvo allí?
Passer-by 3	Treinta . . . treinta días.
Yolanda	¿Estuviste todo el tiempo en Inglaterra?
Passer-by 2	Sí, estuve allí los dos meses completos.

Marruecos	Morocco
¿cuánto tiempo estuviste/estuvo . . .?	how long were you . . .?
quince días	fortnight
todo el tiempo	all the time

▶Spotcheck 1   Who was away longest?

Ⓡ **2**   Ana Schöbel went to Turkey last year . . .

Isabel	Ana, ¿adónde fuiste el año pasado de vacaciones?
Ana	El año pasado estuve en Turquía.
Isabel	¿Y te gustó?
Ana	Me gustó mucho el arte, y la naturaleza, pero no me gustó la miseria y la suciedad.

. . . and Jaime stayed in Spain.

Isabel	¿Adónde fuiste el año pasado?
Jaime	El año pasado estuve en varios sitios de vacaciones. Estuve quince días en el sur de España, y luego también estuve en la zona de Levante.
Isabel	¿Y te gustó?
Jaime	Sí, me gustó mucho. Son playas muy bonitas.

Turquía	Turkey
naturaleza	nature
miseria	poverty
suciedad	dirt
varios	several

▶Spotcheck 2   a   What didn't Ana like about Turkey?
   b   How long did Jaime stay in the south?

To ask where someone went last year:
¿adónde fue/fuiste el año pasado?

To say what you did:
fui a . . .   I went to . . .
estuve en . . .   I stayed in . . .

To ask if someone liked something:
¿te/le gustó . . .?

To say you liked something:
me gustó

® 3   Isabel asked Ana Gamarra about her recent holiday, and where she's thinking of going next year.

Isabel	¿Adónde fuiste el año pasado de vacaciones?
Ana Gamarra	El año pasado en verano estuve en Galicia.
Isabel	Sí, en el noroeste de España. Y este año, ¿adónde piensas ir?
Ana Gamarra	Este año pienso ir a Londres de vacaciones.
Isabel	¿Te gusta Londres?
Ana Gamarra	Me gusta mucho Londres, sí. Voy muchas veces a Londres.

And what about Ana Schöbel? Where's she going to go next year?

Isabel	¿Y adónde vas a ir el año que viene?
Ana Schöbel	El año que viene quiero ir a Estados Unidos.

noroeste	*northwest*
muchas veces	*often*
el año que viene	*next year*

▶ Spotcheck 3   What does Ana Gamarra think of London?

To ask about somebody's plans:
¿adónde piensa(s) ir?

To say what you're thinking of doing:

pienso	ir a ...
	visitar ...

Fishing port
in Galicia

147

Yolanda	¿Adónde quieres ir este año?
Passer-by 1	Quiero ir, pues, a Italia.
Passer-by 2	Pues no sé. Quiero ir al norte de España, a Galicia.

4 Yolanda asked about people's plans for next year.

To say what you want to do:

quiero	ir a . . .
	visitar . . .

The coast
near Málaga

Yolanda	¿Adónde quiere ir este año?
Passer-by 3	Pues, seguramente, a Málaga.
Passer-by 4	Quiero ir a Italia.
Passer-by 5	Si puedo, a la playa.
Passer-by 6	A la playa.
Yolanda	¿Adónde quiere ir este año?
Passer-by 7	A Cádiz.
Yolanda	¿Qué piensa hacer allí?
Passer-by 7	Pasarlo bien, tomar el sol y divertirme.
Passer-by 8	Pasear, bañarme, tomar copas.
Passer-by 1	Sobre todo, visitar Italia, sus ciudades, todo – conocer Italia.

seguramente	*certainly*
si puedo	*if I can*
pasarlo bien	*have a good time*
divertirme	*enjoy myself*
bañarme	*go swimming*
conocer	*to get to know*

▶ **Spotcheck 4** How many people say they're going abroad?

KEYWORDS

visitar	to visit
pensar	to intend, think
conocer	to get to know
¿cuánto tiempo?	how long?
la semana	week
quince días	fortnight
el año que viene	next year
el año pasado	last year
a principios de	at the beginning of
a finales de	at the end of
a mediados de	in the middle of
ayer	yesterday
ahora	now
todavía	still
el sitio	place
el país	country
fui	I went
fuiste	you went
fue	you went; he/she went
estuve	I was
estuviste	you were
estuvo	you were; he/she was

HOW SPANISH WORKS

1 Looking back

When talking about things that happened in the past you use a different form of the verb:

estoy de vacaciones	I'm on holiday
estuve de vacaciones	I **was** on holiday

voy a Inglaterra	I'm going to England
fui a Inglaterra	I **went** to England

As usual, the endings of the verbs change, depending on the subject:

estuve	I was
estuviste	you were
estuvo	you were; he/she was

fui	I went
fuiste	you went
fue	you went; he/she went

2 Looking forward

In Unit 10, you learnt how to say what you're going to do:

voy a ver una película	I'm going to see a film
voy a visitar el museo	I'm going to visit the museum

In this unit you'll find other ways of talking about the future – saying what you **want** to do and what you are **thinking** of doing. Notice that, like *ir a*, the verbs *querer* and *pensar* are both followed by the infinitive when referring to the future:

quiero visitar el museo	I want to visit the museum
pienso ir a Escocia	I'm thinking of going to Scotland

3 Say when

Whether you're talking about the past or the future, you'll often need to be more specific – last year, next year, etc.

Pasado/a is 'last' and *próximo/a* or *que viene* means 'next':

la semana pasada	last week
el año pasado	last year
la semana próxima	} next week
la semana que viene	
el año próximo	} next year
el año que viene	

If you want to say how long ago something happened, the word to use is *hace*:

hace dos días	two days ago
hace dos años	two years ago

SOUND SPANISH

Local accents

In Spain, as in the UK, you may hear a variety of local accents. The variations won't usually stop you understanding what's being said, but it's as well to be prepared for the accent of the south, which has some very particular features. The most obvious are:

1 The 'th' sound as in *cerveza* becomes an 's'
2 The 's' sound is less strong than in northern Spanish and may be missed out altogether – especially at the end of a word; so *buenos días* sounds like *bueno día*.

Some features of this southern accent are also found in the Canary Islands and Latin America.

WORKOUT

1 First impressions

Match these places you've been to recently with the appropriate impression.

a   El verano pasado fui a Roma.
b   La semana pasada fui a Benidorm.
c   El año pasado estuve en Galicia.
d   Ayer fui al restaurante 'La Copita'.

i   Me gustó el paisaje verde y las playas del Atlántico.
ii   Me gustó el segundo plato.
iii Me gustó mucho la playa pero no me gustó el hotel, lleno de ingleses.
iv   Me gustó mucho la ciudad por sus monumentos y por el arte.

2 Jumbled thoughts

Organise these statements in chronological order, going from past to future.

a   Mañana vamos a la playa.
b   La semana pasada estuvimos en la costa.
c   El año que viene quiero tener más tiempo libre.
d   El año pasado fuimos a Santander.
e   El lunes que viene voy otra vez al trabajo.
f   Hace veinte días fuimos a visitar a mi hermano.
g   El martes que viene tengo que trabajar mucho.
h   Esta semana estamos de vacaciones.

3 Perú

Match each question with the most suitable reply.

a   ¿Adónde vas a ir de vacaciones este año?
b   ¡Ah! ¿Fuiste a Perú el año pasado?
c   ¿Y estuviste en la montaña?
d   ¿Cuánto tiempo piensas ir este año?
e   ¿Vas a ir sola?

i   No creo, mi hermano también quiere venir.
ii   Un mes, seguramente.
iii Pues quiero ir a Perú otra vez.
iv   Sí, estuve allí casi dos meses.
v   Claro, estuve en el Machu Picchu.

4 Odd one out

Which is the odd one out?

a   semana, año, tamaño, mes
b   frío, lluvia, llave, nieve
c   el año pasado, la semana que viene, ayer, la semana pasada
d   flan, crema, loción, tableta
e   verano, enero, invierno, primavera
f   muy, demasiado, más, poco
g   playa, campo, costa, mar
h   puerto, aparcamiento, avión, estación

5 As if you were there

On the way out of your hotel, you hand in your key to the friendly receptionist.

Receptionist	Hola, buenos días. ¿Fue a la fiesta ayer?
You	(*Ask what festival.*)
Receptionist	Pues, la fiesta de San Juan – la fiesta local. ¡Es la mejor de la zona!
You	(*Say no. Yesterday you went to the beach – you spent all day there.*)
Receptionist	Hizo mucho calor ayer, ¿no?
You	(*Say yes, but you like the sun. Last week you went to Sevilla and it's extremely hot there.*)
Receptionist	Sí, en Sevilla en verano hace mucho, mucho calor. ¿Y qué tal? ¿Le gustó?
You	(*Say yes, you liked it a lot. You went to the cathedral, the Alcázar and the Barrio de Santa Cruz.*)
Receptionist	¿Y piensa volver allí?
You	(*Say no, but you're thinking of visiting Granada. You want to see the Alhambra.*)
Receptionist	Ah sí, es estupenda. ¿Pero no va a Granada hoy?
You	(*Say no, you're thinking of going tomorrow.*)
Receptionist	Mejor, porque hoy es todavía fiesta en San Juan. ¡Es el día más importante de la fiesta!
You	(*Say good, you're going to go to the village this evening.*)

6 Blankit

All the vowels in these phrases have been blanked out – work out the complete phrases.

a P__ns_ r _ _t_l__.
b _y_r f__ _ l_ pl_y_.
c _st_v_ _n _st_ h_t_l _l _ñ_ p_s_d_.
d H_c_ m_ch_ c_l_r _q__ _n v_r_n_.
e _n t_ñ_ _sm_y h_m_d_.
f Q___r_ j_g_r _l t_n_s _st_ t_rd_.
g V_y _ _r _ l_ p_sc_n_ m_ñ_n_.

7 Send us a postcard!

Here's a postcard sent by someone on holiday in southern Spain. It got a bit smudged, so see if you can fill in the gaps using these words:

gustó   estuve   fui
pasada   quiero   bonito

> Querida Emilia:
> Ahora estoy en Almería pero
> la semana (1) fui a Mojácar,
> un pueblo de la costa. (2)
> en un hotel pequeno y no muy
> caro. También (3) a visitar el
> castillo, que es muy (4)
> Me (5) la plaga del pueblo,
> y su ambiente. Este fin de semana
> (6) ir a la montaña.
> Besos Francisco —

8 Overheard

You overheard these snatches of conversation in a busy restaurant. What you heard were only the answers to a number of questions – what do you think the questions were?

a YO VOY A TOMAR EL MENÚ DEL DÍA Y MI COMPAÑERO VA A TOMAR UNA SOPA Y DESPUÉS UN FILETE.

b SÍ, ME GUSTA MUCHO. LA PAELLA ES MI COMIDA FAVORITA.

c NO, NO FUI A LA PISCINA. ESTÁ CERRADA POR EL MOMENTO.

d BUENO, EL ARROZ A LA CUBANA ES UN ARROZ CON HUEVO FRITO Y CON SALSA DE TOMATE.

e PUES MAÑANA PIENSO IR AL CINE, A VER LA ÚLTIMA PELÍCULA DE JAMES BOND.

ABOUT SPAIN

Fiestas

There are 18 national public holidays in the Spanish calendar. The main ones are: *Semana Santa* (Easter Holy Week), which is celebrated with great religious fervour, particularly in the south of the country; *Los Reyes Magos* (The Three Kings) on 6th January, a favourite with the children because that's the day they get their Christmas presents; and 25th July, the festival of *Santiago* (St James), the patron saint of Spain.

Fiestas with a strong regional flavour are the *Feria de Abril* of Sevilla; the processions and bonfires of the *Fallas* of Valencia in March; the bonfires in Alicante and elsewhere on St John's Day, 24th June; the festival of Moors and Christians in April in Alcoy, province of Alicante; and the bull-running in Pamplona, northern Spain, in the first week of July.

In fact, all towns and villages have their own *fiesta mayor*, when the inhabitants let their hair down with processions, fairs, competitions, music and dancing. Madrid, for instance, celebrates the festival of *San Isidro*, the city's patron saint, on 15th May.

Fiesta de San Isidro, Madrid

Semana Santa in Sevilla

Sevillanos dressed up for *la Feria*

15 Haciendo turismo

Visiting places

Getting information

Buying things to take home

® 1 *El parque de Cazorla* is one of Spain's 'natural' parks. The nearest town to Cazorla is Ubeda, and there Isabel made enquiries at the tourist office.

Cazorla natural park

Isabel ¿Tiene información sobre Cazorla? ¿Hay excursiones desde aquí?

Clerk Bueno, tenemos un folleto sobre la Sierra de Cazorla y Segura. Y desde aquí no hay excursiones; sí hay en Cazorla pueblo, pueden preguntar, hay una cooperativa de guías de la naturaleza –

Isabel ¿Una . . .?

Clerk Cooperativa.

Isabel ¿Y dónde está esta organización?

Clerk En Cazorla pueblo (*sí*), en el pueblo de Cazorla.

At the office in Cazorla, she bought a detailed map of the park.

Isabel ¿Tiene un plano de la Sierra de Cazorla, por favor?

Clerk Sí, sí. Hay este plano. (*he unfolds it*)

Isabel Sí. Estupendo, es muy grande, y veo que están todas las carreteras, todos los itinerarios, los pueblos, los ríos, todo; perfecto. Me llevo éste, por favor.

Clerk De acuerdo. El precio son doscientas pesetas.

Isabel O sea, cuesta doscientas pesetas. (*Sí sí*) Muy bien.

sobre	*about*
folleto	*leaflet*
pueden preguntar	*you can ask*
guías	*guides*
naturaleza	*nature*
veo	*I see*
itinerarios	*routes*
ríos	*rivers*

▶Spotcheck 1
- a What does Isabel actually get from the tourist office in Ubeda?
- b What is she glad to see marked on the map she buys?

Animals in the
Cazorla natural
park

® **2** As she drives through the park towards the *parador nacional*, Isabel comments on the view.

Isabel ¡Caramba, está lloviendo! Pero todo es muy hermoso, muy bonito. Hay flores amarillas, azules, y estamos llegando al parador nacional. Ahí está. Vamos a verlo, y a tomar un café.

At the *parador*, Isabel and her friend are welcomed by the receptionist.

Isabel Hola, buenos días.

Receptionist Buenos días.

Isabel ¿Se puede tomar un café aquí?

Receptionist Sí, sí, sí, ¿cómo no?, sí. Pueden pasar si quieren.

Isabel ¿Hay un bar?

Receptionist Sí, sí, hay un bar, y está a su disposición; pueden ustedes pasar.

Isabel ¿Dónde está?

Receptionist Pasen ustedes aquí, la segunda puerta, la segunda puerta a la izquierda.

Isabel La segunda a la izquierda (*sí*), muy bien, muchísimas gracias.

¡caramba!	*gosh!*
hermoso	*beautiful*
flores	*flowers*
vamos a verlo	*let's go and see it*
pasen ustedes	*go through*
a su disposición	*at your disposal*

▶Spotcheck 2   a   What detail does Isabel spot in the countryside?
                b   Where will they find the bar?

📺 3   Luisa Framis and her husband José enquire about
        flamenco performances at their hotel reception in
        Sevilla.

Luisa	Hola, buenas tardes.
Receptionist	Buenas tardes.
Luisa	Por favor, ¿conoce un buen tablao flamenco por aquí?
Receptionist	Eh, bueno, hay varios. El más próximo es 'El Patio Sevillano', pero hay otros por el barrio de Santa Cruz.

A flamenco
school in Sevilla

Luisa	¿A qué hora abre 'El Patio Sevillano'?
Receptionist	Hay tres pases: el primero a las siete y media, el siguiente a las nueve y media, y luego otro a las once y media.
José	¿Se puede cenar allí?
Receptionist	No, no se puede.
José	¿Y cómo se va?
Receptionist	Mire. (*pointing to map*) Saliendo del hotel hacia la izquierda, luego todo recto hasta llegar al río. Justo aquí está el tablao.
José	Muy bien. Muchas gracias.
Luisa	Adiós.
Receptionist	Adiós. Buenas tardes, señores.

¿conoce . . .?	*do you know?*
tablao flamenco	*flamenco show*
pases	*performances*
siguiente	*following*
¿cómo se va?	*how do we get there?*
hacia	*towards*
hasta llegar	*until you reach*

▶Spotcheck 3 a What time is the last flamenco performance?

b What is the 'Patio Sevillano' right next to?

Spanish ceramics

☑ 4 Pilar Marín has a look in a ceramics shop window in Calle Sierpes, Sevilla. Something catches her eye so she goes in.

Pilar	Buenos días.
Shopkeeper	Buenos días.
Pilar	¿Tiene ese plato de la esquina en otros colores?
Shopkeeper	¿Qué plato? ¿Puede enseñármelo?
Pilar	Sí. (*pointing it out in the window*) Este es.
Shopkeeper	Sí, mire. Este verde es muy parecido.
Pilar	Es bonito. ¿Cuánto cuesta?
Shopkeeper	Dos mil seiscientas noventa.
Pilar	Es un poco caro. ¿Tiene alguno más barato?
Shopkeeper	Sí. (*she lifts down a plate*) Este azul, por ejemplo, es más barato. Vale dos mil trescientas.
Pilar	Este me gusta. ¿Es cerámica sevillana?
Shopkeeper	Sí, es cerámica sevillana.
Pilar	Muy bien, me lo llevo.

plato	*plate*
de la esquina	*in the corner*
enseñármelo	*show it to me*
parecido	*similar*
vale	*it costs*

Shopping in Calle Sierpes, Sevilla

▶Spotcheck 4 a What's wrong with the first plate?

b How much cheaper is the second one?

KEYWORDS

There are no new *Keywords* for this unit as there are no new themes, so this is a good time to take stock.

Try to reinforce what you know by looking back at the *Keywords* for each of Units 1–14, and testing yourself: cover up the Spanish word, then say what it is from the English.

For more vocabulary, turn to the *Word Groups* beginning on p. 205: pick out those extra words you think you may find useful, learn them and test yourself. For example, if you always drink pineapple juice, make sure you know *zumo de piña*.

HOW SPANISH WORKS

This unit is a good opportunity for action replay on the grammar as well. Check through the *How Spanish Works* sections of Units 1–14, and make sure you've understood them all.

If you want a more formal summary of all the grammar in the book, you'll find it on p. 183.

WORKOUT

1   Happy families
Use the family tree to complete the following statements.

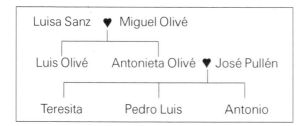

Luisa Sanz ♥ Miguel Olivé

Luis Olivé   Antonieta Olivé ♥ José Pullén

Teresita   Pedro Luis   Antonio

a   Luis Olivé es el .... de Antonieta Olivé.
b   Teresita es la .... de Pedro Luis y Antonio.
c   El .... de Pedro Luis es José Pullén.
d   Luisa Sanz tiene dos ....
e   El nombre completo de Antonio es ....
    ....

2   In shops
Match these sentences with the appropriate translations. You are likely to hear them said in shops.
a   ¿Bolsa grande o pequeña?
b   ¿Qué desea?
c   Está allí.
d   ¿Algo más?
e   Son quinientas veinte.
f   Aquí tiene el cambio.
g   ¿Eso es todo?

i   What would you like?
ii   That's five hundred and twenty.
iii   Here is your change.
iv   Is that all?
v   Large or small packet?
vi   It's there.
vii   Anything else?

3   Ordering drinks and shopping for food
i   Order the following drinks for yourself and some friends.
a   a beer and a tomato juice
b   two coffees and a tea
c   a bottle of mineral water (fizzy) and three beers
d   a white coffee and two red wines
e   an orange juice and a jug of water
f   half a litre of house wine
g   a tonic water and four orange juices

ii   Now ask for the following items at different stalls in the market.
a   a lettuce
b   1/4 kg of cheese
c   a kilo of oranges
d   two tomatoes
e   a large loaf of bread
f   a litre of milk
g   100 grams of ham (naturally-cured)
h   two cans of beer (can = *la lata*)

4   Habitat
Imagine you live in the following places. Explain it in Spanish.
a   Madrid, centre, flat
b   Barcelona, outskirts, small house near beach
c   Here, in a street very close to the hotel
d   England, countryside, house with garden, 50 km from London

5 Survey

Here's a questionnaire for a market research survey on language learning in Spain. Because of a faulty photocopier, all the question words have been left off – what should they be? Choose from these words:

qué   cómo   cuántas
dónde   por qué cuántos

a ¿......... se llama usted?
b ¿......... años tiene?
c ¿........ idiomas habla?   inglés/francés, etc
d ¿......... estudia?   en una academia privada
                        en un centro estatal
                        en casa
e ¿......... horas estudia al día?   menos de una
                                   de una a dos
                                   más de dos
f ¿......... estudia idiomas?   por motivos de
                                   trabajo
                                   por interés cultural
                                   para las vacaciones

6 Paying

Is the change right? Say if the change given is correct in the following situations.

a   – Son mil trescientas veinticinco.
     – Tenga. Dos mil.
     – Aquí tiene el cambio: un billete de quinientas y dos monedas de cien.

b   – Son cuatrocientas ochenta.
     – Tenga: quinientas pesetas.
     – Aquí tiene: veinte pesetas de cambio.

c   – Son cinco mil doscientas.
     – Tenga: seis mil pesetas.
     – Aquí tiene el cambio: un billete de quinientas y tres monedas de cien.

d   – Son cuarenta y cinco pesetas.
     – Tenga: un billete de doscientas.
     – El cambio: ciento cuarenta y cinco pesetas.

7 Some order

If you were the only Spanish-speaker in a group (it *could* happen!), would you be able to order the following? Use the word *ración* when asking for the food.

a

b

c

d

e

f

8 Discovering Salamanca

One of Spain's oldest cities, Salamanca takes some exploring. Follow these sets of directions from the *Oficina de Turismo* (marked with a cross) and see where you end up.

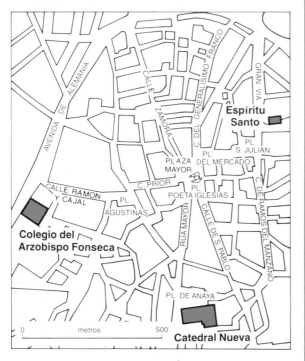

a   Mire, cruce la Plaza Mayor, vaya todo recto por la Calle Prior, cruce la Plaza Agustinas y siga por la Calle Ramón y Cajal. Tome la segunda a la izquierda, y está a mano derecha.

b   Salga de la Plaza Mayor por la izquierda, cruce la Plaza Poeta Iglesias y siga todo recto por la Rúa Mayor. Está al final, a unos quinientos metros, al otro lado de la Plaza de Anaya.

c   Cruce la Plaza del Mercado, aquí detrás, y siga todo recto. Al final, a la izquierda por la Gran Vía, tome la segunda a la derecha, y está a mano izquierda.

9 True/false

Decide if these statements are true (*verdad*) or false (*mentira*).

a   En Venezuela se habla español.
b   Se puede viajar en tren de Málaga a Melilla.
c   En Correos se vende tabaco.
d   En España sólo se habla español.
e   Se venden sellos en un estanco.
f   En Barcelona no hay puerto.
g   En una tienda de comestibles se vende vino.
h   Se dice 'buenas noches' sólo cuando uno se va a dormir.

10 Booking in

With the help of the bill, see if you can complete the conversation.

HOTEL
Almirante Bonifaz
09004 · BURGOS

VITORIA, 22 Y 24 · TELF. (947) 20 69 43 · TELEGRAMAS
ALBOTEL
· TELEX 94303

D. *Antonio Lago.*

Habitación n.º *309*

Personas n.º *2*

Precio: *6.050* Ptas.

Fecha { Llegada *12-8-86*
        Salida *13-8-86*

Conforme: El Cliente, *A. Lago.*

Antonio	Buenas tardes. ¿Tienen una habitación .... ?
Receptionist	¿Para cuántas noches?
Antonio	Para .... noche sólo.
Receptionist	Muy bien. No hay problema.
Antonio	¿Tiene .... la habitación?
Receptionist	Sí, todas las habitaciones tienen baño.
Antonio	¿Y cuánto .... la habitación?
Receptionist	Seis mil .... pesetas por noche. Aquí tiene la llave. Habitación número ....
Antonio	Muchas ....

11 Dirty shirts

These messages were left at the hotel reception for a visiting businessman. Read them through and decide if the statements underneath are true or false.

11.30 Llamó la Sra. Kendall desde
Estados Unidos. Va a llamar otra
vez a la hora de cenar.

Llamó la secretaria del
Sr. Ramos. ¿Puede cenar con
él en el restaurante "La Plata
del Río"? Confirmar en
teléfono. 41 65 42

"Econocoche": su coche está
en el garaje del hotel; llave
en la recepción. ¿Puede
firmar papeles? Coche reservado
por una semana. Matrícula
CO-2354-AB.

Sus camisas no se pueden
lavar esta noche. Lavandería
no funciona hasta mañana a las
7 de la mañana. Pantalones y
chaqueta están listos.

a Mrs Kendall wants you to ring back at supper time.
b She phoned from the United Kingdom.
c Sr Ramos called.
d You have to confirm an arrangement with him.
e He wants you to have lunch with him.
f Unfortunately, your hire car isn't ready yet.
g You've hired the car for a week.
h The computerised reservation number is CO–2354–AB.
i The laundry is open till 7 o'clock tomorrow morning.
j Your shirts aren't ready but your trousers are.

ABOUT SPAIN

National parks

Spain has a number of natural parks (like Cazorla) and seven national parks (*parques nacionales*), where increasingly threatened species of rare flora and fauna can be protected. Most of the *parques nacionales* are found in mountain areas, and the species of animals to be seen include the wild boar, the chamois, the brown bear and the Spanish mountain goat.

Probably the best-known park is El Coto de Doñana, at the mouth of the river Guadalquivir. Its vast area of dunes and saltmarshes provides shelter for migrating birds from Europe and Africa.

El Coto de Doñana

Cattle egrets in the Coto

Souvenirs from Spain

Although Spain is not the cheap country it used to
be, there are still plenty of things worth bringing
back.

Everywhere you go you'll find china and pottery.
Talavera de la Reina, in the province of Toledo,
produces ceramic ware that's very popular within
Spain. (Sevilla and Valencia are also well-known
centres.)

Other traditional crafts, called *artesanía* in Spanish,
include basket-making, leatherwork, lace-making
and carpet-weaving. Particularly popular with tourists is the ornamental metalwork from Toledo.

Don't forget to keep an eye out for local delicacies
like *turrón* (a kind of nougat, originally from
Alicante), *mazapán* (marzipan) and *almendrados*
(biscuits made from almonds and honey).

E×tra dialogues

These are additional dialogues and interviews recorded for the radio and television programmes.

Difficult phrases or grammatical structures are explained; other words can be found in the *Vocabulary*.

UNIT 1

Ⓡ 1   Isabel meets Ana Ubeda.
Isabel   Hola.
Ana   Hola, buenas tardes.
Isabel   ¿Cómo te llamas?
Ana   Ana, mi nombre es Ana.
Isabel   ¿Cómo?
Ana   Ana.

Ⓡ 2   Isabel met José Luis Causapé in Vitoria, in the Basque Country – but he doesn't come from there.
Isabel   ¿Y usted es de aquí de Vitoria?
Sr Causapé   No, no soy de Vitoria, soy de Zaragoza.

Ⓣ 3   Yolanda talks to holidaymakers on the beach at Santander.
Yolanda   Hola, buenos días.
Holidaymaker 1   Hola, buenos días.
Yolanda   Hola, buenos días.
Holidaymaker 2   Hola, buenos días.
Holidaymaker 3   Buenos días.
Holidaymaker 4   Buenos días.
Yolanda   Hola, buenas tardes.
Holidaymaker 5   Buenas tardes.
Yolanda   Hola, buenas tardes.
Holidaymaker 6   Hola, buenas tardes.
Holidaymaker 7   Buenas tardes.
Yolanda   ¿Cómo se llama?
Holidaymaker 7   Me llamo Guillermo Barrallo.
Yolanda   ¿Cómo se llama?
Holidaymaker 5   Paulina.

Yolanda	¿Cómo te llamas?
Holidaymaker 1	Me llamo Juan Manuel.
Yolanda	¿Cómo se llama?
Holidaymaker 4	Me llamo Sofía.
Yolanda	Hola, buenas tardes.
Holidaymaker 8	Hola, buenas tardes.
Yolanda	¿Cómo te llamas?
Holidaymaker 8	Me llamo Mariola San José.

UNIT 2

Ⓡ 1 Isabel met Miguel in the small southern town of Mojácar.

Isabel	Hola, ¿qué tal?
Miguel	Muy bien, ¿y tú?
Isabel	Muy bien. ¿Cómo te llamas?
Miguel	Miguel.
Isabel	Miguel, ¿eres de aquí de Mojácar?
Miguel	Bueno, no soy de Mojácar, soy de Madrid.

Ⓡ 2 Isabel rings the doorbell of Jaime's parents' flat, and has to speak into the entryphone.

Jaime	Sí, ¿quién es?
Isabel	Soy Isabel.
Jaime	Hola, Isabel, ahora te abro.
Isabel	Vale.

ahora te abro   *I'll open the door right now*

Ⓡ 3 At a *cafetería* in Madrid, Isabel and some friends order drinks.

Waiter	¿Qué van a tomar los señores?
Luis	Yo, gin tonic.
Waiter	Gin tonic.
Isabel	Para mí un zumo de naranja.
Waiter	¿Qué va a tomar la señorita?
Ana	Un mosto, por favor.
Waiter	¿Y usted?
Mari Carmen	Yo quiero una tónica, por favor.
Waiter	Tónica. ¿Señor?
Jaime	Para mí una cerveza.

Ⓣ 4 People on the beach at Santander introduce their friends to Yolanda.

Yolanda	¡Hola!
Little girl 1	¡Hola!
Little girl 2	¡Hola!
Yolanda	¿Cómo se llama tu amiga?

Little girl 1	Esta es mi hermana, Beatriz.
Little girl 3	Esta es mi hermana, María Antonia.
Little boy 1	Mi hermano, Juan.
Little boy 2	Este es César, mi hermano.
Holidaymaker 1	Esta es mi amiga, Natalia.
Natalia	Hola.
Holidaymaker 2	Mi amiga, Maite.
Holidaymaker 3	Es mi amigo, Carlos.
Holidaymaker 4	Esta es mi mujer, Panchi.
Holidaymaker 5	Es mi marido, Eusebio.
Little girl 4	Este es mi padre.

UNIT 3

®1   Isabel bought oranges, lemons and tomatoes at the greengrocer's.

Isabel	Hola, buenos días.
Shopkeeper	Buenos días.
Isabel	Un kilo de naranjas, por favor.
Shopkeeper	Sí, sí. (*he weighs the oranges*)
Isabel	Muy bien. Medio kilo de limones.
Shopkeeper	Sí. (*he weighs the lemons*) ¿Algo más?
Isabel	Eh, sí. Medio kilo de tomates para ensalada.
Shopkeeper	(*he weighs the tomatoes*) Medio kilo. ¿Algo más?
Isabel	No, nada más. Eso es todo. ¿Cuánto es, por favor?
Shopkeeper	Doscientas ochenta y cinco.
Isabel	Doscientas ochenta y cinco, muy bien. ¿Tiene cambio?
Shopkeeper	Sí.
Isabel	Muchas gracias.
Shopkeeper	(*counting the change*) Trescientas, quinientas, y quinientas hace mil; uno, dos, tres, y cuatro, cinco mil. Muchas gracias.
Isabel	Muchas gracias a usted. Hasta luego, ¿eh?
Shopkeeper	Adíos, adíos.

hace   *makes*

®2   Jordi asked about Mercedes' extended family.

Jordi	¿Tienes familia en Barcelona?
Mercedes	Sí, tengo todos los hermanos de mi padre, todos los hermanos de mi madre, y la madre de mi madre, o sea mi abuela.
Jordi	O sea, tus tíos y tu abuela. ¿Cuántos tíos tienes en Barcelona?
Mercedes	Por parte de mi padre tengo cuatro tíos, tres de los cuales son señores, y una tía que es la única hija de la familia.

o sea   *that is, in other words*
por parte de mi padre   *on my father's side*
de los cuales   *of whom*

Ⓡ 3   Luis told Isabel about his children.

Isabel	¿Tienes hijos?
Luis	Sí, tengo cuatro hijos.
Isabel	¿Y son todos chicos?
Luis	No, son tres chicos y una chica, la última es una chica. El mayor me parece que tiene veintiocho años, el segundo veintisiete, y luego diecisiete, y la última dieciséis.
Isabel	¿Y cómo se llaman?
Luis	Luis, Juan, Manuel y Ana.

me parece que   *I think* (*that*)

Ⓣⓥ 4   Yolanda speaks to some shoppers in the central market in Santander.

Yolanda	Hola, buenos días.
Passer-by 1	Hola, buenos días.
Yolanda	¿Cómo se llama?
Passer-by 1	Consuelo.
Yolanda	¿Tiene familia?
Passer-by 1	Sí.

Yolanda	Buenos días.
Passer-by 2	Buenos días.
Yolanda	¿Cómo se llama?
Passer-by 2	Angel Gutiérrez Santos.
Yolanda	¿Tiene familia?
Passer-by 2	Sí.

Yolanda	¿Tiene familia?
Passer-by 3	¿Familia? Sí.

Yolanda	¿Tiene familia?
Passer-by 4	Sí, dos hijos.

Yolanda	Buenos días.
Passer-by 5	Hola, buenos días.
Yolanda	¿Cómo se llama?
Passer-by 5	Yo me llamo Irene.
Yolanda	¿Tiene familia?
Passer-by 5	Sí.

Yolanda	¿Tiene familia?
Passer-by 6	No, soy soltero.

Yolanda	¿Tiene familia?
Passer-by 7	¿Yo? No, soy soltera.

UNIT 4

® 1   How to get to the *Museo del Prado*? Isabel asks three people.

Isabel	Por favor, ¿el Museo del Prado?
Man	Pues, bajando la calle del Prado –
Isabel	Sí –
Man	Y justo enfrente del Hotel Ritz está el museo.
Isabel	Muy bien, muchas gracias.
Man	No hay de qué.
Isabel	Hola, buenos días.
Woman	Buenos días.
Isabel	Por favor, ¿dónde está el Museo del Prado?
Woman	El Museo del Prado queda bajando todo derecho, a mano derecha, enfrente.
Isabel	Aha. Muchas gracias, ¿eh?
Woman	De nada.
Isabel	Por favor, ¿el Museo del Prado?
Woman	¡Huy!, lo siento, no soy de aquí.

bajando	*as you go down*
queda	*is (situated)*
no hay de qué	*don't mention it*
lo siento	*I'm sorry*

® 2   Gerónimo Terez now lives in Barcelona, but originally he's from the south of Spain.

Jordi	¿De dónde es usted?
Gerónimo	De Dalías.
Jordi	¿Dónde está Dalías?
Gerónimo	En la provincia de Almería.

® 3   José Luis Causapé lives in Vitoria – where exactly?

Isabel	¿Dónde vive usted?
Sr Causapé	Bueno, vivo aquí en Vitoria, en la calle ... bueno, Plaza de Amárica, Pintor Amárica.
Isabel	¿Está en el centro?
Sr Causapé	Sí, está en el centro, muy cerca de mi oficina.

Ⓣ 4   Yolanda asks people at a campsite where they live.

Yolanda	¿Vive en un piso o en una casa?
Person 1	En un piso.
Person 2	En un piso.
Person 3	En un piso.
Person 4	Vivimos en un piso.
Person 5	En un piso.

Person 6	En un piso.
Person 7	En un piso.
Person 8	En una casa particular, con mi huerta y mi jardín.

UNIT 5

Ⓡ 1   What languages do these people speak?

| Isabel Soto | ¿Usted habla inglés? |
| Isabel | Un poco. |

Isabel	¿Qué idiomas hablas?
Woman	Inglés, latín y griego.
Isabel	¿Griego moderno?
Woman	No, griego antiguo.
Isabel	O sea, hablas castellano, inglés, latín y griego.
Woman	Eso.
Isabel	Cuatro idiomas. ¡Estupendo!

Isabel	¿Hablas inglés?
Woman	Pues, sí.
Isabel	¿Lo hablas muy bien?
Woman	Pues, bastante.

eso   *that's right*

Ⓡ 2   What do people think of Madrid?

Isabel	¿Eres de aquí de Madrid, Cuchi?
Cuchi	Sí, nací en Madrid.
Isabel	¿Y te gusta la ciudad?
Cuchi	Me gusta mucho Madrid, sí. Es una ciudad muy . . . muy divertida y muy . . . muy bonita, me gusta mucho.

nací   *I was born*

Isabel	¿Te gusta Madrid?
Woman	Mucho.
Isabel	¿Sí? ¿Más que Alicante?
Woman	¡No! Alicante es más bonita que Madrid.

Isabel	¿Es usted de Madrid?
Woman	No, pero vivo cincuenta y cinco años ya en Madrid.
Isabel	¿Cincuenta y cinco años? ¿De dónde es usted?
Woman	Yo soy de Toledo.
Isabel	Muy cerca de Madrid, ¿no?
Woman	Cerca, sí.
Isabel	¿Y qué prefiere, Toledo o Madrid?
Woman	Madrid. Es más ciudad y me gusta más la vida de Madrid.

vivo . . . ya   *I've been living . . . now*
es más ciudad   *it's more of a city*

Marga	Vivo en Madrid ya veintidós años.
Isabel	¿Veintidós años? ¿O sea que eres casi española?
Marga	Sí, casi española.
Isabel	¿Y te gusta Madrid?
Marga	Sí. Madrid me gusta mucho. Me apasiona Madrid.

me apasiona   *I adore*

Isabel	¿Qué prefieres, Miguel, Madrid o Mojácar?
Miguel	Prefiero Mojácar. Es más tranquilo, más bonito, hay mejor clima, la gente es más simpática.

UNIT 6

®1   On the way out of the town of Santo Domingo, Isabel directs the driver towards Haro.

Isabel	Bueno, aquí a la izquierda. . . . Y aquí a la derecha, según la indicación, hacia Haro. . . . Y ahora a la derecha. . . . ¡Estupendo! Ya estamos de camino.

ya estamos de camino   *now we're on the way*

®2   In the tourist office in Vitoria, Isabel asks for information.

Isabel	¿Tiene un plano de Vitoria, por favor?
Clerk	Sí. Este es el plano de Vitoria.
Isabel.	Muy bien. ¿Qué monumentos hay en Vitoria?
Clerk	Aquí tenemos la catedral nueva, y ésta que se encuentra en el casco viejo es la catedral vieja.
Isabel	La catedral nueva y la catedral vieja. ¿Y qué otros monumentos o cosas de interés hay en Vitoria?
Clerk	Pues, aquí mismo está una casa que se llama El Portalón, y hoy día es un restaurante muy bonito.
Isabel	¿El Portalón? ¿Está cerca?
Clerk	Sí, está muy cerca de la catedral, a unos cuantos pasos.
Isabel	A unos cuantos pasos. Muy bien.
Clerk	Luego, enfrente del Portalón se encuentra el Museo de Arqueología.

que se encuentra   *which is*
aquí mismo   *right here*
a unos cuantos pasos   *a few yards ('paces') away*

UNIT 7

Ⓡ 1   **What time do people start working? – Ana's a student.**

Isabel   ¿A qué hora empiezas tus clases?

Ana   Empiezo por las tardes a las cuatro, hasta las nueve de la noche, y luego estudio en casa dos o tres horas.

Luis works in a bank.

Isabel   ¿Y a qué hora empiezas?

Luis   Yo trabajo de ocho de la mañana a tres de la tarde.

Ⓡ 2   **At one o'clock in the afternoon, Isabel spoke to a train-driver who'd just come on duty.**

Isabel   ¿A qué hora empieza su trabajo?

Train-driver   Pues, varía de unos días a otros. Hoy, por ejemplo, he empezado, pues, a la una. Otros días empiezo a las siete de la mañana, otros días empiezo a las tres de la tarde, otros días empiezo a las diez de la noche ... varía totalmente.

Isabel   ¿Cuántas horas trabaja al día?

Train-driver   Pues, también depende. Todos los días no es lo mismo. Unos días trabajo cinco horas, otros siete, otros diez, otros doce ... varía constantemente.

Isabel   ¿Y a qué hora termina hoy, por ejemplo?

Train-driver   Hoy aproximadamente sobre las diez de la noche terminaré.

he empezado	*I started*
todos los días	*every day*
lo mismo	*the same* (*thing*)
terminaré	*I'll finish*

Ⓡ 3   **Blas is a loom operator.**

Isabel   ¿Hoy cuántas horas piensas trabajar?

Blas   Nueve o diez.

Isabel   ¿Cuántos años tienes, Blas?

Blas   Diecisiete.

Isabel   Diecisiete, ¡caramba! ¿Y trabajas fines de semana?

Blas   Hasta el sábado por la tarde.

... piensas trabajar?   *... are you intending to work?*

ⓉⓋ 4   **A class of seven- and eight-year-olds learns to tell the time.**

Teacher   Vamos hoy a repasar las horas. Por ejemplo ... (*moving the hands on the clock*) ¿Qué hora es?

Children	Son las diez.
Teacher	¿Qué hora es?
Children	Son las once.
Teacher	¿Qué hora es?
Children	Son las doce.
Teacher	¿Qué hora es?
Children	Es la una.
Teacher	Muy bien. ¿Qué hora es, Joaquín?
Joaquín	Son las nueve y cuarto.
Teacher	Muy bien. ¿Qué hora es, Miguel?
Miguel	Son las nueve y media.
Teacher	¿Qué hora es, Susana?
Susana	Son las diez menos cuarto.

vamos   *we're going*

📺 5   At a primary school in Madrid, Yolanda asked some children about drawings of their parents at work.

Yolanda	¿Cuál es la profesión de tu padre?
1st child	Es fotógrafo.
Yolanda	¿Cuál es la profesión de tu madre?
2nd child	Es periodista.
3rd child	Es barrendero.
4th child	Es taxista.
Yolanda	¿Cuál es la profesión de tu madre?
5th child	Es profesora.
Yolanda	¿Cuál es la profesión du tu madre?
6th child	Es médico.

UNIT 8

® 1   Isabel asked some people about their favourite food.

Isabel	¿Qué te gusta comer? ¿Cuáles son tus cosas favoritas de comer?
Mamie	Arroz, pollo, maíz . . .
Isabel	¿Te gusta el helado?
Mamie	Sí.
Isabel	¡Sí! El helado. ¿Y te gustan los bocadillos?
Mamie	Sí.
Isabel	¿De qué tipo?
Mamie	De . . . de queso y jamón.
Isabel	¿Qué cosas no te gustan?
Mamie	El cocido, y el pumpkin pie.
Isabel	¿El qué?
Mamie	Pumpkin pie.
Isabel	¡Pumpkin pie!

¿cuáles . . . ?   *which . . . ?*

| Isabel | ¿Tu comida favorita? |

Ana   Una de mis comidas favoritas es la paella, que es un plato de arroz con carne y pescado, muy típico español.

Isabel   ¿De qué región es la paella?

Ana   Es de la zona de Valencia.

Isabel   ¿Qué te gusta comer?

Mari Carmen   No tengo ningún problema con la comida, me gusta todo, pero prefiero un plato de legumbres, y después una carne, carne a la brasa, o pescado. Pero me gusta todo – ¡es mi problema!

Isabel   Te gusta todo. ¿Y beber?

Mari Carmen   En verano me gusta mucho la cerveza porque refresca, pero me gusta mucho la leche.

no tengo ningún problema	*I don't have any problem*

Isabel   ¿Qué platos son tus favoritos?

Luis   Las croquetas.

Isabel   Las croquetas – ¿de qué?

Luis   No sé, porque nunca sé lo que tienen dentro.

Isabel   Y aparte de las croquetas, ¿qué es lo que te gusta?

Luis   Me gusta todo generalmente. Me gusta la paella, y me gusta la carne. El pescado quizá menos, pero si hay pescado también lo como. ¡Soy muy buen marido!

Isabel   ¡Ay sí, que lo comes todo!

Luis   ¡Todo!

Isabel   La comida, hay que acompañarla de la bebida, ¿qué es lo que te gusta?

Luis   En efecto. Yo siempre bebo vino con las comidas.

Isabel   ¿Tinto o blanco?

Luis   Tinto. Normalmente bebo Valdepeñas, que es el vino corriente más o menos, un vino que se llama peleón, y lo bebo un poco fresco como casi todo el mundo.

nunca sé	*I never know*
lo que tienen dentro	*what they have inside*
¿qué es lo que . . .?	= ¿qué . . .?
que lo comes todo	*because you eat everything*
hay que acompañarla de	*you have to accompany it with*
peleón	*'plonk'*
como casi todo el mundo	*like nearly everyone*

UNIT 9

Ⓡ 1   Isabel and Ana go to a department store – Isabel wants to buy some tights.

Isabel	Yo necesito la talla pequeña.
Ana	La talla pequeña. (*Sí, y . . .*) ¿De qué color?
Isabel	Color marrón. Mira, aquí están.
Ana	Ah sí, son muy bonitas.
Isabel	A ver qué precio tienen.
Ana	¿Cuánto cuestan?
Isabel	Novecientas cincuenta pesetas.
Ana	Sí. Ah, pues son muy bonitas éstas, Isabel. ¿Por qué no te compras éstas?
Isabel	Pues me las voy a comprar (*sí*). Vamos.
Ana	Marrón (*sí*), solamente marrón. Ah, muy bien. Bueno, pues, vamos a pagar.

qué precio tienen	*what price they are*
¿por qué no te compras . . .?	*why don't you buy (your-self) . . . ?*
me las voy a comprar	*I'm going to buy them*
vamos	*let's go*

Ⓡ 2   In the tourist office, Isabel wants to know if a museum in Vitoria is open today.

Isabel	¿Está abierto hoy, lunes?
Clerk	Los lunes cierran, los demás días de la semana está abierto, y los sábados y domingos únicamente por la mañana. El horario es de once a dos, y por la tarde de cinco a siete.
Isabel	¿Cuánto cuesta la entrada?
Clerk	Todos los museos de Vitoria son gratuitos.
Isabel	Son gratuitos. O sea, no cuestan nada.
Clerk	Nada.

Ⓡ 3   Opening hours at the chemist's . . .

Isabel	¿A qué hora abren?
Chemist	Por la mañana a las nueve y media, y por la tarde a las cinco.
Isabel	¿Y a qué hora cierran?
Chemist	Por la mañana a las dos menos cuarto, y por la tarde a las ocho.
Isabel	¿Y abren los sábados?
Chemist	Los sábados, el horario es de diez a dos menos cuarto. Por la tarde no se abre.

. . . and at the bank.

Isabel	¿El banco, a qué hora abre?
Honorio	Abre a las nueve de la mañana y cierra a las dos de la tarde.
Isabel	¿Y se abre los sábados?
Honorio	Sí, sí, se abre los sábados hasta las dos de la tarde.
Isabel	¿O sea, de nueve a dos?
Honorio	Exacto, de nueve a dos de la tarde.

📺 4 Mariola goes to a tobacconist's to buy stamps.

Mariola	Buenas tardes.
Assistant	Buenas tardes.
Mariola	Dos sellos para Estados Unidos, por favor.
Assistant	¿Para carta o para postal?
Mariola	Para postal.
Assistant	Son ciento cuatro pesetas.
Mariola	Gracias. Adiós.
Assistant	Adiós.

📺 5 Cristina visits *La Pajarita* sweetshop in Madrid's Puerta del Sol.

Cristina	Buenos días.
Assistant	Buenos días. ¿Qué desea?
Cristina	Una caja pequeña de caramelos. Mmm ... me pone cien gramos de éstos. (*the assistant scoops them into a box*) Otros cien de éstos. ¿De qué son los verdes?
Assistant	Los verdes, de menta.
Cristina	Mmm ... ¿Y estos amarillos?
Assistant	Son de piña.
Cristina	Mmm, vale, otros cien gramos.
Assistant	(*she adds them to the box*) ¿Algo más?
Cristina	No, eso es todo. ¿Cuánto es?
Assistant	Son quinientas pesetas.
Cristina	Muy bien. Muchas gracias.
Assistant	Gracias a usted. Adiós.
Cristina	Adiós.

me pone	*give me*
¿de qué son los verdes?	*what are the green ones (made of)?*

📺 6 Isaac Cuende chooses some postcards at a newspaper kiosk.

Isaac	Buenos días.
News-seller	Buenos días.
Isaac	Tres postales. (*he picks up a newspaper*) Y el periódico. ¿Tiene periódicos extranjeros?
News-seller	No, lo siento. Los domingos no tenemos.
Isaac	¿Cúanto es?
News-seller	Son treinta pesetas las postales y noventa el periódico. Ciento veinte pesetas. (*Isaac pays*) Gracias.
Isaac	Adiós.
News-seller	Adiós.

UNIT 10

Ⓡ 1   Jordi asks Mercedes about her hobbies.

Jordi   ¿Cuáles son tus principales aficiones, o dis-
tracciones?

Mercedes   Mis principales aficiones son dormir, dibujar, tocar
el piano, y emborracharme.

Jordi   ¿Tus aficiones ocupan mucho tiempo?

Mercedes   Mis aficiones suelen ocupar entre las once y las tres
de la madrugada.

Jordi   ¿Y cómo puedes luego trabajar por la mañana
siguiente, durmiendo tan poco?

Mercedes   ¡Envejeciendo rápidamente!

emborracharme	to get drunk
suelen ocupar	usually take up
¿cómo puedes luego trabajar?	how can you work then?
durmiendo tan poco	if you sleep so little
envejeciendo	getting old

Ⓡ 2   What are Ana's plans for the evening?

Isabel   ¿Qué vas a hacer esta noche?

Ana   Esta noche me voy a quedar aquí, porque tenemos
una pequeña fiesta donde tocaremos la guitarra y
cantaremos.

Isabel   ¿Pero te gusta salir?

Ana   Me gusta mucho salir, sí.

me voy a quedar	I'm going to stay
tocaremos	we'll play
cantaremos	we'll sing

Ⓡ 3   What do people think of traditional Spanish music?

Jaime   A mí me gusta mucho toda la música del norte de
España – la gallega, la muñeira. El folklore vasco
también me parece fascinante.

Ana   La música vasca es muy bonita, y la música del
centro de España, en Castilla; la jota es muy
conocida y muy bonita.

Isabel   ¿Cuál te gusta más a tí?

Ana   A mí me gusta mucho la jota.

Isabel   Y a mí también.

Luis   La música que se hace en el País Vasco, y naturalmente la música gallega y sobre todo la jota. La
jota es muy característica.

Isabel   ¿Te gusta la jota?

Luis   A mí me gusta, me gusta mucho.

Isabel   ¿La bailas?

Luis	No, no la bailo. No la bailo, pero me gusta.
Isabel	¿Te gusta bailar?
Luis	No, sólo me gusta bailar el pasodoble porque es fácil, pero lo demás . . . soy muy malo para bailar.

a mí me gusta	I (personally) like
que se hace	that they make
pero lo demás	but as for the rest (of them)
malo para bailar	bad at dancing

📺 4 Yolanda asks people in Madrid what sports they play.

Yolanda	¿Qué deporte practica?
Person 1	El tenis.
Yolanda	¿Qué deporte practica?
Person 2	Tenis.
Person 3	Me gusta el baloncesto.
Person 4	Yo, el baloncesto, pero también me gusta el fútbol.
Person 5	Pues yo, la bicicleta, y la natación también me gusta mucho.
Person 6	Me gusta la bicicleta y el tenis.
Person 7	El tenis.

UNIT 11

Ⓡ 1 Isabel checks on train times to Almería at Atocha station in Madrid.

Isabel	Hola, buenos días.
Clerk	Buenos días.
Isabel	Dígame, ¿hay trenes para Almería mañana?
Clerk	Tiene usted dos trenes.
Isabel	¿Cuándo salen?
Clerk	Un momento. (he gets out the timetable)
Isabel	Gracias.
Clerk	Para Almería tiene usted un tren diurno, que sale de Madrid, de la estación de Atocha, a las quince cero cinco, y llega a Almería a las veintidós diecisiete. Y luego también, si usted quiere hacer el viaje por la noche, tiene un expreso, que se llama Expreso Sierra Nevada.

dígame   (can you) tell me

Ⓡ 2 Isabel buys the tickets to Almería.

Isabel	Buenos días.
Clerk	Buenos días.
Isabel	Dos billetes para Almería.
Clerk	¿Ida y vuelta?
Isabel	No, ida solamente.

Clerk	De acuerdo.
Isabel	No fumadores, y mañana por la tarde, por favor.
Clerk	Perfectamente.

de acuerdo   *certainly*

® 3   Teresa wants information about the boats from Barcelona to Mahón in Menorca.

Teresa	Buenos días.
Clerk	Buenos días, señorita. Usted dirá.
Teresa	¿Hay un barco cada día a Menorca? A mí me interesa para el mes de julio.
Clerk	Para el mes de julio, bueno. Tiene el martes, miércoles, viernes, sábado y domingo, a las veintitrés treinta.
Teresa	O sea, martes, miércoles, viernes, sábado y domingo ...
Clerk	Sábado y domingo, a las veintitrés treinta. Estos son los servicios durante la temporada de verano para Mahón.

usted dirá   *can I help you? ('you will say')*

a mí me interesa   *I'm interested in*

⊤ᴠ 4   In Sevilla, Juan and Guadalupe ask about river boat trips on the Guadalquivir.

Boat captain	Buenos días.
Juan	Buenos días ¿A qué hora sale el próximo barco?
Captain	Hay uno dentro de quince minutos, a las tres y media.
Juan	¿Y más tarde?
Captain	El último sale a las siete.
Guadalupe	¿Y cuánto dura el viaje?
Captain	Una hora justa.
Guadalupe	¿Y cuánto cuesta el billete?
Captain	Quinientas pesetas.
Juan	Bien, dos billetes para el próximo barco.
Captain	Son mil pesetas.

¿cuánto dura el viaje?   *how long does the trip last?*

una hora justa   *one hour exactly*

UNIT 12

® 1   Isabel phones a hotel to make a reservation.

Isabel	Sí, buenas tardes. Quisiera hacer una reserva para dos habitaciones individuales. (*she listens to the clerk on the other end of the line*) Para la noche de mañana, eso es, la noche del ... del domingo. .... Sí. .... Dos individuales. .... Eso es, para una

noche. .... Isabel Soto. .... No, no cenamos, sólo tomamos el desayuno. .... ¿Qué precio tiene la habitación individual, por favor? .... Dos mil cuatrocientas diez. Muchas gracias, ¿eh? Adiós.

quisiera   *I would like*

Ⓡ 2   Isabel arrives in Mojácar and tries to get a couple of rooms for the night.

Isabel	Hola, buenas tardes.
Receptionist	Hola, buenas tardes.
Isabel	¿Tiene habitaciones?
Receptionist	Sí. ¿Qué es, doble?
Isabel	No, dos individuales, por favor.
Receptionist	De acuerdo, un momentito. (*noting down the details*) ¿Me deja el carnet de identidad, por favor?
Isabel	Sí, sí, ¿cómo no? Tenga.
Receptionist	Gracias.
Isabel	¿Tiene baño la habitación?
Receptionist	Sí, tiene.
Isabel	¿Y aire acondicionado?
Receptionist	No, no tiene acondicionado.
Isabel	Bien. ¿Cuánto cuesta la habitación individual?
Receptionist	Tres mil trescientas, por persona.
Isabel	¿Tres mil trescientas por persona?
Receptionist	Sí.
Isabel	¿Incluye el desayuno?
Receptionist	Sí.

tenga   *here you are*
por persona   *per person*
¿incluye ...? *does that include ...?*

Ⓡ 3   What is there to do in the small town of Haro?

Mick	¿Qué se puede hacer, qué hay para hacer en Haro para un turista como yo?
Nati	En Haro se puede descansar muy bien, y se puede ver paisaje, monumentos como las iglesias, casas muy bonitas; y la parte vieja que llamamos es muy típica y muy bonita – calles estrechas donde se va con los amigos en cuadrilla a tomar vasitos de vino muy pequeños, chiquitos que se llaman aquí.
Mick	¿Y se bebe vino de Rioja, supongo?
Nati	Por supuesto, estamos en esta tierra que es donde mejores vinos de mesa hay en toda España.
Mick	Doña Carmen, ¿qué más se puede hacer en Haro?
Carmen	Mucha cosa no se puede hacer porque es un pueblo muy tranquilo, pero tiene sitios naturales donde uno disfruta mucho.

como yo	*like me*
que llamamos	*as we call it*
donde se va	*where you go*
por supuesto	*of course*
mucha cosa	*a lot of things*

UNIT 13

®1 Isabel went to a chemist's to buy suntan cream, something for sunburn, something for a headache, and some tissues.

Isabel Hola, buenos días.

Assistant Hola, buenos días.

Isabel Quiero una crema bronceadora, por favor.

Assistant Sí, un momentito. Mire, tiene ésta que es leche hidratante.

Isabel ¿Qué factor de protección tiene?

Assistant Tiene el factor número tres.

Isabel Ah, estupendo. ¿Y cuánto cuesta?

Assistant Pues vamos a ver. Ochocientas setenta y cinco pesetas.

Isabel Muy bien. ¿Y tiene algo para las quemaduras de sol?

Assistant Mire, esto es una emulsión que es muy buena porque es calmante y además hidrata (*ah, perfecto*). Aplicarlo después del sol.

Isabel Muy bien. Entonces, la crema bronceadora y la loción esta calmante. Y ahora, ¿tiene algo para el dolor de cabeza?

Assistant Pues, ¿para quién es? ¿Para un adulto o para un niño?

Isabel Sí, sí, es para mí, es para mí, un adulto.

Assistant Para usted. Mire, este producto es muy bueno porque lleva paracetamol y no perjudica el estómago.

Isabel Muy bien, me lo llevo. Una cosa más, ¿tiene Kleenex?

Assistant Sí, sí, puede cogerlo usted misma.

Isabel (*she gets two packets*) Estos dos.

Assistant Muy bien. ¿Alguna cosa más quería?

Isabel No, gracias. ¿Cuánto cuesta todo?

Assistant Mil quinientas veinte.

Isabel Mil quinientas veinte.

leche hidratante	*moisturising milk*
aplicarlo	*apply it*
¿para quién es?	*who is it for?*
lleva	*it contains*
puede cogerlo	*you can get it*
usted misma	*yourself*
. . . quería?	*. . . did you want?*

® 2   What's the best month to be in Madrid? ·

Isabel   ¿Cuál es el mejor mes en Madrid?

Sra Suárez   Octubre.

Isabel   ¿Por qué?

Sra Suárez   Por la temperatura, es mucho más agradable.

Isabel   ¿Hace menos calor?

Sra Suárez   Bastante menos, o sea las noches son de las más agradables para pasear, con una chaqueta, inclusive.

Isabel   ¿Y para dormir?

Sra Suárez   Eso sobre todo, porque durante el verano no hay quien duerma en Madrid, de calor.

por la temperatura	*because of the temperature*
son de las más	*are some of the most*
no hay quien	*there isn't anyone who*
de calor	*because of the heat*

UNIT 14

® 1   Julián and his wife Marisa prefer the countries of northern Europe to the Mediterranean.

Isabel   ¿Adónde fuiste el año pasado de vacaciones?

Julián   El año pasado estuve en Suiza.

Isabel   ¿En toda Suiza?

Julián   Pues, Ginebra, Lausanne, Berna, y luego la parte de los lagos.

Isabel   ¿Y adónde piensas ir el año que viene?

Julián   Iremos a Alemania.

Isabel   ¿Es la primera vez?

Julián   No, la segunda.

Isabel   ¿Os gustan los países nórdicos?

Julián   Sí, porque no hace mucho calor.

Isabel   ¿Y la cocina nórdica también?

Julián   Sí, es muy exquisita.

Isabel   ¿Y la bebida?

Julián   La cerveza, por supuesto.

iremos	*we'll go*
¿os gustan . . .?	*do you like . . .?*

® 2   Where does a travel agent spend his holidays?

Isabel   ¿Adónde fue usted el año pasado de vacaciones?

Sr Méndez   Yo normalmente elijo un sitio tranquilo, es . . . se llama Las Fuentes, está en Alcocéber, provincia de Castellón.

Isabel   ¿Está en la costa?

Sr Méndez	Está en la costa de Castellón, sí, sí.
Isabel	¿Y piensa ir el año que viene?
Sr Méndez	Sí, desde luego, sí.
Isabel	¿Y va a un apartamento alquilado o …?
Sr Méndez	A un apartamento alquilado, un apartamento alquilado, sí.
Isabel	¿Y va con su familia?
Sr Méndez	Sí, sí, efectivamente.
Isabel	¿Y cuánto tiempo pasan ustedes en la costa?
Sr Méndez	Quince a veinte días.
Isabel	¡Qué poquito!
Sr Méndez	Sí, claro, es lo más que se puede permitir uno en verano en una agencia de viajes.

yo elijo	*I choose*
desde luego	*of course*
lo más que	*the most that*
se puede permitir uno	*one can allow oneself*

Ⓡ 3   At Bilbao airport Isabel spoke to a rather disgruntled traveller.

Isabel	¿Adónde vas?
Man	Voy a Valencia.
Isabel	¿A Valencia?
Man	A Valencia, sí.
Isabel	¿Qué vas a hacer en Valencia?
Man	Pues, voy a asistir a un congreso.
Isabel	¿No vas de vacaciones?
Man	No voy de vacaciones, no, voy a trabajar.
Isabel	Vas a trabajar. *(Mmm)* ¿Vas a participar tú?
Man	Pues, yo iba a participar esta tarde, pero han cancelado el vuelo del avión y no sé si voy a llegar.
Isabel	¿Vas a ir en tren?
Man	Voy a ir en avión hasta Madrid, y de Madrid a Valencia voy a ir en tren.

yo iba a	*I was going to*
han cancelado	*they have cancelled*

UNIT 15

Ⓡ 1   By the lake of El Tranco in the Parque de Cazorla, Isabel met a family picnicking.

Isabel	Hola, buenas tardes.
Woman	Hola.
Man	Buenas tardes.
Isabel	¿Estáis de vacaciones aquí?
Woman	No.
Man	No, no estamos de vacaciones, trabajamos aquí.

Isabel	¿En qué trabajáis?
Man	Pues, en una central hidroeléctrica que hay, de empleado de electricidad.
Isabel	¿De dónde sois?
Woman	Yo de Jaén.
Isabel	De Jaén. Y ...
Man	Yo soy de un pueblo cercano aquí, a dieciséis kilómetros, que se llama Hornos.
Isabel	Hornos.
Man	Sí.
Isabel	El agua hoy está estupenda, francamente estupenda. ¿Os vais a bañar?
Woman	Pues, hoy no.
Isabel	¿Pero os gusta bañaros?
Man	Sí, nos gusta bastante.
Isabel	Cuando hace más calor.
Man	Cuando hace más calor, sí.

de empleado de electricidad	*as an electricity worker*
... sois?	*... are you?*
¿os vais a bañar?	*are you going swimming?*
¿pero os gusta bañaros?	*but you like to go swimming?*

Grammar in a Nutshell

It **is** possible to speak a language perfectly without consciously knowing a word of grammar, but most people believe it's a useful shortcut to know at least something about the 'rules' that hold a language together.

In the main units of this book, grammar is only introduced in small doses, as necessary. In the section that follows, these notes are brought together and expanded a little. They don't cover the whole of Spanish grammar, but should be sufficient at this stage of your learning to help form a picture of how Spanish works.

NOUNS

In Spanish, as in English, a noun is a word that tells you what something or someone is: *una ciudad* (a city), *una mujer* (a woman), *un coche* (a car).

Gender

In Spanish every noun has a gender, either feminine or masculine: *chica* (girl) and *cerveza* (beer) are both feminine; *chico* (boy) and *tomate* (tomato) are masculine.

As a general rule, words ending in -*a* are feminine and those ending in -*o* are masculine. Of course there are exceptions: *mano* (hand) is feminine, *mapa* (map) is masculine. And there are some words that end in letters other than -*a* and -*o*: *leche* (milk) – feminine, *pastel* (cake) – masculine.

Articles

There are two words for 'a' – *una* and *un*. You use *una* with feminine nouns, *un* with masculine nouns.

Similarly, there are two words for 'the' – *la* and *el*, depending on the gender of the noun: *la chica*, *la cerveza*, but *el chico*, *el tomate*.

Note that if the words *a* or *de* come before *el*, the two words run together: **al** *lado* **del** *banco*.

In Spanish the definite article *la* or *el* is used when talking about things in general, whereas in English it isn't:
no me gusta la cerveza   I don't like beer
juego al fútbol   I play football

Plurals

When there are two or more of something, it's called a plural. There are two simple rules for making a noun plural in Spanish:

1   If it ends in a vowel, simply add -*s*:
    una patata   *tres patata***s**
    un kilo   *dos kilo***s**

2   If it ends in a consonant, add -*es*:
    una mujer   *dos mujer***es**
    un hotel   *cinco hotel***es**

Before a plural noun the word for 'the' changes from *la* or *el* to *las* or *los*:

las *chicas*   (feminine noun)
los *chicos*   (masculine noun)

The plural form of the indefinite article is used to mean 'a few', 'some':
¿quiere unas aceitunas?   would you like some olives?

ADJECTIVES

An adjective describes people, places or things. It normally goes next to a noun:
un vestido **rojo**   a **red** dress

or after 'is' or 'are':
este vestido es **bonito**   this dress is **pretty**

Position

In English, when an adjective and a noun come together, the adjective comes first, eg 'a **small** loaf'. In Spanish the adjective usually follows the noun:

*una bolsa **grande***	a large bag
*los zapatos **rojos***	the red shoes

Agreement

Adjectives have to 'agree' with nouns they describe. They usually have four possible forms: feminine singular and plural, and masculine singular and plural:

*una camisa **roja***	a red shirt	(fem. sing.)
*un coche **rojo***	a red car	(masc. sing.)
*dos camisas **rojas***	two red shirts	(fem. pl.)
*dos coches **rojos***	two red cars	(masc. pl.)

The endings are usually similar to the ending of the noun they describe; adjectives which don't end in -*o* or -*a* have only one singular and one plural form:

*una chaqueta **gris**, un pantalón **gris***	a grey jacket, a pair of grey trousers
*unas chaquetas **grises**, unos pantalones **grises***	some grey jackets, some pairs of grey trousers
*una manzana **verde**, un melón **verde***	a green apple, a green melon
*unas manzanas **verdes**, unos melones **verdes***	some green apples, some green melons

Adjectives of nationality that don't end in -*o*/-*a* behave slightly differently, in that they **do** change in the feminine:

*un chico **español***	*una chica **española***
*un coche **inglés***	*una bicicleta **inglesa***

When an adjective describes any mixtures of masculine and feminine nouns, it's used in the masculine plural:

María y José son españoles
el pan y la fruta son muy baratos

(See also POSSESSIVES and DEMONSTRATIVES opposite.)

A way of making an adjective more forceful is to add -*ísimo* or -*ísima* to the end:

una comida buena	a good lunch
*una cena **buenísima***	a really good dinner

POSSESSIVES

Possessive adjectives are 'my', 'your', 'his', 'her' etc:

mi	my
tu	your (informal)
su	your (formal); his, her, its
nuestro/a	our
vuestro/a	your (informal, plural)
su	your (formal, plural); their

Because they're adjectives, they agree with the noun they go with:

mi hermano	my brother
mis hermanos	my brothers
su coche	his car (*or* her car *or* their car)
sus coches	his cars (*or* her cars *or* their cars)

The English **'s** (apostrophe s) doesn't exist in Spanish. Instead you have to turn the words around and use *de* (of):

los hijos de mi amigo	my friend's children
la casa de Alfonso	Alfonso's house

DEMONSTRATIVES

The words for 'this' and 'that' can be either adjectives or pronouns. There is one word for 'this' and two for 'that' in Spanish. One of the words for 'that' refers to something very recent or close to you, the other to something distant in time or place.

As **adjectives**, all these words agree with the noun they describe. The different words are shown in these examples:

this	*esta camisa, este plato, estas camisas, estos platos*
that (close)	*esa camisa, ese plato, esas camisas, esos platos*
that (distant)	*aquella camisa, aquel plato, aquellas camisas, aquellos platos*

As **pronouns**, meaning 'this one' or 'that one', they may be written with an accent: *ésta, ésa, aquélla*.

When the gender of the thing hasn't been established, *esto* and *eso* are used without an accent: *¿qué es esto?, eso es todo*.

PRONOUNS

These are the 'shorthand' way of referring to people (or things): 'I', 'you', 'he', 'she', etc.

Subject pronouns

These are the subject of a verb – '**I** go', '**she** lived', '**we** are arriving':

yo	I
tú	you (informal, singular)
usted*	you (formal, singular)
ella	she
él	he
nosotros/as	we
vosotros/as	you (informal, plural)
ustedes*	you (formal, plural)
ellos/as	they

(*usted and ustedes are often short-ened in writing to Vd and Vds)

Notes:

1   Having learnt these pronouns, the next thing to do is to remember not to use them all the time! Very often, the ending of the verb (see VERBS below) will tell you who is being referred to. For example: *¿dónde vives?* means 'where do you live?' – *tú* is not necessary as *vives* can only refer to *tú*.

2   The word for 'it' is, technically, *ella* (for a feminine thing) or *él* (for a masculine thing), but in practice these words are rarely used as subject pronouns.

Object pronouns

These are the objects of verbs. They are direct objects ('I saw **her**', 'I'll take **it**', 'I want **them**'), or indirect objects ('I'll give it **to you**', 'show it **to me**'):

me	me, *or* to me
te	you, to you (informal, singular)
le	you, to you (formal, singular); him, to him; her, to her
la	her; it (feminine)
lo	him; it (masculine)
nos	us, to us
os	you, to you (informal, plural)
les	you, to you (formal, plural); them, to them
las	them (feminine)
los	them (masculine)

Notes:

1   These pronouns usually come **in front of** the verb:

no **la** veo	I can't see **her**
no **te** veo	I can't see **you**
me **las** llevo	I'll take **them** (feminine)

2   The pronouns to use with the verb *gustar* are *me, te, le, nos, os, les*:

me gusta el español	I like Spanish ('Spanish pleases me')
le gustan los espárragos	he likes asparagus ('asparagus pleases him')
nos gusta el fútbol	we like football ('football pleases us')

Reflexive pronouns

Some Spanish verbs can be used with an extra pronoun – they are called reflexive. The pronouns are the same as the indirect object pronouns, except for the third person (singular and plural) which is *se*, eg:

(yo) **me** llamo
(tú) **te** llamas
(usted, él, ella) **se** llama
(nosotros/as) **nos** llamamos
(vosotros/as) **os** llamáis
(ustedes, ellos, ellas) **se** llaman

There are quite a few of these reflexive verbs, and in dictionaries they are listed with *se* on the end of the infinitive, eg *bañarse, quedarse, divertirse*.

QUESTIONS

One way of asking a question is to put a question word at the front, eg:

¿cómo?	how?	¿qué?	what?
¿cuándo?	when?	¿cuál?	which?
¿dónde?	where?	¿quién?	who?
¿adónde?	where (to)?	¿cuánto?	how much?
¿por qué?	why?	¿cuántos/as?	how many?

When you use these interrogatives, the subject (if there is one) comes after the verb:
¿cuántos hijos tiene **usted**?
¿dónde está **el hotel**?
¿cuál es **su profesión**?
¿a qué hora sale **el tren**?

If the question doesn't begin with an interrogative, you can raise the tone of your voice to turn a statement into a question:

Enrique tiene dos coches   *¿Enrique tiene dos coches?*

Or you can make a statement and check that it's true by adding *¿no?* or *¿verdad?* at the end:
Enrique tiene dos coches, ¿verdad?

You can also reverse the order of the subject (if there is one) and the verb:
¿tiene Enrique dos coches?

VERBS

Spanish verbs are listed in dictionaries in their infinitive form, eg *trabajar* – to work, *tener* – to have, *vivir* – to live. Each verb has a number of different forms, and the form used depends on a number of factors. The three most important ones are:

1   Which category is the verb in? Does the infinitive end in *-ar*, *-er* or *-ir*? (Each of these groups has a slightly different pattern.) Or is the verb in question an 'irregular', which breaks the rules at some point?

2   Is the action in the present, the past or the future? In other words, what 'tense' is it in? The present is the main one used in *España Viva*, though we've also touched on the past tense.

3   Who is performing the action? Who is the 'subject' – I, you, she etc?

Verb patterns in the present tense
A   REGULAR VERBS

1   *-ar* verbs, eg *trabajar* (to work)

yo	trabaj**o**	*nosotros/as*	trabaj**amos**
tú	trabaj**as**	*vosotros/as*	trabaj**áis**
usted *él, ella* } trabaj**a**		*ustedes* *ellos/as* } trabaj**an**	

2   *-er* verbs, eg *comer* (to eat, have lunch)

yo	com**o**	*nosotros/as*	com**emos**
tú	com**es**	*vosotros/as*	com**éis**
usted *él, ella* } com**e**		*ustedes* *ellos/as* } com**en**	

3   *-ir* verbs, eg *vivir* (to live)

yo	viv**o**	*nosotros/as*	viv**imos**
tú	viv**es**	*vosotros/as*	viv**ís**
usted *él, ella* } viv**e**		*ustedes* *ellos/as* } viv**en**	

B   Some verbs don't just change their endings – they have a slight, predictable change in the middle of some of their forms as well, eg:

	querer (to want)	*jugar* (to play)
yo	qu**ie**ro	j**ue**go
tú	qu**ie**res	j**ue**gas
usted; él, ella	qu**ie**re	j**ue**ga
nosotros/as	queremos	jugamos
vosotros/as	queréis	jugáis
ustedes; ellos/as	qu**ie**ren	j**ue**gan

These verbs are known as radical-changing verbs and are shown as *querer* (ie), *jugar* (ue) in the *Vocabulary* at the back of the book.

C   IRREGULAR VERBS

ser (to be)

soy	eres	es	somos	sois	son

estar (to be)

estoy	estás	está	estamos	estáis	están

ir (to go)

voy	vas	va	vamos	vais	van

dar (to give)

doy	das	da	damos	dais	dan

decir (to say)

digo	dices	dice	decimos	decís	dicen

hacer (to do)

hago	haces	hace	hacemos	hacéis	hacen

tener (to have)

tengo	tienes	tiene	tenemos	tenéis	tienen

venir (to come)

vengo	vienes	viene	venimos	venís	vienen

The present tense

Strictly speaking, there are two present tenses. The most common one is the Simple Present:

trabajo de nueve a siete **I work** from nine to seven

ahora trabajo en Madrid **I'm working** in Madrid now

So this can mean 'I work' or 'I'm working', depending on the sentence.

The other present tense is the Present Continuous, which is used to stress what someone is actually doing at the moment. It's made up of two parts: the correct form of *estar* (to be), plus the *-ndo* part (the present participle) of the main verb – this second part doesn't change:

estoy trabajando con mi cuñado **I'm working** with my brother-in-law

¿estás aprendiendo español? **are you learning** Spanish?

The past tense

This describes something that someone **did** some time ago:

el año pasado fuimos a Cantabria last year **we went** to Cantabria

¿cuánto tiempo estuviste allí? how long **were you** there?

The future

One of the ways of talking about the future – the equivalent to the English 'I **will** do' – is not covered in this book. But you can get on quite well by using the equivalent of 'I'm going to . . .':

el año que viene vamos a visitar Gran Bretaña next year we're going to visit Britain

This construction consists of the correct form of *ir* (to go), plus *a*, plus the infinitive of the verb describing the action.

You can also say what you're thinking of doing, using *pensar* plus an infinitive:

pienso ir a Mallorca I'm thinking of going to Majorca, I intend to go to Majorca

Negatives

A straight *no* in front of the verb is all that's required to make a positive statement negative:

tengo hermanos *no tengo hermanos*

mi marido está aquí *mi marido no está aquí*

If the words for 'nothing', 'nobody' or 'never' follow the verb, you still need the *no* in front of it:

no tengo nada I have nothing, I don't have anything

no voy nunca al cine I never go to the cinema

no me gusta nadie I don't like anyone

ADVERBS

Adverbs describe a verb or an adjective, eg 'slowly', 'sadly', 'quickly'. In English many adverbs end in '-ly'. In Spanish a lot of them end in *-mente*:

normalmente ceno a las ocho I normally have supper at eight

probablemente probably

Some common adverbs don't end in *-mente*:

bien	well	*demasiado*	too
mal	badly	*más*	more
muy	very	*menos*	less
bastante	quite, fairly		

PREPOSITIONS

Prepositions are words like 'near', 'along', 'after', which link with nouns to show where or when an action takes place. These are some examples of the more important ones, in two categories:

Place

en la costa	on the coast
en el restaurante	in the restaurant
delante de la catedral	in front of the cathedral
detrás de la iglesia	behind the church
cerca de la plaza	near/close to the square
lejos de la playa	far from the beach
por la calle	along the street

Time

después de la comida	after the meal
antes de la cena	before supper
a mediodía	at midday
sobre las cinco	at about five o'clock
por la mañana	in the morning

Pronouncing Spanish

Fortunately for learners of Spanish, Spanish spelling and pronunciation go much more closely together than English; so if you see a certain letter or combination of letters, you can be reasonably sure of how to say them.

Here is a list of Spanish letters and a guide to the sounds they represent:

Letter(s)	Rough English equivalent sound	Example
VOWELS		
a	'a' as in northern English 'cat' (between southern English 'cat' and 'cut')	gamba
e	'e' as in 'hen'	tres
i	'ee' as in 'seek'	vivo
o	'o' as in 'rob'	dos
u	'oo' as in 'boot'	uno
CONSONANTS		
b	'b' as in 'boot'	bueno
c + e/i†	'th' as in 'thick'	cerveza
ch*	'ch' as in 'church'	mucho
c + other letters	'c' as in 'come'	¿cómo?
d at beginning of word	'd' as in 'deed'	día
d between vowels, and at end of word	'th' as in 'other', lightly pronounced	cerrado Madrid
f	'f' as in 'farm'	farmacia
g + e/i	'ch' as in Scottish 'loch'	ginebra
g + other letters	'g' as in 'get'	grande
h	never pronounced	helado
j	'ch' as in Scottish 'loch'	jamón
k	'k' as in 'kill'	kilo
l	'l' as in 'look'	leche
ll*†	'lli' as in 'bullion'	Sevilla
m	'm' as in 'mother'	madre
n	'n' as in 'never'	noche
ñ*	'ni' as in 'onion'	mañana
p	'p' as in 'pen'	por favor
qu	'k' as in 'key'	¿qué?
r at beginning of word, and rr	strongly rolled 'r' as in Scottish 'bairn'	rojo Correos

r between vowels	only slightly rolled	caro
s	's' as in 'six'	sí
t	't' as in 'tin'	patata
v	similar to 'b' as in 'bar'	vino
x	's' as in 'best'	expreso
y	'y' as in 'yes' (but with a touch of . 'j' as in 'jam')	ya
z†	'th' as in 'thin'	cerveza

*   In the dictionary, **ch** comes at the end of entries under **c**, **ll** at the end of the **l**'s, and **ñ** after the **n**'s.

†   In Southern Spain and Spanish-speaking America, the following is normal:
– the **c** + **e**/**i** and **z** sounds are usually pronounced 's' instead of 'th'
– the **ll** and **y** sounds are usually pronounced more like an English 'j'.

Pronouncing words

In words of more than one syllable, one syllable is emphasised more strongly than the other(s). There are a few simple rules for working out which is the stressed syllable:

1   If the word has a written accent on it, the accented vowel will be stressed. For example: _café_; _ración_; _médico_.

2   If the word ends in a vowel, an **n** or an **s**, the stress falls on the next to last syllable. For example: _servicios_; _naranja_; _llaman_.

3   If the word ends in any consonant except **n** or **s**, the stress falls on the last syllable. For example: _final_; _Madrid_; _trabajar_.

PUNCTUATION

The only things to remember here are the upside-down question mark (¿) and exclamation mark (¡). All they do is help you by telling you early on that you're reading a question or an exclamation.

Key: Spotcheck

These are answers to the **Spotcheck** questions that follow the **Spanish Live** dialogues.

UNIT 1

1 The neighbour on the stairs.
2 The brother and sister, Santiago and Mercedes Peralta.
3 All of them.
4 Only Jaime was from Madrid, and Marga was not a Spaniard.
5 Two are from the north (León and Bilbao) and one from the south (Sevilla). The others are from the middle of Spain (Madrid and Segovia).

UNIT 2

1 One (una cerveza).
2 a Sister.
　b One (Antonio).
3 a Four.
　b Julián.
4 Four (tea, tea with milk, black coffee, white coffee).

UNIT 3

1 a Three (oranges, tomatoes, lettuce).
　b One.
2 a No.
　b 590 pesetas.
3 a Medium.
　b 100 grams.
4 Friends.
5 a Salvador.
　b Eight.

UNIT 4

1 At the end of the street.
2 a Right.
　b On the left-hand side.

3 The lighthouse.
4 At the end of the Calle del Prado.
5 The second on the right.
6 a Isabel.
　b Ana Schöbel.

UNIT 5

1 a No.
　b Madrid.
2 One.
3 Holidaymaker 3.
4 The beach.
5 Lively (*divertido*) and quiet (*tranquilo*).

UNIT 6

1 Left.
2 Before.
3 935 pesetas.
4 a A mineral water and a white coffee.
　b Chocolate, strawberry and lemon.
5 The cathedral.

UNIT 7

1 Madrid is six hours ahead.
2 a Passers-by 1 and 2.
　b Passers-by 4 and 5.
3 a Miguel.
　b Studying languages.
5 a Blas, Isabel and Olga.
　b Julián.

UNIT 8

1 The ham.
2 a A dry sherry, a white wine and a vermouth.
　b Emilio.
3 a Vegetable soup, followed by grilled chicken.
　b Fizzy mineral water and ordinary water.
4 The Orduña omelette.
5 Sweet *anís*.

UNIT 9

1 a   Eleven.
   b   England.
2   Because of the colour.
3 a   Fuchsia.
   b   Because it's fashionable.
4 a   The bank.
   b   Two o'clock.

UNIT 10

1 a   Atlético Fortpienc.
   b   Español (from Barcelona).
2   Three (passers-by 1, 2 and 5).
3 a   Jaime.
   b   (Wild) asparagus.
4   One (passer-by 6).

UNIT 11

1 a   57.
   b   No, there's one just coming.
2 a   8.38 pm.
   b   11.00 pm.
3 a   No.
   b   4300 pesetas.
4 a   Two tickets.
   b   Line number one.
5 a   Three buses.
   b   On the underground.

UNIT 12

1   Leave her passport and sign her name.
2 a   With bathroom.
   b   5000 pesetas.
   c   In a nearby car park, in the Paseo de Colón
3 a   By credit card.
   b   15,613 pesetas.
4 a   From 1.30 to 3.30.
   b   An aperitive.
5 a   There are more of them and they're cheaper
   b   You can go for walks in the country, the children can play in the street, and it's easier to get to sleep at night.

UNIT 13

1 a   The large one.
   b   A small boy.
2 a   It's very hot, and it's horrendous.
   b   The cold and the damp.
3 a   38 degrees.
   b   January.
4 a   It's not as hot as in summer nor as cold as in winter.
   b   Sleeping – having a siesta.

UNIT 14

1   Passer-by 2 (two months).
2 a   The poverty and the dirt.
   b   A fortnight.
3   She likes it very much.
4   Two (passers-by 1 and 4).

UNIT 15

1 a   A brochure about the Cazorla and Segura mountain area.
   b   Main roads, routes, towns and rivers.
2 a   The yellow and blue flowers.
   b   Through the second door on the left.
3 a   11.30 pm.
   b   The river.
4 a   It's a bit expensive.
   b   390 pesetas.

Key: Workout

UNIT 1

1 As if you were there

a Buenos días.

b Buenas tardes. *or* Buenas noches.

c Hola.

d (Adiós.) Hasta luego.

e Buenas noches.

f You'd repeat your name.

2 Answerback

a ¡Hola!

b Me llamo(+ your name). *or* Just say your name.

c No.

d No, soy (+ your nationality, eg: inglés/inglesa, escocés/escocesa).

e Me llamo (+ your name). *or* Just say your name.

f No, no soy de aquí, soy de (+ the place you're from).

3 Factfinding

a am – meeting

b pm – leaving

c pm – meeting

d pm – leaving

4 Bubbles

a ¿Cómo te llamas?

b ¿Eres española?

c ¿De dónde es usted?

d ¿Cómo se llama usted?

5 Identikit

a Zamora Vicente Spanish Sevilla

b Valdano Diego Colombian Bogotá

c Borges Eduardo Argentinian Mendoza

d Núñez Luisa Spanish Vigo

6 Syllablocks

a Me llamo Víctor.

b ¿Cómo te llamas?

c No soy de aquí.

d ¿De dónde eres?

7 Vertico

   BUENASTARDES

  A**Q**UI

   D**E**

    INGLESA

   H**O**LA

  HA**S**TALUEGO

 DON**D**E

  A**D**IOS

BUENA**S**

  NO**S**OYDEAQUI

8 Stringalong

¿Eres de aquí?

¿Cómo te llamas?

No, no soy de aquí, soy de Madrid.

9 Scriptwriter

Interviewer	Hola, buenos días. ¿Cómo te llamas?
Pablo	Hola, me llamo **Pablo**.
Interviewer	¿Y de dónde eres?
Pablo	Soy de Vitoria.
Interviewer	Y tú, ¿de dónde eres?
Beatriz	Soy de **Sevilla**, y me llamo Beatriz.
Interviewer	Buenos días, señora, ¿de dónde es usted?
Montse	Soy de Barcelona.
Interviewer	¿Y cómo se llama?
Montse	Me llamo **Montse**.
Interviewer	Y usted, señor, ¿cómo se llama?
Carlos	Me llamo Carlos, y soy de **Madrid**.

10 Key Wordsearch

B	U	E	N	A	S
U	O	U	S	L	A
E	T	S	E	O	I
N	U	T	R	H	D
O	R	E	E	M	S
S	E	D	R	A	T

11 Lo típico

a – 3 Valencia
b – 2 Barcelona
c – 5 La Mancha
d – 4 San Sebastián
e – 1 Jerez

UNIT 2

1 Just imagine

a Mucho gusto. *or* Encantado *or* Encantada (depending on whether you're male or female).
b Hola, (¿qué tal? *or* ¿cómo estás?).
c Mucho gusto.
d Bien, (gracias). ¿Y tú?
e Hola, ¿cómo estás?
f Hola, (buenos días). ¿Cómo está usted?

2 Answerbook

a Una tónica, por favor.
b Un zumo de tomate, un café solo y una cerveza.
c Mucho gusto. *or* Encantado/a. *or* Hola, ¿qué tal?
d Esta es Jane, ésta es Christine, y éste es David.

3 The big match

a – iii b – vi c – i d – v e – ii f – iv

4 Barred

E	H	C	E	L	O	M
A	R	N	B	G	S	T
T	O	M	A	T	E	R
C	E	R	V	E	Z	A
A	S	A	N	C	U	P
F	O	N	M	H	M	E
E	L	J	R	E	O	D
D	O	A	S	T	L	N

The missing word is *tónica*.

5 Beginnings and ends

a Buenos días
b Adiós
c Hola
d Hasta luego
e ¿Qué tal?
f Buenas noches

6 Family ties

Across
4 hermano 5 madre 6 marido

Down
1 hermana 2 padre 3 hijo 4 hija 5 mujer

7 A question of family

a La Princesa Cristina.
b El Príncipe Felipe.
c El Rey Juan Carlos.
d La Princesa Elena.
e Este es mi marido el Rey de España; éste es mi hijo, el Príncipe Felipe; ésta es mi hija, la Princesa Cristina, y ésta es mi hija, la Princesa Elena (*or* y éstas son mis hijas, la Princesa Cristina y la Princesa Elena).

8 Casting

Waiter ¿El zumo de naranja, por favor?
Rosa Para mí.
Waiter ¿Y el café solo?
Rafael Para mí, por favor.
Waiter ¿Las cervezas?
Maribel Para mí, y para el señor.
Waiter Y el café con leche para usted, ¿no?
Miguel Sí, gracias.
Waiter De nada.

9 Odd one out

a una hija
b una tónica
c por favor
d soy irlandés
e mujer

UNIT 3

1   As if you were there
a   Buenos días. ¿Tiene naranjas?
b   Dos kilos, por favor.
c   Medio kilo de tomates, por favor.
d   No, gracias. *or* Nada más.
e   ¿Cuánto es?
f   290 pesetas.
g   Gracias. Adiós.

2   Matching numbers
a – 3   b – 5   c – 6   d – 1   e – 4   f – 2

3   Mix-up

Shopkeeper	Buenas tardes.
Customer	Buenas tardes. ¿Tiene queso?
Shopkeeper	Sí, tenemos queso manchego, queso gallego . . .
Customer	Doscientos cincuenta gramos de queso manchego, por favor.
Shopkeeper	Manchego, muy bien. ¿Algo más?
Customer	Sí, cien gramos de jamón.
Shopkeeper	¿Serrano o de York?
Customer	Serrano, por favor.
Shopkeeper	¿Algo más?
Customer	Nada más, gracias. ¿Cuánto es?
Shopkeeper	Son cuatrocientas cuarenta y cinco pesetas.
Customer	Aquí tiene quinientas.
Shopkeeper	Y cincuenta y cinco son quinientas. Adiós.
Customer	Adiós, buenas tardes.

4   Family tree
a   Jesús es el **marido** de Maite.
b   Maite y Jesús tienen **tres** hijos.
c   Tienen dos **hijos** y una **hija**.
d   Maite García **Izquierdo** es la **madre** de Nacho, Teresa y Manolo. Jesús Pita es el **padre**.
e   Nacho y Teresa son **hermanos**.
f   Su hermano pequeño es **Manolo**.

5   Weigh-in
a   trescientos cincuenta gramos
b   medio kilo
c   un kilo
d   dos
e   dos barras grandes

6   Sieve
You've forgotten the lettuce and the melon.

7   Anagrams
a   Eso es todo.
b   Por favor.
c   ¿Tiene?
d   Nada más.
e   ¿Algo más?
f   ¿Cuánto es?

8   Overheard
mother (Cristina) 36; father (Julio) 37; daughters: Mercedes 4, Amparo 9; son (Pablo) 7

9   Interference

Waiter	Hola. ¿Qué quieres?
Woman	Un café con **leche**, **por** favor.
Waiter	¿**Eres** de aquí?
Woman	No, **soy de** Cuenca.
Waiter	¿**Tienes** familia aquí?
Woman	Sí, **tengo un** hermano aquí.
Woman	Y éstos son mis **hijos**.
Waiter	¿Cómo se llaman?
Woman	**Se llaman** Pedro y María.
Waiter	Hola, María. ¿Cuántos **años** tienes?
María	**Tengo** siete, y mi hermano **tiene** cuatro.
Waiter	¿Qué van a tomar?
Woman	Dos **zumos** de naranja, **por favor**.
Waiter	Ahora mismo.

10   Odd one out
a   jamón serrano
b   cien gramos
c   cincuenta pesetas
d   lechuga
e   una botella
f   leche

UNIT 4

1 Getting there

a Por favor, ¿dónde está el Parador Nacional?
b Por favor, ¿dónde está el Hotel Rhin?
c Por favor, ¿dónde está la calle Cervantes?
d Por favor, ¿dónde están los servicios?
e Por favor, ¿dónde está el centro comercial?
f Por favor, ¿dónde está la Plaza Mayor?
g Por favor, ¿dónde está la catedral?
h Por favor, ¿dónde está la oficina de turismo?

2 Pathfinder

a – 3   b – 2   c – 1   d – 2   e – 3

3 No way out

Your part of the conversation:
No, tengo un amigo aquí.
Se llama Santiago Jiménez. Vive en el segundo piso.
No, tiene mujer y una hija.
¿Y tiene familia?
No, soy inglés y vivo en Bristol.
No, está en Escocia, a seiscientos kilómetros.

4 On the map

a – D   b – A   c – B   d – C   e – E

5 Tracking

TODO RECTO

6 Break-up

Coja la primera calle a la derecha.
Siga todo recto.
Está cerca del centro

7 Eavesdropping

a – 4   b – 3   c – 1   d – 2   e – 1   f – 2

8 On the right track

b is the correct set of directions

9 Odd one out

a lejos
b en un supermercado
c una cerveza
d todo recto
e a los servicios
f en las afueras

10 Mmm . . .

a Madrid
b Menorca
c Mojácar
d Málaga
e Mondragón

UNIT 5

1 Wish you were here

a – 6
b – 1
c – 3
d – 4
e – 5
f – 2

2 As if you were there

Your part of the conversation:
Sí, hablo un poco.
No, soy escocesa.
Soy de Dundee – es una ciudad cerca de
Edinburgh/Edimburgo. (Y tú,) ¿de dónde eres?
Me gusta mucho/muchísimo. Las playas son limpias
y el campo es muy bonito.
No es muy tranquilo pero es bastante divertido.
Gracias.

3 Being negative

a No, no me gusta la playa.
b No, no hablo bien español.
c No, no soy de aquí.
d No, no estoy de vacaciones.
e No, no vivo aquí.
f No, no hablo idiomas.
g No, no me gusta el vino.
h No, no tengo hermanos.

4 Keeping your distance

a ¿Le gusta la playa?
b ¿Habla bien español?
c ¿Es (usted) de aquí?
d ¿Está (usted) de vacaciones?
e ¿Vive (usted) aquí?
f ¿Habla (usted) idiomas?
g ¿Le gusta el vino?
h ¿Tiene (usted) hermanos?

5 Overheard in a bar in Benidorm

a ¿Tiene cerveza inglesa?
b ¿Vive(s) aquí cerca?
c ¿Vive(s) en el centro?
d ¿Le/Te gusta la playa?
e ¿Este es su/tu hermano?
f ¿Está(s) de vacaciones?
g ¿Habla(s) inglés?
h ¿Es (usted)/ Eres español?

6 Missing words

Estoy **aprendiendo** idiomas en Madrid. **Hablo**
francés un poco **pero** no me gusta mucho. Hablo
italiano muy bien porque no es **difícil**, y portugués
bastante bien. Me **gustan** muchísimo estos dos
idiomas.

7 Match

a – iv   b – v   c – ii   d – vi   e – iii   f – vii   g – i

8 Turismo

a chorizo
b una playa
c una galesa
d Hablo bastante bien inglés.
e Estoy de vacaciones en España.
f una ciudad grande

9 Going round in circles

¿Por qué no te gusta el pueblo? – Porque es muy
pequeño.
¿Qué estás estudiando? – Estoy estudiando castellano.

10 A matter of taste

a Me gusta muchísimo la montaña. (a moun-
    taineer)
b Me gustan las playas. (a surfer)
c No me gusta el vino. (a teetotaller)
d Me gusta el campo. (a rambler)
e Me gustan mucho los museos. (an archae-
    ologist)
f No me gusta el jamón. (a vegetarian)

11 In the wrong place

a – vii   f – x
b – ix   g – iii
c – viii   h – ii
d – vi   i – v
e – i   j – iv

UNIT 6

1 Nearly there?

a ¿Hay una gasolinera cerca / por aquí?
b ¿Hay una oficina de turismo cerca / por aquí?
c ¿Hay un bar cerca / por aquí?
d ¿Hay un hotel cerca / por aquí?
e ¿Hay un supermercado cerca / por aquí?

2 Orders

a Un bocadillo de jamón, por favor.
b Una cerveza, por favor.
c Dos bocadillos de queso, por favor.
d Un agua mineral sin gas, por favor.
e Dos cafés con leche, por favor.
f Un helado de vainilla, por favor.

3 Directions

a – 4   b – 2   c – 5   d – 1   e – 3   f – 6

4 Nice

a – iii   b – vi   c – ii   d – v   e – i   f – iv

5 How far?

El Bar Marcelino, el Hotel Sardinero, la playa de la
Magdalena, Torrelavega, Santillana del Mar.

6 Getting around

a el Camping El Cid
b la Oficina de Turismo
c el Hotel Felipe III
d una gasolinera
e el Bar Vivar
f la carretera de Burgos

7 Oddball

a jamón
b queso
c carretera
d gasolinera
e queso
f bocadillo

8 Do it with numbers

a – 4   b – 2   c – 3   d – 5   e – 6   f – 1   g – 7

9 City search

```
O A D G I R V M E U
T C U A O P A Z S P
C L N S A Z A L P B
U M D O N T N B U D
D I G L E S I A E F
E S R I D Q A R N L
U M O N U M E N T O
C A T E D R A L R R
A S T R H U U A Y S
L B K A J P F V A C
```

ACUEDUCTO is the one that's very particular to Segovia.

10 Forever asking

a ¿Hay bocadillos?

b ¿Tiene un plano de la ciudad?

c ¿Tiene agua mineral?

d ¿Hay servicios?

e ¿Tiene helados de fresa?

f ¿Hay pan?

11 Printout

a 13 kilometres.

b Plaza del Doctor Marañón.

c Take the first turning on the left into José Abascal.

UNIT 7

1 Got the time?

a Son las siete.

b Son las diez.

c Es la una.

d Son las tres y cuarto.

e Son las once y media.

f Son las cinco menos cuarto.

g Son las ocho y cuarto.

h Son las doce (de la noche).

2 Beginnings . . . and endings

a Empiezo a las seis y media.

b Empiezo a las ocho.

c Empiezo a las ocho menos cuarto.

d Empiezo a las nueve y cuarto.

e Termino a las siete y media.

f Termino a las ocho y cuarto.

g Termino a las nueve.

h Termino a las tres.

3 Confused conversation

a – iii b – iv c – i d – vi e – vii f – v g – ii

4 Getting to know you

Your part of the conversation:

Soy de York, en Inglaterra.

Sí, me gusta mucho.

Hay una catedral, una muralla y muchos museos.

Sí, muchos/muchísimos, y la cerveza es muy buena.

Trabajo en una oficina.

Empiezo a las nueve y cuarto.

(Termino) a las cinco y media.

El trabajo no es muy divertido, pero no es muy difícil.

5 Spanish inquisition

a ¿Cómo te llamas?

b ¿Estás de vacaciones?

c ¿Te gusta el hotel?

d ¿Hay una playa bonita cerca / por aquí?

e ¿Hay una discoteca buena en el pueblo?

f ¿De dónde eres?

g ¿En qué trabajas?

h ¿A qué hora terminas el trabajo?

i ¿Tienes coche?

6 Vowel trouble

a banco

b fábrica

c oficina

d gasolinera

e museo

f ayuntamiento

g supermercado

h bar

7 Happy birthday

a – iii b – ii c – iv d – i e – v

8 What's my line?

a Teacher of German

b Bilingual secretary (Spanish/French)

c Gardener

d Taxi-driver

e Telephonist

f Optician

g Lawyer

h Baker

i Mechanic

j Doctor

k Engineer

9 Right choice

a Sí, me gusta mucho.
b Empiezo a las siete de la mañana.
c Siga recto hasta el puente.
d No, no me gustan los idiomas.
e Sí, tengo siete.
f Son quinientas pesetas.
g Es la una y cuarto.
h Sí, estoy en el camping aquí cerca.

UNIT 8

1 ¿Hay . . . ?

a ¿Hay calamares? Una ración de calamares, por favor.
b ¿Hay queso? Una ración de queso, por favor.
c ¿Hay champiñones? Una ración de champiñones, por favor.
d ¿Hay patatas fritas? Una ración de patatas fritas, por favor.
e ¿Hay aceitunas? Una ración de aceitunas, por favor.
f ¿Hay tortilla española? Una ración de tortilla española, por favor.
g ¿Hay jamón? Una ración de jamón, por favor.

2 Going down well

a Es muy buena. *or* Es buenísima.
b Es muy bueno. *or* Es buenísimo.
c Son muy buenos. *or* Son buenísimos.
d Es muy bueno. *or* Es buenísimo.
e Son muy buenas. *or* Son buenísimas.
f Es muy buena. *or* Es buenísima.

3 A perfect match

helados variados
vino tinto
agua mineral
patatas fritas
tortilla española
queso manchego

4 As if you were there

Your part of the conversation:
Un zumo de naranja, dos cervezas, un vino tinto y un vino blanco. ¿Y hay tapas?
Una ración de calamares, una de queso y una de aceitunas (por favor).
(Es) para mí.
¿Cuánto es?
Gracias.
The bill was 1400 pesetas.

5 Don't mix your drinks

a café solo
b té con leche
c cerveza
d vino tinto
e zumo de naranja
f agua mineral

6 ¡Buen provecho!

Ana – Menu B   Bernarda – Menu D
Conchita – Menu A   Diego – Menu E
Enrique – Menu C

7 Bad copy

	MENU DEL DIA 510 ptas
Primero	Calamares a la romana
	Ensalada mixta
	Tortilla francesa
Segundo	Filete de cerdo
	Pollo al ajillo
	Pescado frito
Postre	Fruta del tiempo
	Flan
	Pan y vino
	Servicio e impuestos incluidos

8 Problems, problems!

Your part of the conversation:
De primero una sopa de pescado y una ensalada.
Pues, sopa de ajo.
De segundo, paella para dos.
¿Hay (*or* Tiene) mariscos?
Calamares, y pollo con patatas fritas.
El vino tinto de la casa.
Pues, una botella de agua mineral.
Grande, y con gas, por favor.

9   All tastes

Felipe	solomillo
Nicolás	lenguado a la plancha
Lola	tortilla de jamón
Pilar	tortilla española
Cristina	piña en almíbar
Ramón	flan

UNIT 9

1   As if you were there

a   ¿Tiene postales?
b   Quiero éstas, por favor.
c   Diez sellos para Inglaterra y dos para Estados Unidos.
d   ¿Cuánto es?
e   ¿Hay un buzón cerca / por aquí?
f   ¿Cómo?
g   Gracias. Adiós.

2   Mix and match

vino tinto
sellos para Inglaterra
gasolina normal
agua mineral sin gas
bocadillos de queso
menú del día
café con leche
tomates para ensalada

3   Going red

a   Sí, pero me gusta más la roja.
b   Sí, pero me gustan más las rojas.
c   Sí, pero me gusta más el rojo.
d   Sí, pero me gusta más la roja.
e   Sí, pero me gusta más el rojo.

4   Many a slip

The assistant got the price of the jacket wrong.

5   Right size

a   La cuarenta y dos.
b   La treinta y ocho.
c   La cuarenta y cuatro.
d   La treinta y seis.
e   La cuarenta.

6   Just looking

a   ¿La tiene en azul?
b   ¿La tiene en la talla cuarenta?
c   ¿Lo tiene en negro?
d   ¿Lo tiene en amarillo?
e   ¿La tiene en la talla cuarenta y cuatro?

7   Over the top

a   Me parece demasiado grande.
b   Me parece demasiado pequeña.
c   Me parece demasiado grande.
d   Me parece demasiado caro.
e   Me parece demasiado grande.
f   Me parece demasiado pequeño.

8   Opposites

blanco – negro
abierto – cerrado
pequeño – grande
lejos – cerca
bien – mal
aquí – allí
con – sin
trabajo – paro
nada – todo
poco – mucho
caro – barato

9   Clockwise

a   In the tourist office.
b   In the tobacconist's.
c   Tobacconist's.
d   Tourist office.
e   Tourist office.
f   Tourist office.

UNIT 10

1   Non-trivial

a – vi   b – i   c – iv   d – ii   e – iii   f – v

2   Preferences

Teresa	Prefiero el cine.
Manuel	Prefiero los deportes, sobre todo el baloncesto.
Luisa	Prefiero la lectura.
Ramón	Prefiero hacer footing. *or* Prefiero el footing.

3   ¿Qué vas a hacer mañana?

El lunes, voy a **estudiar** francés. El martes, voy a **ir** al cine. El miércoles, voy a **jugar** al tenis. El jueves, voy a **tomar** unas copas en el barrio viejo. El viernes, voy a **cenar** al restaurante 'Caserío'. El sábado, voy a **ver** la televisión en casa. El domingo, voy a **hacer** un poco de deporte.

4   As if you were there

Your part of the conversation:
¿Qué vas a hacer esta tarde?
¿Te gustan los museos?
No, no mucho. Prefiero (*or* Me gusta más) ir a la playa.
¿Dónde está?
Gracias, voy a ir allí esta tarde.
Bueno, no me gusta la natación – prefiero leer o dormir.

5   Odd one out

a   la película
b   leer
c   una biblioteca
d   en una iglesia
e   trabajar
f   sello
g   carta

6   Just say

a   Me gusta jugar al fútbol.
b   No me gusta el tenis.
c   Soy aficionado/a al fútbol.
d   Me gusta escuchar música, pero prefiero bailar.
e   Me gusta vivir en el campo.
f   Me gusta hablar español.
g   Me gusta mucho (*or* Me encanta) viajar por España.

7   Ask me another

a – iv   b – vii   c – ii   d – viii   e – vi   f – i
g – v   h – iii

8   Routine change

a   Me gusta estar tranquilo en casa, pero hoy voy a **salir con mis amigos**.
b   Me gusta ver películas extranjeras, pero hoy voy a **ver una película española**.
c   Me gusta mucho pasear, pero hoy voy a **ver la tele**.
d   Me gusta ir al cine, pero hoy **voy a ir al teatro**.
e   Me gusta escuchar música, pero esta tarde **voy a jugar al fútbol**.
f   Normalmente ceno en una cafetería, pero hoy **voy a cenar en casa**.

9   A taste of Spain

Statement **b** is true, the rest are false.

10   Happy days

sábado

UNIT 11
1   Just the ticket

a   Un billete de ida y vuelta para Sevilla, por favor; de segunda clase, no fumador.
b   Un billete de ida para Córdoba, por favor; de segunda clase, no fumador.
c   Un billete de ida y vuelta para Granada, por favor; de primera clase, fumador.
d   Un billete de ida y vuelta para Cádiz, por favor; de segunda clase, no fumador.
e   Un billete de ida para Málaga, por favor; de primera clase, no fumador.

2   Asking the right questions

a   una parada de autobús
b   una estación de tren
c   un aeropuerto
d   una gasolinera
e   una oficina de turismo

3   False start

d is wrong – the number 60 goes from the Plaza de Pizarro.

4   Information

a   ¿De dónde sale el número 33?
b   ¿A qué hora llega a Sevilla el expreso?
c   ¿Hay otro autobús más tarde?
d   ¿Dónde está la parada del 28?
e   ¿El tren de Granada sale esta tarde/noche?
f   ¿Hay restaurante en el expreso?
g   ¿Cuánto es?
h   ¿Este tren va a Segovia?

5   Getting about

Lola – e   Rodrigo – a   Asunción – d
Francisco – b Pastora – f   Juan – c

6   Getting there

a   un autobús
b   una postal
c   un horario de trenes
d   una parada
e   el Talgo que llega a las diecinueve quince
f   Hay restaurante en este tren.

7   As if you were there

Your part of the conversation:
¿Hay un autobús para el aeropuerto?
Gracias. ¿Qué número es?
¿Va al aeropuerto?
¿Hay un autobús para el aeropuerto?
¿Hay una parada de taxis por aquí?
¿Y dónde está el Hotel Carlos III?
¿El hotel está a mano izquierda o (a mano) derecha?
Gracias . . .

8   Taking flight

a   ¿A qué hora sale el próximo vuelo?
b   20 minutes.
c   *Fumador* for smoking, *no fumador* for non-smoking.
d   Go to departure gate number 15.
e   ¿Este es el vuelo para Barcelona? (*or* ¿Este vuelo va a Barcelona?)

9   Timetables

a   a las once y cinco de la noche
b   a las seis menos veintiocho de la tarde
c   a las siete menos veinte de la tarde
d   a la una y cuarto de la tarde
e   a las ocho menos diez de la tarde

10   The trains in Spain . . .

a – ii
b – ii
c – i

11   No way out

a   no fumador
b   un billete
c   de primera clase
d   de ida y vuelta
e   de segunda clase
f   la parada de autobús

UNIT 12

1   Somewhere to sleep

a   Una habitación doble con baño, para dos noches.
b   Una habitación individual con ducha, para una noche.
c   Una habitación individual con lavabo, para tres noches.
d   Una habitación doble con ducha, para dos noches.
e   Una habitación doble y una individual, para una noche.

2   As if you were there

a   Hola, buenas tardes. ¿Tienen una habitación doble?
b   Para una noche.
c   Quiero (*or* Queremos) una habitación con baño.
d   ¿Cuánto es?
e   5900 pesetas a night.
f   ¿Es con desayuno?

3   Matchmaker

a – iii   b – i   c – vi   d – v   e – ii   f – iv

4   Cans and can'ts

a – i   b – iv   c – ii   d – vii   e – ix   f – viii
g – vi   h – v   i – iii

5   Missing link

a   ¿**Tienen** equipaje? – more than one
b   ¿**Vive** en España? – one
c   ¿Me **deja** su pasaporte? – one
d   ¿**Quiere** cenar? – one
e   ¿**Viajan** en coche? – more than one
f   ¿Me **firman** aquí? – more than one

201

6 We . . .

a **Vamos** a Portugal.
b **Tenemos** un piso en el centro.
c **Hacemos** muchas cosas.
d **Somos profesores** de alemán.
e **Aceptamos** todas las tarjetas de crédito.
f **Vivimos** en el sur de Inglaterra.
g **Estamos** muy bien.
h **Jugamos** al baloncesto.

7 All mod cons

a una habitación doble y una con tres camas
b aire acondicionado
c baño
d un ascensor
e cena de 8 a 10.30
f un garaje

8 Short stay

a 213
b two
c 530 pesetas
d 6445 pesetas
e 890 pesetas
f breakfasts

9 Hotel information

a – v b – ii c – viii d – iv e – i f – ix
g – vii h – iii i – vi

UNIT 13

1 Today's weather

a – 7 b – 1 c – 4 d – 5 e – 2 f – 3 g – 6

2 Who says?

a – 3 b – 6 c – 4 d – 2 e – 5 f – 1

3 Feeling bad

a Me duele el estómago.
b Me duele la cabeza.
c Me duele aquí.
d Mi hijo no está bien. *or* Mi hijo está mal.
e ¿Tiene algo para las quemaduras de sol?
f Me duele, pero no demasiado.

4 The three Ms

a mejor
b menos
c más
d más
e mejor
f menos

5 Which?

a ¿Queréis cenar?
b Vamos al cine.
c Viven cerca de aquí.
d ¿Tiene habitaciones?
e Somos de Folkestone.
f Están allí al fondo.
g ¿Vivís aquí?

6 Split months

agosto
abril
febrero
mayo
junio
diciembre

7 As if you were there

Your part of the conversation:
Hace calor, ¿no? (*or* ¿verdad?)
Hace demasiado calor para mí.
No me gusta el calor.
Sí, llueve bastante.
Llueve más en invierno, pero llueve en verano también.

8 Timesearch

L	O	N	B	C	A	E	N	E	R	O
P	O	Z	R	A	M	S	E	T	I	T
E	R	B	M	E	I	V	O	N	J	O
M	E	R	B	U	T	C	O	D	U	Ñ
P	R	I	M	A	V	E	R	A	N	O
S	B	J	U	L	I	O	R	F	I	Y
S	E	T	I	E	M	B	R	E	O	A
E	F	S	O	O	T	S	O	G	A	M

The missing season is INVIERNO, and the missing months are ABRIL and DICIEMBRE.

9 All weathers

Juan García – Pirineos
Luis Gómez – Barcelona
Teresa Vázquez – Islas Canarias
Elvira Zapata – Madrid

10 Opposites

Hace mucho calor. – Hace mucho frío.
En invierno. – En verano.
Llega el tren. – Sale el tren.
En el norte. – En el sur.
Estoy bien. – Estoy mal.
Un poco más. – Un poco menos.
El grande. – El pequeño.
El día. – La noche.

UNIT 14

1 First impressions

a – iv   b – iii   c – i   d – ii

2 Jumbled thoughts

d, f, b, h, a, e, g, c

3 Perú

a – iii   b – iv   c – v   d – ii   e – i

4 Odd one out

a   tamaño
b   llave
c   la semana que viene
d   flan
e   enero
f   poco
g   campo
h   avión

5 As if you were there

Your part of the conversation:
¿Qué fiesta?
No. Ayer fui a la playa – estuve todo el día allí.
Sí, pero me gusta el sol. La semana pasada fui a
Sevilla y hace muchísimo calor allí.
Sí, me gustó mucho. Fui a la catedral, al Alcázar y al
Barrio de Santa Cruz.
No, pero pienso visitar Granada. Quiero ver la
Alhambra.

No, pienso ir mañana.
Bien, voy a ir al pueblo esta tarde.

6 Blankit

a   Pienso ir a Italia.
b   Ayer fui a la playa.
c   Estuve en este hotel el año pasado.
d   Hace mucho calor aquí en verano.
e   En otoño es muy húmedo.
f   Quiero jugar al tenis esta tarde.
g   Voy a ir a la piscina mañana.

7 Send us a postcard!

Querida Emilia:
Ahora estoy en Almería
pero la semana **pasada**
fui a Mojácar, un pueblo
de la costa. **Estuve**
en un hotel pequeño y no
muy caro. También **fui**
a visitar el castillo, que
es muy **bonito**. Me **gustó**
la playa del pueblo, y su
ambiente. Este fin de semana
quiero ir a la montaña.
Besos, Francisco

8 Overheard

a   ¿Qué van a tomar los señores?
b   ¿Te gusta la paella?
c   ¿Fuiste a la piscina?
d   ¿Qué es el arroz a la cubana?
e   ¿Qué piensas (*or* vas a) hacer mañana?

UNIT 15

1 Happy families

a   hermano
b   hermana
c   padre
d   hijos
e   Antonio Pullén Olivé

2 In shops

a – v   b – i   c – vi   d – vii   e – ii   f – iii
g – iv

3 Ordering drinks and shopping for food

i

a una cerveza y un zumo de tomate
b dos cafés y un té
c una botella de agua mineral con gas y tres cervezas
d un café con leche y dos vinos tintos
e un zumo de naranja y una jarra de agua
f medio litro de vino de la casa
g una tónica y cuatro zumos de naranja

ii

a una lechuga
b un cuarto (de) kilo de queso
c un kilo de naranjas
d dos tomates
e una barra grande de pan
f un litro de leche
g cien gramos de jamón serrano
h dos latas de cerveza

4 Habitat

a Vivo en el centro de Madrid, en un piso.
b Vivo en las afueras de Barcelona, en una casa pequeña cerca de la playa.
c Vivo aquí, en una calle muy cerca del hotel.
d Vivo en Inglaterra, en una casa con jardín, en el campo a cincuenta kilómetros de Londres.

5 Survey

a ¿**Cómo** se llama usted?
b ¿**Cuántos** años tiene?
c ¿**Qué** idiomas habla?
d ¿**Dónde** estudia?
e ¿**Cuántas** horas estudia al día?
f ¿**Por qué** estudia idiomas?

6 Paying

a not correct (25 pesetas too much)
b correct
c correct
d not correct (10 pesetas too little)

7 Some order

a Una tónica, y una ración de queso.
b Una cerveza, y una ración de jamón (serrano).
c Un zumo de naranja, y una ración de calamares.
d Un vino tinto, y una ración de gambas.
e Un café con leche, y una ración de patatas fritas.
f Un vino blanco, y una ración de aceitunas.

8 Discovering Salamanca

a Colegio del Arzobispo Fonseca
b Catedral Nueva
c Espíritu Santo

9 True/false

a verdad
b mentira
c mentira
d mentira
e verdad
f mentira
g verdad
h mentira

10 Booking in

Antonio	Buenas tardes. ¿Tienen una habitación doble?
Receptionist	¿Para cuántas noches?
Antonio	Para una noche sólo.
Receptionist	Muy bien. No hay problema.
Antonio	¿Tiene baño la habitación?
Receptionist	Sí, todas las habitaciones tienen baño.
Antonio	¿Y cuánto cuesta la habitación?
Receptionist	Seis mil cincuenta pesetas por noche. Aquí tiene la llave. Habitación número trescientos nueve.
Antonio	Muchas gracias.

11 Dirty shirts

a False – she is going to ring you.
b False – she phoned from the United States.
c False – it was his secretary.
d True.
e False – it's dinner.
f False – it **is** ready.
g True.
h False – that's the car's registration number.
  False – it's open **from** 7 o'clock in the morning.
j True.

Word groups

This reference list of vocabulary gives you words grouped into areas of meaning. It will allow you to brush up on and expand areas which you find particularly useful.

List of topics

1 Numbers / *Números*
2 Days, months, seasons / *Días, meses, estaciones*
3 Drinks / *Bebidas*
4 Appetisers and sandwiches / *Tapas y bocadillos*
5 Restaurant / *Restaurante*
6 Food / *Comestibles*
7 Shops / *Tiendas*
8 Shopping / *Compras*
9 Clothes / *Ropa*
10 Colours / *Colores*
11 Accommodation / *Alojamiento*
12 Travelling around / *De viaje*
13 Countries and nationalities / *Países y nacionalidades*
14 Jobs / *Profesiones*
15 Spare time / *Tiempo libre*
16 The family / *La familia*
17 The body / *El cuerpo*

1 Numbers / *Números*

0	**cero**	12	**doce**
1	**uno**	13	**trece**
2	**dos**	14	**catorce**
3	**tres**	15	**quince**
4	**cuatro**	16	**dieciséis**
5	**cinco**	17	**diecisiete**
6	**seis**	18	**dieciocho**
7	**siete**	19	**diecinueve**
8	**ocho**	20	**veinte**
9	**nueve**	21	**veintiuno**
10	**diez**	22	**veintidós** etc
11	**once**		

30	**treinta**	100	**cien**
31	**treinta y uno** etc	101	**ciento uno**
40	**cuarenta**	150	**ciento cincuenta**
50	**cincuenta**		etc
60	**sesenta**	200	**doscientos/as**
70	**setenta**	1000	**mil**
80	**ochenta**	2000	**dos mil** etc
90	**noventa**		

1,000,000 **un millón**
2,000,000 **dos millones (de . . .)** etc

1987 **mil novecientos ochenta y siete**

first	**primero/a** (but **primer piso**)
second	**segundo/a**
third	**tercero/a** (but **tercer piso**)
last	**último/a**

2 Days, months, seasons / *Días, meses, estaciones*

Monday	**lunes**
Tuesday	**martes**
Wednesday	**miércoles**
Thursday	**jueves**
Friday	**viernes**
Saturday	**sábado**
Sunday	**domingo**
January	**enero**
February	**febrero**
March	**marzo**
April	**abril**
May	**mayo**
June	**junio**
July	**julio**
August	**agosto**
September	**se(p)tiembre**
October	**octubre**
November	**noviembre**
December	**diciembre**

spring	**la primavera**
summer	**el verano**
autumn	**el otoño**
winter	**el invierno**

3 Drinks / *Bebidas*

beer	**la cerveza**
draught beer	**la cerveza de barril** (**una caña** – glass of draught beer)
brandy	**el coñac, el brandy**
champagne (French) (Spanish)	**el champán** **el cava**
gin	**la ginebra**
gin and tonic	**el gin tonic**
rum	**el ron**
rum and coke	**el cubalibre**
sherry, dry sherry	**el jerez, el fino**
vermouth	**el vermú** (or **vermut**)
whisky (and soda)	**el whisky (con soda)**
wine white/red/rosé	**el vino blanco/tinto/rosado**
bottle/glass of . . .	**una botella/un vaso de . . .**
with ice	**con hielo**

Spanish specialities: **el anís** (aniseed liqueur); **la sangría** (mixture of red wine and fruit).

soft drinks	*refrescos*
fruit juice	**el zumo de fruta**
freshly-squeezed	**el zumo natural**
lemon/orange	**de limón/naranja**
pineapple/tomato	**de piña/tomate**
lemonade	**la limonada**
'white' lemonade	**la gaseosa**
mineral water	**el agua mineral**
fizzy/still	**con gas/sin gas**
orangeade	**la naranjada**
tonic water	**la tónica**
chocolate	**el chocolate**
coffee	**el café**
black/white	**solo/con leche** (**un cortado** – small espresso coffee with dash of milk)

cold, hot	**frío/a, caliente**
milk	**la leche**
milkshake	**el batido**
tea (with lemon/ milk)	**el té (con limón/ leche)**

A Spanish speciality: **la horchata** (milky drink made from tiger nuts).

4 Appetisers and sandwiches / *Tapas y bocadillos*

a portion of . . .	**una ración de . . .**
a sandwich	**un bocadillo (de . . .)** – made with French bread **un sandwich (de . . .)** – made with sliced bread
a toasted sandwich	**un sandwich (caliente)**

fishy appetisers	
anchovies	**las anchoas** (salted) **los boquerones** (pickled)
clams	**las almejas**
mussels	**los mejillones**
octopus	**el pulpo**
prawns	**las gambas**
sardines	**las sardinas**
squid	**los calamares**
tuna	**el atún**

meaty ones	
ham cured/cooked	**el jamón** **serrano/de York**
salami	**el salchichón**

others	
cheese	**el queso**
crisps	**las patatas fritas**
mushrooms	**los champiñones**
olives	**las aceitunas**
peanuts	**los cacahuetes**
Russian salad	**la ensaladilla rusa**

Spanish specialities: **el chorizo** (pork sausage highly seasoned with garlic and paprika); **los churros** (a sweet snack – type of fritters, often eaten for breakfast with hot chocolate).

5 Restaurant / *Restaurante* (see also 3, 6)

breakfast	el desayuno
lunch	la comida, el almuerzo
tea	la merienda
supper/dinner	la cena
bill	la cuenta
course/dish	el plato
for 1st/2nd course	de primero/segundo
menu	el menú, la carta
set menu	el menú del día
waiter, waitress	el camarero, la camarera
fried eggs	los huevos fritos
hors d'œuvres	los entremeses (variados)
mayonnaise	la mayonesa
omelette (Spanish)	la tortilla (española)
plain omelette	la tortilla francesa
rice	el arroz
sauce	la salsa
soup	la sopa
fish/garlic	de pescado/ajo
clear soup	el consomé

fish and seafood	*pescado y mariscos*
cod	el bacalao
crab	el cangrejo
hake	la merluza
lobster	la langosta
monkfish	el rape
red mullet	el salmonete
salmon	el salmón
sole	el lenguado
trout	la trucha

meat and poultry	*carne y aves*
chicken	el pollo
chop	la chuleta
lamb	el cordero
pork	el cerdo
loin/steak	el lomo
rabbit	el conejo
sausages	las salchichas
steak	el bistec
sirloin	el solomillo
stew	el cocido
veal escalope	el escalope de ternera

boiled	hervido/a
fried	frito/a
grilled	a la parrilla
	a la plancha (cooked on a griddle)
rare, medium, well done	poco hecho, normal, bien hecho
roast	asado/a
stewed	cocido/a

vegetables	*verduras*
asparagus	los espárragos
broad beans	las habas
carrots	las zanahorias
green beans	las judías verdes
peas	los guisantes
potatoes	las patatas
chips	las patatas fritas
salad (green/mixed)	la ensalada (verde/mixta)
spinach	las espinacas

desserts	*postres*
cream	la nata
crème caramel	el flan
fruit (fresh)	la fruta del tiempo
(tinned)	la fruta en almíbar
fruit salad	la macedonia
ice-cream (vanilla)	el helado (de vainilla)

Spanish specialities: **el gazpacho** (cold soup of tomatoes, cucumber, green pepper, onion); **la paella (a la) valenciana** (rice with seafood and chicken); **la zarzuela** (spicy fish/seafood stew).

6 Food / *Comestibles* (see also 4, 5)

biscuits	las galletas
bread	el pan
butter	la mantequilla
cooked meats	los fiambres
eggs	los huevos
salt, pepper	la sal, la pimienta
sugar	el azúcar
yoghurt	el yogur

fruit	*fruta*
apple	la manzana
apricot	el albaricoque
banana	el plátano
cherries	las cerezas

grapes	las uvas
lemon	el limón
melon	el melón
water-melon	la sandía
orange	la naranja
peach	el melocotón
pear	la pera
pineapple	la piña
strawberries	las fresas

salad	*ensalada*
celery	el apio
cucumber	el pepino
lettuce	la lechuga
radishes	los rábanos
spring onions	las cebollas tiernas
tomato	el tomate

7   Shops / *Tiendas* (see also 8, 9)

bank	el banco
bread shop	la panadería
cake shop	la pastelería
chemist's	la farmacia
clothes shop	la tienda de ropa
department store	los grandes alma-cenes
fruit shop	la frutería
grocer's	la tienda de comes-tibles/ultramarinos
hairdresser's	la peluquería
hypermarket	el hipermercado
market	el mercado
newspaper stand	el quiosco
post office	Correos
shoe shop	la zapatería
supermarket	el supermercado
tobacconist's	el estanco
tourist office	la oficina de turismo
travel agent's	la agencia de viajes

Note: **la farmacia** sells pharmaceutical products; go to **la perfumería** for toiletries, cosmetics.

8   Shopping / *Compras*

aspirins	las aspirinas
baby food	la comida para bebés
cigarettes	los cigarrillos
film	el rollo (de película)
magazine	la revista

matches	las cerillas
nappies	los pañales
newspaper	el periódico
postcard	la postal
razor blades	las hojas de afeitar
sanitary towels	las compresas
tampons	los tampones
shampoo	el champú
shaving cream	la crema de afeitar
soap	el jabón
stamp	el sello
sticking plaster	el esparadrapo
suntan cream	la crema bronceadora
sweets	los caramelos
tissues	los pañuelos de papel
toilet paper	el papel higiénico
toothpaste	la pasta de dientes

presents and souvenirs	*regalos y recuerdos*
bracelet	la pulsera
gold/silver	de oro/plata
castanets	las castañuelas
cigarette lighter	el mechero
doll	la muñeca
earrings	los pendientes
fan	el abanico
guitar	la guitarra
handbag	el bolso
necklace	el collar
perfume	el perfume
pottery	la cerámica
purse	el monedero
toy	el juguete
watch	el reloj

Spanish souvenirs: **el botijo** (earthenware jug); **el porrón** (glass wine jar with long spout).

9   Clothes / *Ropa* (see also 10)

belt	el cinturón
blouse	la blusa
coat	el abrigo
dress	el vestido
gloves	los guantes
hat	el sombrero
jacket	la chaqueta
jeans	los vaqueros
jumper	el jersey
panties (women's)	las bragas

raincoat	**el impermeable**
sandals	**las sandalias**
shirt	**la camisa**
shoes	**los zapatos**
skirt	**la falda**
socks	**los calcetines**
stockings	**las medias**
suit	**el traje**
swimsuit	**el traje de baño**
tennis/training shoes	**los tenis**
tie	**la corbata**
tights	**las medias**
trousers	**el pantalón**
T-shirt	**la camiseta**
underpants (men's)	**los calzoncillos**

10 Colours / *Colores*

black	**negro/a**
blond(e)	**rubio/a**
blue	**azul**
navy blue	**azul marino**
brown	**marrón**
(hair/complexion)	**moreno/a**
green	**verde**
grey	**gris**
orange	**color naranja**
pink	**color de rosa**
red	**rojo/a**
white	**blanco/a**
yellow	**amarillo/a**
light, dark	**claro/a, oscuro/a**

11 Accommodation / *Alojamiento*

apartment	**el apartamento**
boarding-house	**la pensión**
campsite	**el camping**
caravan	**la caravana**
flat	**el piso**
hotel	**el hotel**
house	**la casa**
(semi-)detached	**el chalet**
tent	**la tienda**
villa	**el chalet**
bathroom	**el cuarto de baño**
bedroom	**el dormitorio**
dining-room	**el comedor**
kitchen	**la cocina**

lounge	**el salón, el cuarto de estar**
room (in hotel)	**la habitación**
single/double	**individual/doble**
air conditioning	**el aire acondicionado**
balcony	**el balcón**
bath, with bath	**el baño, con baño**
bed, twin beds	**la cama, dos camas**
chair	**la silla**
door	**la puerta**
fridge	**la nevera, el frigorífico**
garden	**el jardín**
heating	**la calefacción**
key	**la llave**
light, lamp	**la luz, la lámpara**
shower	**la ducha**
swimming pool	**la piscina**
table	**la mesa**
tap	**el grifo**
telephone	**el teléfono**
television	**la televisión**
terrace	**la terraza**
toilet	**el wáter**
washbasin	**el lavabo**
window	**la ventana**
it doesn't/they don't work	**no funciona(n)**

12 Travelling around / *De viaje*

aeroplane	**el avión**
airport	**el aeropuerto**
bicycle	**la bicicleta**
boat	**el barco**
bus	**el autobús**
bus stop	**la parada (de autobús)**
car	**el coche**
car park	**el aparcamiento**
coach	**el autocar**
crossroads	**el cruce**
customs	**la aduana**
driving licence	**el permiso de conducir**
flight	**el vuelo**
hitchhiking	**el autostop**
lorry	**el camión**

map	el mapa
street map/plan	el plano
motorbike	la motocicleta
motorway	la autopista
petrol station	la gasolinera
railway	el ferrocarril
Spanish Railways	la RENFE
road (main)	la carretera
service station	la estación de servicio
station (train)	la estación (de tren)
taxi	el taxi
ticket	el billete
single/return	de ida / de ida y vuelta
timetable	el horario
toll	el peaje
traffic lights	el semáforo
train	el tren
underground	el metro
van	la furgoneta
car	*el coche*
air	el aire
clutch	el embrague
brakes	los frenos
engine	el motor
headlight	el faro
ignition	el contacto
indicator	el intermitente
oil	el aceite
petrol	la gasolina
2-star/4-star	normal/súper
puncture	el pinchazo
steering-wheel	el volante
tyre	el neumático
pressure	la presión
windscreen	el parabrisas
it doesn't/they don't work	no funciona(n)
to check	controlar
to hire	alquilar
to repair	reparar

13 Countries and nationalities / *Países y nacionalidades*

(names of countries are feminine singular unless indicated)

Australia, Australian	Australia, australiano/a
Austria, Austrian	Austria, austríaco/a
Belgium, Belgian	Bélgica, belga
Canada, Canadian	Canadá (m), canadiense
Denmark, Danish	Dinamarca, danés/esa
England, English	Inglaterra, inglés/esa
Europe, European	Europa, europeo/a
France, French	Francia, francés/esa
Germany, German	Alemania, alemán/ana
Great Britain, British	Gran Bretaña, británico/a
Greece, Greek	Grecia, griego/a
Holland, Dutch	Holanda, holandés/esa
Ireland, Irish	Irlanda, irlandés/esa
Italy, Italian	Italia, italiano/a
Norway, Norwegian	Noruega, noruego/a
Portugal, Portuguese	Portugal (m), portugués/esa
Scotland, Scottish	Escocia, escocés/esa
South America, South American	América del Sur, sudamericano/a
Spain, Spanish	España, español/ola
Sweden, Swedish	Suecia, sueco/a
United Kingdom	Reino Unido (m)
United States, American	Estados Unidos (mpl), americano/a
USSR/Russia, Russian	Unión Soviética/ Rusia, ruso/a
Wales, Welsh	Gales (m), galés/esa
east, west	el este, el oeste
north, south	el norte, el sur

Languages: use the masculine singular form of the adjective, eg **el español**, **el inglés**.

14 Jobs / *Profesiones*

(masculine and feminine forms are given where both exist)

accountant	contable
architect	arquitecto
bricklayer	albañil
businessman	hombre de negocios
businesswoman	mujer de negocios
carpenter	carpintero
civil servant	funcionario / a
clerk	administrativo / a, oficinista

computer operator	**operario/a de computadoras**
programmer	**programador/ora**
dentist	**dentista**
designer	**diseñador/ora**
doctor	**médico/a**
electrician	**electricista**
engineer	**ingeniero/a**
executive	**ejecutivo/a**
farmer	**agricultor/ora**
head, boss	**jefe**
lawyer, solicitor	**abogado/a**
lorry driver	**camionero/a**
manager/director	**director/ora**
managing director	**director/ora gerente**
nurse	**enfermero/a**
owner/proprietor	**propietario/a**
plumber	**fontanero**
sales rep.	**representante**
secretary	**secretario/a**
shop assistant	**dependiente/a**
social worker	**asistente/a social**
teacher	**profesor/ora**
technician	**técnico**
worker	**obrero/a**

15 Spare time / *Tiempo libre*

hobbies	*aficiones*
art	**el arte**
exhibition	**la exposición**
gallery	**la galería**
cinema	**el cine**
film	**la película**
to collect	**coleccionar**
antiques/stamps	**antigüedades/ sellos**
cookery	**la cocina**
to knit	**hacer punto**
music (classical/pop)	**la música (clásica/ pop)**
concert	**el concierto**
reading, to read	**la lectura, leer**
fiction, poetry	**las novelas, la poesía**
sewing, to sew	**la costura, coser**
theatre	**el teatro**
play	**la comedia, la obra (dramática)**

games and sports	*juegos y deportes*
athletics	**el atletismo**
basketball	**el baloncesto**
chess	**el ajedrez**
football	**el fútbol**
jogging	**el footing, el jogging**
skiing, to ski	**el esquí, esquiar**
swimming, to swim	**la natación, nadar**
tennis	**el tenis**
water-skiing	**el esquí acuático**
windsurfing	**el windsurf**
to play (piano/violin)	**tocar (el piano/violín)**
to play (cards/golf)	**jugar (a las cartas/al golf)**

sightseeing	*turismo*
beach	**la playa**
botanical gardens	**los jardines botánicos**
castle	**el castillo, el alcázar**
cathedral	**la catedral**
church	**la iglesia**
museum	**el museo**
palace	**el palacio**
park	**el parque**
town hall	**el ayuntamiento**

16 The family / *La familia*

brother, sister	**el hermano, la hermana**
brother/sister-in-law	**el cuñado, la cuñada**
cousin	**el primo, la prima**
father, mother	**el padre, la madre**
grandfather, grandmother	**el abuelo, la abuela**
grandson, granddaughter	**el nieto, la nieta**
nephew, niece	**el sobrino, la sobrina**
son, daughter	**el hijo, la hija**
uncle, aunt	**el tío, la tía**

Note: to say 'brother(s) and sister(s)', 'children' etc, use the masculine plural form, eg **los hermanos**, **los hijos**.

17 The body / *El cuerpo*

ankle	**el tobillo**
arm	**el brazo**
back	**la espalda**

blood	**la sangre**	mouth	**la boca**
chest	**el pecho**	muscle	**el músculo**
ear	**la oreja** (outer part)	nose	**la nariz**
	el oído (inner part)	shoulder	**el hombro**
eye	**el ojo**	skin	**la piel**
face	**la cara**	stomach	**el estómago**
finger	**el dedo**	throat	**la garganta**
foot	**el pie**	thumb	**el pulgar**
hair	**el pelo**	toe	**el dedo del pie**
hand	**la mano**	wrist	**la muñeca**
head	**la cabeza**	it hurts, they hurt	**me duele, me duelen**
heart	**el corazón**	broken	**roto/a**
knee	**la rodilla**	burned	**quemado/a**
leg	**la pierna**	sprained/twisted	**torcido/a**

Vocabulary

Notes

1 The English translations apply to the words as they are used in this book.
2 Adjectives which have different endings for masculine and feminine are shown thus: **bueno/a**.
3 Verbs: regular verbs follow the patterns shown on p. 186(A). Irregular verbs: for those followed by (**ie**) or (**ue**), see p. 186(B); for those marked *, see p. 186(C); for reflexive verbs (eg **divertirse**), see p. 185.
4 Remember that **ch**, **ll** and **ñ** are separate letters in the Spanish alphabet, following **c**, **l** and **n** respectively.
5 Abbreviations: *f* – feminine, *m* – masculine, *pl* – plural.

A

a *at; to; on* a las . . . *at . . . (o'clock)* a . . . minutos/kilómetros *. . . minutes/kilometres away*
abierto/a *open*
abril *April*
abrir *to open*
abstracto/a *abstract*
la abuela *grandmother*
la academia *academy, school*
la aceituna *olive*
aceptar *to accept*
la actriz *actress*
el acueducto *aqueduct*
de acuerdo *of course, certainly; fine*
además *also*
adiós *goodbye*
¿adónde? *where (to)?*
el adulto *adult*
el aeropuerto *airport*
la afición *hobby*
aficionado/a (a) *keen (on)*
las afueras *outskirts, suburbs*
la agencia de viajes *travel agency*
agosto *August*
agradable *pleasant*

el agua (*f*) *water* el agua mineral *mineral water*
ahí *(over) there*
ahora *now* ahora mismo *right away*
el aire acondicionado *air conditioning*
el ajo *garlic* al ajo/ajillo *cooked in/with garlic*
al = a + el
alcanzar *to reach*
el alcázar *castle*
el alemán *German*
Alemania (*f*) *Germany*
algo *anything; something* ¿algo más? *anything else?* algo así *thereabouts*
alguno/a (algún *before a masculine singular noun*) *any; some*
la almeja *clam*
en almíbar *in syrup (ie tinned)*
el almuerzo *lunch*
el alojamiento *accommodation*
alquilado/a *rented*
allí *there*
amarillo/a *yellow*
el ambiente *atmosphere*
la amiga, el amigo *friend*
andando *on foot*
antes *previously* antes de *before*
antiguo/a *ancient*
anunciar *to announce, make known*
el año *year* tener . . . años *to be . . . years old* cumplir años *to have a birthday*
el aparcamiento *car park*
aparcar *to park*
el apartamento *apartment*
aparte *separate* aparte de *apart from*
apasionar: me apasiona *I adore (it)*
el aperitivo *aperitive*
aplicar *to apply*
apreciado/a *valued*
aprender *to learn*
aprovechar: ¡que aproveche! *bon appétit!, have a good meal!*
aproximadamente *approximately, more or less*
aquí *here* por aquí *near hear, around here*
argentino/a *Argentinian*

la arqueología   *archaeology*
el/la arquitecto   *architect*
el arroz   *rice*
el arte   *art*
   asado/a   *roast*
el ascensor   *lift*
   así: algo así   *thereabouts*
   asistir a   *to attend*
el Atlántico   *Atlantic*
el autobús   *bus*
la autopista   *motorway*
la avenida   *avenue*
el avión   *plane*
   ¡ay!   *oh!*
   ayer   *yesterday*
   azul   *blue*

   B
   bailar   *to dance*
el baloncesto   *basketball*
   bañarse   *to go swimming*
el baño   *bath(room)*
el bar   *bar*
   barato/a   *cheap*
el barco   *boat*
la barra   *(stick) loaf*
el barrendero   *sweeper*
el barrio   *district, quarter*
   bastante   *quite, fairly; quite a lot*
   beber   *to drink*
la bebida   *drink*
   Berna   *Bern*
el beso   *kiss*
la biblioteca   *library*
la bicicleta   *bicycle*
   bien   *well, fine; right*   muy bien   *right, very*
      well/good
el billete   *ticket; (bank)note*
el bistec   *steak*
   blanco/a   *white*
el bocadillo   *sandwich*
la bolsa   *bag*
el bonito   *tunny*
   bonito/a   *pretty, attractive, nice*
las botas   *boots*
la botella   *bottle*
a la brasa   *(charcoal-)grilled*
a la brava   *in spicy sauce*
   bronceadora: la crema bronceadora   *suntan cream*
   bueno   *right; well*
   bueno/a (buen *before a masculine singular*
      noun)   *good*   buenas = buenos días

   C
la cabeza   *head*
   cada   *each, every*
el café   *coffee; café*   el café solo   *black coffee*
      el café con leche   *white coffee*
la cafetería   *café, coffee bar*
la caja   *box*
los calamares   *squid*
los calcetines   *socks*
   calmante   *soothing*
el calor   *heat*   hace (mucho) calor   *it's (very) hot*
la calle   *street*
la cama   *bed*
el cambio   *change; exchange*
la camisa   *shirt*
la camiseta   *T-shirt*
el camping   *campsite*
el campo   *country(side)*
la capital   *capital, main town*
   característico/a *characteristic*
   ¡caramba!   *gosh!*
el caramelo   *sweet*
   cargado/a   *charged*
la carne   *meat*
el carnet de identidad   *identity card*
   caro/a   *dear, expensive*
la carretera   *(main) road*
la carta   *letter; menu*
la casa   *house; home*   en casa   *at home*
el casco viejo   *old quarter*
   casi   *nearly, almost*
   caso: en caso contrario   *otherwise*
el castellano, castellano/a   *Castilian*
el castillo   *castle*
el catalán   *Catalan*
la catedral   *cathedral*
   catorce   *fourteen*
la cebolla   *onion*
la cena   *supper, dinner*
   cenar   *to have supper/dinner*
la central   *power station*
el centro   *centre*   el centro ciudad   *town/city centre*
la cerámica   *pottery, ceramics*
   cerca   *nearby, close*   aquí cerca   *near here*   cerca
      de   *near, close to*
   cercano/a   *nearby*
el cerdo   *pork*
   cero   *zero, 0*
   cerrado/a   *closed*
   cerrar (ie)   *to close*
la cerveza   *beer*
   cien, ciento   *a/one hundred*
   cinco   *five*

cincuenta *fifty*
el cine *cinema*
la ciudad *town, city*
claro *of course*
claro/a *clear*
la clase *class*
el cliente *client*
el clima *climate*
el cocido *stew*
la cocina *cooking*
el coche *car*
el cofre *safe deposit box*
coger *to take; to catch, to get*
colgar (ue) *to hang*
el color *colour*
comer *to eat; to have lunch*
comercial *commercial*
comestibles: la tienda de comestibles *food shop, grocer's*
la comida *food; meal*
como *like; as*
¿cómo? *how?; pardon?* ¡cómo no! *of course*
¿cómo está(s)? *how are you?* ¿cómo te llamas?, ¿cómo se llama? *what is your name?*
el compañero *companion*
completo/a *complete, full*
comprar *to buy*
de compras *(out) shopping*
la comunicación *communication*
con *with*
confirmar *to confirm*
el congreso *conference*
conocer *to know*
conocido/a *well-known*
constantemente *constantly*
la construcción *construction, building*
continuar *to continue*
contrario: en caso contrario *otherwise*
la cooperativa *cooperative*
la copa *glass, drink*
el cordero *lamb*
correcto/a *correct*
Correos *Post Office*
correr *to run*
corriente *ordinary, everyday*
la cosa *thing*
la costa *coast*
costar (ue) *to cost* ¿cuánto cuesta(n)? *how much does it/do they cost?*
creer *to think*
la crema *cream*
la croqueta *croquette, type of rissole*
cruce – *see* cruzar

el cruce *crossroads*
cruzar *to cross*
la cuadrilla *group/gang*
¿cuál?, ¿cuáles? *what?, which?*
cuando *when*
¿cuándo? *when?*
¿cuánto? *how much?; how long?* ¿cuánto es/cuesta? *how much is it?* ¿cuánto tiempo? *how long?*
¿cuántos/as? *how many?* ¿cuántos años tienes? *how old are you?*
cuarenta *forty*
el cuarto *quarter* … menos cuarto *a quarter to …* … y cuarto *a quarter past …*
cuatro *four* cuatrocientos/as *400*
a la cubana *Cuban-style*
cuelgue – *see* colgar
la cuenta *bill*
cuesta(n) – *see* costar
cultural *cultural*
el cumpleaños *birthday*
cumplir años *to have a birthday*

CH

el chalet *(detached) house*
el champiñón *mushroom*
la chaqueta *jacket*
la chica *girl*
el chico *boy*
chiquito/a *tiny*
el chocolate *chocolate*
el chorizo *type of spicy pork sausage*
la chuleta *chop*
los churros *kind of fritters*

D

de *of; from*
decir* *to say*
dejar *to leave* ¿me deja …? *can you let me have …?*
del = de + el
demás *other, rest of the*
demasiado *too; too much*
el/la dentista *dentist*
dentro *inside* dentro de *in, within*
depender *to depend*
el deporte *sport*
depositado/a *deposited*
derecha: a mano derecha *on the right*
la derecha *right* a la derecha *to/on the right*

derecho, todo derecho *straight on*
desayunar *to have breakfast*
el desayuno *breakfast*
descansar *to relax*
desde *from*
desear *to want (would like)* ¿qué desea? *what would you like?*
después *then, afterwards* después de *after*
detrás *behind*
el día *day* al día *a/per day* buenos días *good morning, good day* hoy día *nowadays*
diario/a *daily*
dibujar *to draw*
dice – *see* decir
diciembre *December*
dieciséis, diecisiete, dieciocho, diecinueve *16, 17, 18, 19*
diez *ten*
difícil *difficult*
la dirección *management; address*
dirigir *to manage*
la discoteca *disco(thèque)*
diseñar *to design*
disfrutar *to enjoy oneself*
la distracción *leisure activity*
diurno/a *day, daytime*
divertido/a *enjoyable; lively*
divertirse (ie) *to enjoy oneself*
doble *double*
doce *twelve*
el dolor *pain* el dolor de cabeza *headache* el dolor de estómago *stomach-ache*
el domingo *Sunday*
donde *where*
¿dónde? *where?* ¿de dónde? *where from?*
doña *polite form of address used with first name*
dormir (ue) *to sleep*
dos *two* doscientos/as *200*
la ducha *shower*
duele: me duele el/la ... *my ... hurts*
duerme – *see* dormir
durante *during*
durar *to last*

E

e = y (*before word beginning with* i *or* hi)
efectivamente *that's right*
en efecto *yes indeed*
ejemplo: por ejemplo *for example*
el *the*
él *he; him; it*
el electricista *electrician*

eléctrico/a *electrical*
ella *she*
el embalse *reservoir*
emborracharse *to get drunk*
empezar (ie) *to begin*
la empresa *company*
la empresaria *businesswoman*
la emulsión *emulsion*
en *in; on* en autobús/coche etc *by bus/car etc*
encantado/a *pleased to meet you*
encantar: me encanta *I love (it)*
enero *January*
enfrente *opposite, in front* enfrente de *opposite*
la ensalada *salad*
entonces *so*
la entrada *admission*
entre *among; between*
entregar *to hand in*
los entremeses *hors d'œuvres*
el equipaje *luggage*
eres, es – *see* ser
el escalope *escalope*
Escocia (f) *Scotland*
escuchar *to listen to*
ese/a *that* ése/a *that (one)*
eso *that* eso (es) *that's right*
España (f) *Spain*
el español, español/ola *Spanish; Spaniard*
los espárragos *asparagus*
el espectáculo *show*
el esquí *skiing*
esquiar *to ski*
la estación *station* la estación de tren *railway station*
Estados Unidos (mpl) *United States*
el estanco *tobacconist's*
estar* *to be* ¿cómo está(s)? *how are you?*
estatal *(of the) State*
el este *east*
este/a *this* éste/a *this (one)*
esto *this*
el estómago *stomach*
estos/as *these* éstos/as *these (ones)*
estrecho/a *narrow*
la estrella *star*
estudiar *to study*
estupendo/a *marvellous, great*
estuve, estuviste, estuvo – *past tense of* estar
exactamente *exactly*
exacto *exactly*
excepto *except*
excesivo/a *excessive, too much*
la excursión *excursion, tour*

el expreso   *fast train (usually night)*
exquisito/a   *delicious*
extranjero/a   *foreign*

F
fácil   *easy*
el factor   *factor*
la falda   *skirt*
la familia   *family*
famoso/a   *famous*
fantástico/a   *fantastic*
el faro   *lighthouse*
fascinante   *fascinating*
favor: por favor   *please; excuse me*
favorito/a   *favourite*
febrero   *February*
la fecha   *date*
el festival   *festival*
la fiesta   *festival; party*
el filete   *(fillet) steak*
el fin de semana   *weekend*
el final   *end*   al final   *at the end*
el fino   *type of dry sherry*
firmar   *to sign*
el flan   *crème caramel*
la flor   *flower*
el folklore   *folklore*
el folleto   *leaflet*
fondo: al fondo   *at the back*
el footing   *jogging*
la foto   *photo*
el fotógrafo   *photographer*
francamente   *frankly*
el francés, francés/esa   *French*
Francia *(f)*   *France*
la fresa   *strawberry*
fresco/a   *chilled*
el frío   *cold*   hace (mucho) frío   *it's (very) cold*
frío/a   *cold*
frito/a   *fried*   las patatas fritas   *crisps*
la fruta   *fruit*   la fruta del tiempo   *fresh fruit (in season)*
fucsia   *fuchsia(-coloured)*
fue, fui, fuiste – *past tense of* ir
fumador, no fumador   *smoking, non-smoking*
fumar   *to smoke*
funcionar   *to operate, to work*
el fútbol   *football*
el futbolista   *footballer*

G
Gales *(m)*   *Wales*
galés/esa   *Welsh*

gallego/a   *Galician*
la gamba   *prawn*
el garaje   *garage*
la garganta   *throat*
gas: con gas   *fizzy*   sin gas   *still*
la gasolina   *petrol*
la gasolinera   *petrol station*
la gastronomía   *gastronomy, food*
generalmente   *generally, usually*
la gente   *people*
el gin tonic   *gin and tonic*
Ginebra   *Geneva*
girar   *to turn*
el golf   *golf*
gracias   *thank you*   muchas/muchísimas gracias   *thank you very much*
el grado   *degree*
el gramo   *gram*
grande (gran *when before a noun*)   *big, large*
gratuito/a   *free*
Grecia *(f)*   *Greece*
el griego   *Greek*
gris   *grey*
la guitarra   *guitar*
gustar: me gusta(n)   *I like*
¿te/le gusta(n) …?   *do you like …?*
me gusta más   *I prefer*
gusto: mucho gusto   *pleased to meet you*

H
la habitación   *room*
hablar   *to speak*
hacer*   *to do; to make*   hacer fotos   *to take photos*   hace … … *ago*   hace calor/frío/sol/viento   *it's hot/cold/sunny/windy*
hacia   *towards*
hago – *see* hacer
hasta   *as far as, up to; to, until*   hasta luego   *see you later*
hay   *there is/are*   ¿hay?   *is/are there?*
el helado   *ice-cream*
la hermana   *sister*
el hermano   *brother*
hidratante   *moisturising*
hidratar   *to moisturise*
hidroeléctrico/a   *hydroelectric*
la hija   *daughter*
el hijo   *son*   los hijos   *children*
la historia   *history*
hizo – *past tense of* hacer
hola   *hello*
el hombre   *man*

la hora   *hour; time*   ¿qué hora es?   *what time is*
   it?   ¿a qué hora?   *(at) what time?, when?*
el horario   *timetable; opening hours*
horrible   *horrible, dreadful*
el hospital   *hospital*
el hotel   *hotel*
hoy   *today*   hoy día   *nowadays*
la huerta   *vegetable garden*
el huevo   *egg*
húmedo/a   *damp*
¡huy!   *oh!, phew!*

I

ida: (de) ida   *single, one-way*   (de) ida y
   vuelta   *return*
el idioma   *language*
la iglesia   *church*
importante   *important*
el importe   *cost*
el impuesto   *tax*
incluido/a   *included*
incluir   *to include*
inclusive   *included*
incluye – *see* incluir
la indicación   *sign*
individual   *individual; single*
la información   *information*
Inglaterra   *(f)   England*
el inglés, inglés/esa   *English*
intensivo/a   *intensive*
el interés   *interest*   de interés   *useful*
interesante   *interesting*
el interior   *interior*
el invierno   *winter*
ir*   *to go*   ir otra vez   *to go back*   ir a   (+ *in-*
   finitive)   to be going to   vamos a ver   *let's see*
   vaya   *go*
irse*   *to go (off)*
irlandés/esa   *Irish*
la isla   *island*
Italia   (f)   *Italy*
el italiano   *Italian*
I.V.A.   *V.A.T.*
izquierda: a mano izquierda   *on the left*
la izquierda   *left*   a la izquierda   *to/on the left*

J

el jamón   *ham*   el jamón de York   *cooked ham*
   el jamón serrano   *naturally cured ham*
el jardín   *garden*
la jarra   *jug*
el jerez   *sherry*
la jornada   *working day*

la jota   *folk dance from Aragon*
las joyas   *jewellery*
   juega(s) – *see* jugar
el jueves   *Thursday*
jugar (ue)   *to play*   jugar a   *to play (a sport)*
julio   *July*
junio   *June*
justo   *right*
justo/a   *exact*

K

el kilo   *kilo*
el kilómetro   *kilometre*

L

la   *the; it; her*
lado: al lado de   *next to*   al otro lado (de)   *on the*
   other side (of)
el lago   *lake*
las   *the; them*   las ..., a las ...   *... o'clock, at ...*
   o'clock
el latín   *Latin*
el lavabo   *washbasin*
la lavandería   *laundry*
lavar   *to wash*
le   *(to) you; (to) him, (to) her*
la lectura   *reading*
la leche   *milk*
la lechuga   *lettuce*
leer   *to read*
las legumbres   *pulses*
lejos   *far*   lejos de   *far from, a long way from*
el lenguado   *sole*
les   *(to) you; (to) them*
libre   *free*   dejar libre   *to vacate*   el tiempo
   libre   *spare time*
el limón   *lemon*
limpio/a   *clean*
la línea: en línea recta   *straight on*
listo/a   *ready*
el litro   *litre*
lo   *him; it*   lo que   *what*   lo + *adjective   the ...*
   thing
local   *local*
la loción   *lotion*
el lomo   *steak; loin (of pork)*
Londres   *London*
los   *the; them*
luego   *then*   hasta luego   *see you later*
el lugar   *place*
el lunes   *Monday*

LL

llamar *to call*

llamarse *to be called* ¿cómo te llamas?, ¿cómo se llama? *what is your name?*

la llave *key*

la llegada *arrival*

llegar (a) *to arrive (at); to get to* ¿cómo se llega a ...? *how do I/you get to ...?*

lleno/a *full* lleno *a full tank*

llevar *to take* me la/lo llevo *I'll take it*

llover (ue): llueve *it rains, it's raining* está lloviendo *it's raining*

la lluvia *rain*

M

la madre *mother*

los madrileños *inhabitants/people of Madrid*

la madrugada *early morning*

el maíz *sweet corn*

mal *badly; unwell*

malo/a *bad*

Mallorca *Majorca*

manchego/a *of/from La Mancha*

la mano *hand* a mano derecha/izquierda *on the right/left*

la mantequería *grocer's*

la manzana *apple*

mañana *tomorrow*

la mañana *morning* de/por la mañana *in the morning*

el mapa *map*

el mar *sea*

el marido *husband*

marinera *cooked with onions, tomatoes, herbs and wine*

los mariscos *shellfish, seafood*

marrón *brown*

el martes *Tuesday*

marzo *March*

más *more; else; plus* más que *more than* más o menos *more or less* el/la más ... *the most ..., the ...-est*

la matrícula *registration number*

mayo *May*

la mayonesa *mayonnaise*

mayor *main* el mayor *the oldest*

la mayoría *majority*

máximo/a *maximum*

me *(to) me* *reflexive pronoun – see p. 185*

media: ... y media *half past ...*

el/la médico *doctor*

medio/a *half*

el mediodía *midday*

los mejillones *mussels*

mejor *better; rather* el/la mejor *the best*

el melón *melon*

Menorca *Minorca*

menos *less; least* ... menos cuarto *a quarter to ...*

la menta *peppermint*

el menú del día *set menu*

el mercado *market*

la merluza *hake*

el mes *month*

mesa: el vino de mesa *table wine*

el metro *metre; underground (railway)*

mi, mis *my*

mí *(to) me*

el miércoles *Wednesday*

mil *a thousand*

mineral: el agua mineral *mineral water*

mínimo *minimum*

el minuto *minute*

mirar *to look*

mismo: ahora mismo *right away* aquí mismo *right here*

mixto/a *mixed*

el modelo *model, style*

moderno/a *modern*

el molino de viento *windmill*

el momento *moment* un momento, un momentito *just a moment*

la moneda *coin*

la montaña *mountains*

montar (en) *to ride*

el monumento *old building*

el mosto *grape juice*

el motivo *reason*

mucho *much, a lot* muchísimo *very much, enormously*

mucho/a *much, a lot (of)* mucho gusto *pleased to meet you*

muchos/as *a lot (of), lots of* muchas/muchísimas gracias *thank you very much*

la mujer *woman; wife*

la muñeira *folk dance from Galicia*

el museo *museum*

la música *music* la música rock *rock music*

muy *very*

N

nací (*past tense of nacer*) *I was born*

nacional *national*

nada *nothing* no ... nada *not ... at all* de nada *not at all, don't mention it*

la naranja *orange*

la natación *swimming*
natural *natural*
la naturaleza *nature*
naturalmente *naturally, of course*
Navidad *Christmas*
necesitar *to need*
negro/a *black*
nevar (ie) *to snow* nieva *it snows, it's snow-ing* está nevando *it's snowing*
la nieve *snow*
el niño *child*
no *no; not* ¿no? *right?*
la noche *night* de/por la noche *at night* esta noche *tonight, this evening*
buenas noches *good evening, goodnight*
el nombre *name* a nombre de *in the name of*
nórdico/a *Nordic*
normal *two-star (petrol)*
normalmente *normally*
el noroeste *north-west*
el norte *north*
nos *(to) us reflexive pronoun – see p. 185*
novecientos/as *900*
noventa *ninety*
la novia *girlfriend*
noviembre *November*
el novio *boyfriend*
nueve *nine*
nuevo/a *new*
el número *number*

O

o *or* o sea (que) *so; that is, in other words*
el objeto *object*
la obra *work*
ochenta *eighty*
ocho *eight* ochocientos/as *800*
octubre *October*
ocupar *to take up*
la oficina *office*
once *eleven*
la organización *organisation*
el oro *gold* el tiempo es oro *time is money, time is precious*
os *(to) you reflexive pronoun – see p. 185*
otro/a *another, other* otra vez *again*
otros/as *other, others*

P

el padre *father* los padres *parents*
la paella (valenciana) *dish of rice with seafood and chicken*

pagar *to pay*
el país *country*
el País Vasco *Basque Country*
el paisaje *countryside, scenery*
el palacio *palace*
el pan *bread*
el pantalón *(pair of) trousers*
el papel *paper*
para *for; to*
el paracetamol *paracetamol*
la parada *stop; rank*
el parador *State-owned hotel*
parecer: me parece (que) *I think (that)* ¿qué te/le parece …? *what do you think of …?*
la pared *wall*
el paro *unemployment* en paro *unemployed*
el parque *park*
a la parrilla *grilled*
la parte *part*
participar *to take part*
particular *private* en particular *in particular*
pasado/a *last*
el pasajero *passenger*
el pasaporte *passport*
pasar *to go (through); to spend*
pasear *to go for walks*
el pasodoble *type of dance*
la patata *potato* las patatas fritas *crisps*
el patio *courtyard*
la película *film*
pensar (ie) (+ infinitive) *to intend to, to be thinking of*
pequeño/a *small, little*
la pera *pear*
perdón, perdone *excuse me*
perfectamente *perfectly*
perfecto *perfect, fine*
el periódico *newspaper*
el/la periodista *journalist*
perjudicar *to harm*
pero *but*
la persona *person* las personas *people*
el pescado *fish*
la peseta *peseta*
el piano *piano*
piensa(s), pienso – *see* pensar
la pimienta *pepper*
la piña *pineapple*
los Pirineos *Pyrenees*
la piscina *swimming pool*
el piso *floor; flat*
a la plancha *grilled (on a griddle)*
el plano *plan, street map*

la planta *plant*
el plato *plate; course; dish*
la playa *beach, seaside*
la plaza *square*
un poco *a bit; slightly*
  poco/a *little* poca gente *not many people*
  poder (ue) *to be able (can)* ¿se puede ... (+ infinitive)? *is it possible to ...?, can I/one ...?*
el policía municipal *policeman*
el polo *ice-lolly*
el pollo *chicken*
un poquito *a little (bit)*
  por *along; for; per* por aquí *near here, around here* por la mañana *in the morning* por favor *please; excuse me*
  ¿por qué? *why?*
  porque *because*
el portugués *Portuguese*
la posibilidad *possibility*
la postal *postcard*
el postre *dessert, pudding* de postre *for dessert/ pudding*
  practicar *to do; to play*
el precio *price* ¿qué precio tiene? *what price is it?, how much is it?*
  precisamente *to be precise, precisely*
  preferir (ie) *to prefer*
  presentar *to introduce*
la primavera *spring*
el primero *starter, first course* de primero *as a starter, for the first course*
  primero/a (primer *before a masculine singular noun*) *first*
la princesa *princess*
  principal *main*
el príncipe *prince*
  privado/a *private*
el problema *problem*
el producto *product*
la profesión *job, profession*
el profesor, la profesora *teacher*
la protección *protection*
  provecho: ¡buen provecho! *bon appétit!*
la provincia *province*
  próximo/a *next*
el pudin *pudding*
el pueblo *(small) town, village*
  puede(s), puedo – *see* poder
el puente *bridge*
la puerta *door; (departure) gate*
el puerto *port*
  pues *well, then; er ...*

Q

que *who; that, which* más que *more than*
¿qué? *what?, which?*
¡qué ...! *how ...!*
quedar *to be (situated)*
quedarse *to stay*
las quemaduras de sol *sunburn*
querer (ie) *to want (would like)*
querido/a *dear*
el queso *cheese*
¿quién? *who?*
quiere(s), quiero – *see* querer
quince *fifteen* quince días *fortnight*
quinientos/as *500*
el quiosco *newspaper stand*
quizá, quizás *perhaps, maybe*

R

la ración *portion*
rápidamente *quickly, rapidly*
la recepción *reception*
el/la recepcionista *receptionist*
recta: en línea recta *straight on*
recto, todo recto *straight on*
refrescar *to refresh*
la región *region*
la reina *queen*
el reloj *clock, watch*
repasar *to revise*
la reserva *reservation, booking*
reservado/a *booked*
responder (de) *to be responsible (for)*
el restaurante *restaurant*
los restos *remains*
el rey *king*
rico/a *delicious*
el río *river*
rojo/a *red*
Roma *Rome*
romano/a *Roman* calamares a la romana *squid fried in batter*
la ropa *clothes*
rosado/a *rosé*
ruega: se ruega a ... *... are requested*

S

el sábado *Saturday*
saber *to know* no (lo) sé *I don't know*
salga – *see* salir
la salida *departure*
salir (de) *to go out (of); to leave* salga *go out*
la salsa *sauce*

se *one, you, people reflexive pronoun – see p. 185*
sé – *see* saber
sea: o sea (que) *so; that is, in other words*
la secretaria *secretary*
los segovianos *inhabitants/residents of Segovia*
seguir *to carry on* siga *carry on; follow*
según *according to*
el segundo *main/second course* de segundo *for the main/second course*
segundo/a *second*
seguramente *certainly*
seis *six* seiscientos/as *600*
el sello *stamp*
el semáforo *traffic lights*
la semana *week* la Semana Santa *Holy Week*
la señal *road sign*
el señor *man, gentleman; sir; Mr*
la señora *lady; madam; Mrs*
los señores *ladies and gentlemen*
la señorita *young lady; miss*
se(p)tiembre *September*
ser* *to be* son ... pesetas *that's ... pesetas* será *will be*
serrano: el jamón serrano *naturally cured ham*
el servicio *service*
los servicios *toilets*
sesenta *sixty*
setecientos/as *700*
setenta *seventy*
setiembre (or septiembre) *September*
sevillano/a *of/from Sevilla*
los sevillanos *inhabitants/residents of Sevilla*
si *if*
sí *yes*
siempre *always*
siento: lo siento *I'm sorry*
la sierra *mountain range, mountains*
la siesta *siesta, (afternoon) nap*
siete *seven*
siga – *see* seguir
siguiente *following*
simpático/a *nice, pleasant*
sin *without*
el sitio *place*
situado/a *situated*
sobre *on; (at) about* sobre todo *above all, in particular, particularly*
sois – *see* ser
el sol *sun* tomar el sol *to sunbathe*
solamente *only*
sólo *only*
solo/a *alone* el café solo *black coffee*
el solomillo *sirloin steak*

soltero/a *single, unmarried*
la sombra *shade*
son – *see* ser
la sopa *soup*
soy – *see* ser
su, sus *your; his, her, its; their*
el suéter *sweater*
Suiza (f) *Switzerland*
súper *four-star (petrol)*
el supermercado *supermarket*
el supositorio *suppository*
supuesto: por supuesto *of course*
el sur *south*

T

el tabaco *tobacco*
la tableta *pill*
tal: ¿qué tal? *how are things?; how is/was ...?; how well ...?*
el Talgo *fast train*
la talla *size*
el tamaño *size*
también *also, as well, too*
tanto/a *so much*
la tapa *appetiser, snack*
tarde *late* más tarde *later*
la tarde *afternoon, evening* de/por la tarde *in the afternoon/evening* buenas tardes *good afternoon/evening*
la tarjeta *card* la tarjeta de crédito *credit card*
el taxi *taxi*
el/la taxista *taxi-driver*
te *(to) you reflexive pronoun – see p. 185*
el té *tea*
el teatro *theatre*
telefonear *to telephone*
el teléfono *telephone*
la televisión *television* la tele *telly*
la temperatura *temperature*
la temporada *season*
tener (ie)* *to have* ¿qué precio tiene? *what price is it?, how much is it?* ¿qué talla tiene(s)? *what size are you?* tenga, aquí tiene *here you are, here is* tener ... años *to be ... years old* tener que (+ infinitive) *to have to*
tenga, tengo – *see* tener
el tenis *tennis*
tercero/a *(tercer before a masculine noun) third*
terminar *to finish*
la ternera *veal*
la terraza *terrace*
tí *(to) you*
la tía *aunt*

el tiempo *time; weather* ¿cuánto tiempo? *how long?* el tiempo libre *spare time* ¿qué tiempo hace? *what is the weather like?*
la tienda *shop*
tiene(s) – *see* tener
la tierra *land*
tinto/a *red* (*wine*)
el tío *uncle* los tíos *uncles and aunts*
típicamente *typically*
típico/a *typical*
el tipo *type* ¿de qué tipo? *what sort?*
tocar *to play*
todavía *still*
todo derecho, todo recto *straight on*
todo *all, everything* eso es todo *that's all* sobre todo *above all, in particular, particularly*
todo/a *all, the whole* (*of*)
todos/as *all; every*
tomar *to have; to take* tomar el sol *to sunbathe* ¿qué va(n) a tomar? *what would you like?*
el tomate *tomato*
la tónica *tonic water*
la tortilla *omelette*
en total *in total, altogether*
totalmente *completely*
trabajar *to work* ¿en qué trabaja(s)? *what job/work do you do?*
el trabajo *work, job*
el traje *suit*
tranquilo/a *quiet*
tras *after*
trece *thirteen*
treinta *thirty*
el tren *train*
tres *three* trescientos/as *300*
la trucha *trout*
tu, tus *your*
tú *you*
el turismo *tourism* la oficina de turismo *tourist office*
el/la turista *tourist*

U

¡uf! *ugh!, phew!*
último/a *last; latest*
un, una *a*
únicamente *only*
único/a *only*
uno/a *one* la una *one o'clock*
unos/as *some, a few* unos . . . (kilómetros) *about . . . (kilometres)*
usted, ustedes *you*

V

va – *see* ir
las vacaciones *holidays* de vacaciones *on holiday*
la vainilla *vanilla*
vale *OK*
valenciano/a *of/from Valencia*
los valores *valuables*
vamos, van – *see* ir
variado/a *assorted*
variar *to vary*
varios/as *several*
vas – *see* ir
vasco/a *Basque*
el vasito *little glass*
vaya – *see* ir
¡vaya! *well!, well now!*
veces – *see* vez
veinte *twenty*
veintiuno/a *twenty-one* las veintiuna *2100 (hours)*
vender *to sell*
venir (ie)* *to come* . . . que viene *next . . .*
ver *to see; to watch* (vamos) a ver *let's see*
el verano *summer*
la verdad *truth, true* ¿verdad? *isn't that right/true?, . . right?*
verde *green*
la verdura *vegetable*
la vez *time* otra vez *again* a veces *sometimes* muchas veces *often*
viajar *to travel*
el viaje *journey* ¡buen viaje! *have a good trip!*
la vida *life*
viejo/a *old*
viene – *see* venir
viento: hace viento *it's windy*
el viernes *Friday*
el vino *wine* el vino de la casa *house wine* el vino de mesa *table wine*
visitar *to visit*
vivir *to live*
volver (ue) *to go back*
voy – *see* ir
el vuelo *flight*
vuelta: (de) ida y vuelta *return*

W

el windsurf *windsurfing*

Y

y *and*

ya   *now; yes of course*
yo   *I*
York: el jamón de York   *cooked ham*

Z
la zona   *region*
el zumo   *juice*